Professor Geoff Beattie is Head of School and Dea... ...
logical Sciences at the University of Manchester. He obtained
his PhD in Psychology from the University of Cambridge (Trinity
College) and is a Fellow of the British Psychological Society
(BPS). He was awarded the Spearman Medal by the BPS for
'published psychological research of outstanding merit'. Geoff
was President of the Psychology section of the British Association
for the Advancement of Science in 2006.

Geoff is widely regarded as one of the leading international
figures on non-verbal communication. He has published
seventeen books, many of which have either won or been shortlisted for major international prizes.

Geoff was the resident on-screen psychologist on ten 'Big
Brother' series. He was the presenter of BBC1's *Family SOS* and
co-presenter of BBC1's *Life's too Short*. He was also the
psychologist and presenter of *The Farm of Fussy Eaters* (UKTV
Style) and Channel 4's *Dump Your Mates in Four Days*. He is
currently the on-screen psychologist on ITV2's series *Ghost
Hunting with* . . . On the run-up to the General Election in 2005
he had a regular slot on the main ITV news called *The Body
Politic*, in which he analysed the body language of all the senior
politicians involved in the election.

His academic publications have appeared in a wide variety of
international journals including *Nature*, *Semiotica*, and the
Journal of Language and Social Psychology. But he has been
keen to show how psychology can illuminate many aspects of
human experience and consequently he has written for a diverse
range of newspapers and magazines including the *Guardian*,
The Times, the *Independent*, the *Sunday Telegraph*, the
Observer, the *New Statesman*, and *Marie Claire*.

'GET THE EDGE is packed with useful advice that brilliantly illustrates the power of rapid change.'

Richard Wiseman, author, 59 SECONDS

'GET THE EDGE provides wonderful advice based on the wisdom of a lifetime combined with lessons firmly rooted in psychological research. This book is not only profoundly informative, but also a pleasure to read.'

Aaron T. Beck, Professor of Psychiatry,
University of Pennsylvania and founder of
Cognitive Behaviour Therapy (CBT)

GET THE EDGE

GEOFF BEATTIE

headline
business plus

Copyright © 2011 Geoff Beattie

The right of Geoff Beattie to be identified as the Author
of the Work has been asserted by him in accordance with the
Copyright, Designs and Patents Act 1988.

First published in 2011
by HEADLINE PUBLISHING GROUP

1

Cataloguing in Publication Data is available from the British Library

ISBN 978 7553 6037 6

Typeset in Sabon by Avon DataSet Ltd,
Bidford-on-Avon, Warwickshire

Printed in the UK by CPI Mackays, Chatham, ME5 8TD

Headline's policy is to use papers that are natural, renewable and
recyclable products and made from wood grown in sustainable forests.
The logging and manufacturing processes are expected to conform to the
environmental regulations of the country of origin.

HEADLINE PUBLISHING GROUP
An Hachette UK Company
338 Euston Road
London NW1 3BH

www.headline.co.uk
www.hachette.co.uk

This book is dedicated to my mother and my father.

CONTENTS

ACKNOWLEDGEMENTS

There are a number of people in that I need to thank profusely for this book. Firstly, Robert Kirby, my agent from United Agents who got me thinking about this topic in the first place, and prompted me with ever so delicate suggestions. Secondly, Val Hudson, then at Headline, whose instantaneous, enthusiastic reaction to the original pitch was everything that I had hoped for and more, and her enthusiasm just grew from there. (I clearly *need* enthusiastic people, although this is probably an important admission on my part.) John Moseley took the project over with equal enthusiasm and great professionalism. And lastly, I would like to thank Laura McGuire, who was absolutely invaluable from start to finish; she assisted me with great fortitude and without ever once complaining, in that painstaking process of researching a book like this. Many other people have taught me important (and sometimes painful) lessons along the way, and I thank them indirectly and vaguely for their own unique contributions to my personal, psychological development and hence, in turn, to this volume. Some parts of the recollections of my father's death first appeared in a slightly different form in my memoir *Protestant Boy*, and I thank Granta for their permission to reproduce parts of it here.

1. FIRST STEPS/FIRST IMPRESSIONS

'I do not judge men by anything they can do. Their greatest deed is the impression they make on me.'

Thoreau, *Journal*, 18 February 1841

Why do some people feel instinctively comfortable interacting with complete strangers while others do not? What can you actually do about it? Let me begin with a story from my own life.

I was a shy child, although I did have many close friends from the dull mill streets of Belfast on which I grew up. I was shy with strangers, particularly adults that I didn't know. I would be in the centre of town with my mother on a Saturday afternoon and she would regularly bump into some of her old friends; people I didn't recognize, whom maybe she knew before my father and she were married. I would be introduced and I would stand there looking down at the ground, refusing to make eye contact, except with the cracks on the pavement, feeling awkward and stiff. I can't remember now what was going on in my head in any real detail but I can vividly remember the *look* (partly because it was commented on so much), and the *feel* of my stiff body posture. 'He's a lovely, shy, wee boy,' the friend would say, somehow equating 'shyness' with 'loveliness', which I thought even then might be significant. My hands would be clenched tightly behind my back, not because of any latent aggressive impulses, as far as I can now tell, but because I didn't like accepting money from strangers, which was always part of these exchanges. I like it now as a social custom, but as a child I think I disliked the idea that people could buy my affection; I didn't want to be beholden to anyone. Perhaps I was thinking about it too much in a particular kind of way, and steadfastly not seeing the bigger picture. It was, after all, about working-class people who didn't have much, sharing what they did have. I thwarted their plan by simply refusing to hold out my hand to accept the money; I didn't accept their invitation to participate in this exchange. And then a long ritual would commence of them trying to get me to accept a few coins or a pound note. It was embarrassing for everybody once it had started. The friend would be put on the spot by my refusal to accept the money, and would try to prise open my tightly closed hand (they were assuming, of course, that I was just being polite). I would stand there, resisting and shaking with the sheer physical effort of being a refusenik. My mother would look away with embarrass-ment. 'He's not like this normally,' she would say. But I was always the same, always determined in my own peculiar way. 'He'd normally snatch your hand off, like any boy would; he's in a wee bit of a quiet mood today,' she would add. On the bus on the way home my mother would complain about my behaviour and my social ineptness, and how embarrassing it was for all concerned, and remind me that my brother Bill would not have stood there like that, refusing to shake hands, refusing to talk, refusing to accept the pound note. 'You can be a really odd boy, when you want to be,' she would say. By 'odd' she meant socially awkward. 'When are you going to grow out of it?' she would ask.

Even as an adult, for years I found it difficult entering a room full of total strangers and talking freely. Thankfully this only lasted for a while, because later, as much out of necessity as any-thing else, I started to change, until my mother hardly recognized what she saw. The fact that I was studying psychology was also surely a major factor in this process of change. 'My God, you don't shut up these days,' she would say, with a slight look of surprise on her face; and with almost a tutting sound in her voice. 'You'll talk to anybody; you're not a bit self-conscious anymore. You could bloody well win prizes for chatting up women.' (It's important to point out that to her mind chatting to any passing female between the ages of say eighteen and fifty, in a reasonably friendly or charming way, was effectively a process of 'chatting up'). I tried to point out the difference to her many times, but to no avail. I think, however, that she believed that I had gone too far in the opposite direction. I had ended up far 'too forward'. 'You don't refuse money these days either,' she would say; 'you've changed in a lot of ways.'

Perhaps my personal shortcomings drew me to psychology in the first place. I wanted to understand the relationship between the debilitating sort of self-consciousness which can constrain personal and social development, and social interaction. I believe I needed to understand the connection between those distracting self-absorbed thoughts and those nagging self-doubts, which can pop into our heads at any time, and our actual behaviour towards other people.

So how can you interact with others more effectively? What should you be consciously aware of when you talk to others and what role do unconscious processes play in meeting and getting on with other people? Can you manipulate the unconscious to better effect? Can you nudge it in certain key directions? Can you train yourself to be more skilled at interaction?

I spent many years studying some of the basic processes of social interaction, first for my PhD at Cambridge and then at other leading universities. I came to recognize the power of small behaviours, and sometimes the incredible significance of small details, that could hold the key to successful outcomes in interaction. Some of this study must have rubbed off on me because my own behaviour started to change. No longer shy, my odd and distinctive stammer ('do you put that on for effect to get people to feel sorry for you?' my mother would ask) has gone, I trust, for ever. I came to think that life is a little too short for this sort of constraint that locked me into a social claustrophobia.

So what is the secret of freeing yourself from such social awkwardness? In my view, the science of psychology can inform many important everyday processes. In this book, I will discuss some of the more interesting findings from this vibrant and expanding discipline. The choice is eclectic; these are things that I found useful and informative and sometimes things that surprised me. This book is not a training manual, but sometimes a little knowledge can be all that you need to start the process of change, to help you 'get the edge'. I have made the book personal at times, sometimes very personal, because it's important to show that the kind of psychology I discuss impacts directly on *real lives*, including my own. It is part of my concern with demonstrating the relevance and significance of psychology as a discipline for *all* our lives.

How to make the perfect entrance

First things first: how do you make the perfect entrance into a social gathering? There will be a collection of individuals all ready to interact with you and yet prepared to make a whole series of rapid, and sometimes unconscious, social judgements about you. Of course, at a party, or indeed any type of social gathering, many people tend to be quite self-conscious. This makes them more than a little aware of their own behaviour and also more ready to think about why other people behave in the way they do. This increase in the spiral of self-consciousness is what used to terrify me.

The first thing to think about when making the perfect entrance is the timing. It's a simple enough decision. If you arrive early you have the advantage that you will have longer to talk to people and thereby feel more familiar and comfortable with them. On the downside, people may wonder why you are there so early – 'Has this person nothing better to do?' If you arrive at a party early, of course, you can watch others arriving, which might seem like an obvious advantage. The disadvantage is that you will have to temporarily break the social bonds that you are forming to watch the new arrivals and this can make the person you are talking to uncomfortable – 'Why aren't they interested in me? Why do they keep watching the door?' If you arrive late at a party, it may send out an implicit message that you are not desperate to be there. A possible downside of arriving late is that social bonds will already be starting to form and sometimes it is harder to break into a social group when it has already been established or partly established. Therefore, in terms of timing it is important to arrive *not too early* and *not too late*. The best time is at that stage of the evening when people have had some time to talk, but when guests will also be looking for new stimulation.

Social gatherings like parties are often all about first impressions because people make quick and sometimes instantaneous decisions about who to interact with and who to avoid.

It is possible to take risks at parties in terms of approaching new people, in ways that are not possible in many other situations. You have an opportunity to talk to others who you might not approach in any other context so it is important that your appearance reflects your intention to impress unfamiliar faces. At the outset of many forms of interaction, the fear of rejection can be the predominant emotion and can inhibit what people do. But at a party the implicit rule is that by being there you are open at least to some social interaction. So if someone approaches you, put them at their ease immediately, smile in a welcoming, non-threatening way, pay them a compliment and concentrate on the emotional tone of any short sentence you use. In short, make them feel welcome. Smiles are an extremely contagious social signal, particularly when they are open and natural, and help increase the enjoyment of interaction.

At a party, tell people about yourself, but don't overdo it. Men quite often tend to tell people far too much about themselves in too short a period in order to position themselves in a social hierarchy (which is often their prime concern). This can be off-putting. You need to be interesting in what you say but also attentive. Signal how attentive you are through a high level of eye contact and through the use of 'back-channel' communications such as 'mmm' and 'yeah'. These will fall naturally into the brief pauses in the speech of the person talking and will encourage the flow of conversation and stop embarrassing silences from developing. If you use back-channel signals like this effectively, the person speaking to a group will direct a lot of their talk your way, and this will help you stand out because you will be the speaker's focus of attention.

You need to be attentive to your current social group but at the same time you need to notice who else has arrived. These glances around the room need to be brief and you can even comment on them to your current conversational partners to turn the whole thing into a cooperative activity, for example by saying 'I wonder who is going to be here tonight?' If you accompany your glance around the room with a verbal statement in this way, you are less likely to be perceived as bored with the current conversation.

In these sorts of ways you will have made the perfect entrance.

- Remember that your behaviour is not permanently fixed. You can change how you interact with others

- At a party, think about the timing of your arrival beforehand

- Be a good listener. Make others want to talk to you

- Avoid telling people too much about yourself too early. Do not 'over-present'. Balance what you tell others with what they are telling you

- Make yourself rewarding to talk to by using lots of back-channels (like 'mmm' and 'yeah') to encourage others to speak

- These back-channels will get you a lot of attention from whoever is speaking, and they will turn you into a primary focus in the conversation

How to establish instant rapport

The quickest way to establish an instant rapport with someone is to display synchrony in movement with that person. You don't have to match exactly the form of the movement with the other person (which can sometimes look a little odd if it's not done well), but you should mirror their timing. This is normally an unconscious sign of rapport but it can be consciously manipulated with a little practice. As they pick up the menu, reach for your glass; as they stroke their hair, touch your face, and so on. Also try to focus on the words being said and the natural rhythm of the speech itself. This should become the mechanism for you both to achieve perfect coordination. You should allow your bodily movements to be affected by the stress points in the speech. Consciously time your movements in the early part of the conversation so that there is some degree of rapport early on, but then allow the rhythms of the speech to take over. This will produce feelings of rapport in a matter of minutes, sometimes even quicker.

- Establish rapport with another person, by copying the timing of their movements

- Focus in on the changes in the rhythm in the speech, and let that coordinate the 'interactional synchrony' between the two of you. It should be as if you are both moving naturally together to the rhythm of speech (if it doesn't happen naturally as quickly as you would like, then do it deliberately)

How to have a smooth conversation

If you have just met someone for the first time, there is nothing more embarrassing than a long silence developing in conversation. The only problem is that what can seem like a long silence is probably only one or two seconds long (sometimes even a lot shorter than this; we often start to notice gaps of around 600 milliseconds in conversation and find these uncomfortable). These kinds of silences develop for a number of reasons but one of the most important reasons is that people are often unable to anticipate or predict when someone is about to finish talking. So in order to have a smooth conversation, help your conversational partner out by using the following two devices to allow them to anticipate when you are about to stop talking. The first device is the **three-part list**. Say things like 'I've got a lot of hobbies like running, going to the cinema and reading'. Don't finish after 'cinema' and don't add a fourth example to the list because it violates the three-part rule. Your conversational partner will be able to anticipate the end point of your sentence when you list three items, and come in immediately without any perceptible delay.

The second technique is to use a **two-part contrast**. Say things like 'I enjoy the cinema but it's not as good as live theatre'. Once you've started a construction like this, your conversational partner will be able to anticipate when it ends and they will be able to respond without any embarrassing silence. If there is an awkward pause after you have used either the three-part list or the two-part contrast in your conversation, then you have a bigger problem – you may need to change your hobbies, your appearance or your conversational partner because the reason for the embarrassing silence may be much deeper.

- Embarrassing silences often occur in conversation because people don't know whose turn it is to speak

- Prevent awkward moments by helping your conversational partner to anticipate the end points of your sentences

- Use three-part lists (A, B and C) and two-part contrasts (not A but B) to structure what you are saying

How to pay a compliment

The problem with most compliments is that they stick to a very strict formula with a simple syntactic structure and they rely on a limited range of words. In terms of structure they are built on things like 'You are very nice'. Embarrassingly, the word 'nice' appears in nearly a quarter of all compliments made and the word 'you' in three-quarters of all compliments. The problem with formulaic language like this is that it can be accessed from the brain in a routine and automatic way and without any real thought. As a consequence, such compliments are seen as very easy to generate and may not appear genuine, even when they are fully meant. When I first met Cheryl Cole and the rest of Girls Aloud for the television programme *Ghosthunting with Girls Aloud* for ITV2, Cheryl paid me a compliment more or less immediately. The girls were sitting waiting for dinner in a hotel restaurant in North Wales. They were sipping white wine in this heady, perfumed, and very private space. I was running late as usual, and was the last to get there. I had been driven from Lincoln where I had been filming *The Farm of Fussy Eaters*. I was slightly exhausted from working all day. As I walked in I could see that the girls recognized me. I have to admit that it felt really good. It turned out that they were all fans of *Big Brother*. The fact that they knew what I did for a living was going to make my job that much easier. I was going to be analysing them over the next few days and nights. It helps if people think that you might have something interesting to say. 'I love listening to your analysis,' said Cheryl, the first to speak, and then added, 'You've got a really nice voice.' Her compliment had both 'you' and 'nice' in it. That was the first thing I noticed. It didn't ruin it for me, but it could have done. I replied spontaneously, and without much thought, 'You've got an accent that is really ni— (but then I corrected myself) amazing too.' It seemed almost over the top, but I had my reasons, which thankfully I kept to myself.

But there is still an important point here. To pay a compliment effectively, you must break the mould, use a different structure and avoid the words 'nice' and 'you'. Say things like 'I couldn't help noticing your hair, it looks absolutely fantastic'. Even 'your' is better than 'you' because it requires some (i.e. a tiny amount of) thought. Think about what's appropriate to comment on and then get the structure right. Avoid the 'compliment formula' because it can seem very insincere (although, interestingly enough, everything that Cheryl says does seem sincere and that's probably her greatest asset).

- Pay original-sounding compliments (they will seem more genuine)

- Avoid the word 'nice' in compliments, whenever possible. It's just too commonly used

- Avoid the 'You are . . .' structure. Never say 'You are very nice'

How to 'read' someone in a tenth of a second

My mother was always very quick to arrive at a judgement about other people. She prided herself on the speed with which she could do this. 'He's a nice wee boy,' she would say, before my new friend had barely opened his mouth. Or, on another occasion, 'He's a bad 'un, he'll never be any good.' All said before my friend was even out of earshot. 'Give them a chance!' I would say. Even then I thought that there might be more to the process of judging another person than one brief look at the narrowness of the eyes, or the sloping of the forehead, or the way that the mouth creases peculiarly at one side but not the other. 'But you know that I'm always right,' she would say. 'You can't fool me. All your friends know that I can read any of them like a book.'

Years later, I introduced my mother, without much forewarning, to a close female friend in Sheffield. It was a last-minute thing, or that's how I tried to make it seem, but my mother's instantaneous judgement in the streetlights on that cold winter night was written all over her face (she sensed what was going on all right). 'There's just something about her I don't like. Don't ask me what it is. She'd be no good for you,' she said, as she hurried back to the car without even looking at me. 'Take me back to your house now.'

So can you learn to read someone accurately in a tenth of a second? Can you tell what they're really like in a blink of an eye? How can you tell how trustworthy someone is just by glancing at them? In the light of what I know now, I think that I can safely say that the single best psychological tip that I can give here is that you *can't*. It simply cannot be done. But this doesn't stop the vast majority of people (and not just my highly biased late mother) doing it. So if you want to perceive someone accurately when you first meet them then you need to take conscious steps to override your natural impulse to make instant, unconscious judgements. It turns out that people tend to judge others across a whole range of characteristics within a tenth of a second, including things like how

'attractive'
'likeable'
'trustworthy'
'competent'
'aggressive'

they are. However, you cannot judge such characteristics seriously in this short time. But that doesn't stop our brain from trying. If you want to read someone accurately, therefore, you have to fight against this natural but essentially destructive tendency. If you don't, there is a real danger that you will misjudge people badly on the basis of first impressions, and then unconsciously not want to correct your first impressions. (Who, after all, wants to be proven wrong about something?) The problem is that if we make up our minds about someone that quickly, when we have more time to interact with them we will look for additional evidence to confirm (rather than refute) our original impression. We will not keep an open mind, and we will not be interested in any information that might contradict our original impression. So the tip for reading someone accurately is to try to slow down, or inhibit, these natural, unconscious judgemental processes. Easier said than done, of course, but you have to try.

The science behind all of this is based on research carried out by Janine Willis and Alexander Todorov of Princeton University, who found that making judgements about someone that we have met for the first time is something that most people do readily, naturally and very quickly. They argue that we make inferences about the personal characteristics of people in a process essentially routed in the unconscious. They wanted to investigate how quick this process really is, so they presented participants with photographs of people and asked them to judge how 'attractive', 'likeable', 'competent', 'trustworthy' and 'aggressive' they were. The photographs consisted of head shots of the individuals with a neutral expression. Half of the subjects were men and half were women. Participants in the experiment were specifically told that it was a study of first impressions and that they should make their decisions as quickly as possible. In some trials, the faces were just presented for 100 milliseconds (a tenth of a second), in others for 500 milliseconds (half a second) and in others for 1 second. Now, one possible outcome for a study like this is after a 100-millisecond exposure to a face, the participants would be unable to make any judgements. Perhaps, at a push, a participant could make an instantaneous judgement of 'attractiveness'. But what about the other characteristics; surely longer is needed to take all the information in from the face to form a complete opinion?

But this is not how people's brains seem to work. Even after an exposure of one-tenth of a second to a picture of a human face, judgements of personality traits were made which were very similar to judgements made when individuals had significantly more time at their disposal. Extraordinarily, the highest correlations are for judgements of 'trustworthiness'. In other words, after seeing a face for one-tenth of a second, people have already made up their mind about how trustworthy a person is. What Willis and Todorov also found was that increasing the exposure time (from one-tenth to a half a second) did not significantly increase the statistical correlation for *any* of the traits that they examined, namely 'attractiveness', 'likeability', 'trustworthiness', 'competence' and 'aggressiveness'. However, allowing participants more time to look at the faces (even just half a second!) had some effect on judgements, in that the judgements tended to become more negative and the participants became more confident in their decisions. This increasing negativity with additional exposure time suggested to the researchers that there may be some kind of positivity bias operating in social judgement which operates with the smallest of exposures.

What this research demonstrates is that we make up our minds extraordinarily quickly about some aspects of the personality of other people on the basis of facial features. This is done so quickly that it bypasses any conscious decision-making processes. It is not that we identify certain facial features and make a reasoned character judgement in the manner of researchers like John Lavater (1772–1880), who detailed the relationship between facial features and personality, as in 'the nearer the eyebrows are to the eyes, the more earnest, deep, and firm the character'. It is more that we can't stop ourselves making judgements about personality from facial features. Our unconscious basically takes over and makes judgements on the basis of the tiniest amounts of information.

The question of why we are more inclined to do this with the dimension of 'trustworthiness', compared with other personality traits, is an interesting and important one. The researchers argue that this is a process directed by the fundamental mechanism of evolution. In evolutionary terms, one of the most important things to find out when you meet a person for the very first time is how trustworthy they are. Basically, you need to know whether they are a friend or a foe. In certain circumstances, an individual's survival may have depended upon these kinds of things and therefore on the process of instantaneously judging intention and trustworthiness. Brain-imaging studies have shown that the detection of trustworthiness is a spontaneous and automatic process linked to activity in the amygdala, one of the very primitive parts of the human brain.

The researchers go on to speculate that a tenth of a second may not even be required for these unconscious judgements to be made; we may actually do this much quicker than that! They point to studies on object detection which seem to demonstrate that objects can be categorized as quickly as they can be detected. In other words, as soon as you know they are there, you know what it is. In the words of Willis and Todorov, 'Maybe, as soon as a face is there, you know whether to trust it.'

So how do you read a face in a tenth of a second? Maybe the question 'How do you stop yourself trying to read a face in a tenth of a second?' is a better one. Our minds make these fast, intuitive and unconscious judgements immediately without any of our conscious help. What information could possibly be contained in one's facial features which would be an accurate and valid indicator of competence or trustworthiness? The answer is none, but our unconscious processes do not work like this. Reading people accurately, therefore, may involve, not so much speeding the brain up, but slowing it down.

Of course, the results of the Willis and Todorov study are slightly alarming in a number of ways. They suggest that after the most minimal exposures, we have already made our mind up about another person. The expression 'making our mind up' may be entirely the wrong one in this context, because the researchers suggest that the processes involved are so fast that consciousness never comes into it. The implications of this set of results for subsequent social interaction are quite frightening because human beings, after all, often like to find confirming evidence that back up their original judgements rather than evidence that contradict it or prove it wrong. So having made your mind up about someone's lack of trustworthiness or competence, what are you then prepared to do (consciously or more probably unconsciously) to prove yourself right? However, I have one issue with the fundamental style of the study and others like it. This study presented head shots of people with neutral expressions to control the stimulus to which their participants were exposed. But in real life, when we meet strangers for the first time, we get a complex set of messages from the facial features, the facial expressions, bodily movement, interpersonal distance, tone of voice, speech patterns and micro-movements. So how do we combine all of this information in a tenth of a second to form a lasting and accurate judgement about personality characteristics? Perhaps in real life, it is not quite as quick and not quite as blind as the research of Willis and Todorov might suggest. Perhaps we need several seconds to compile all of this information and work out whether this stranger in front of us is a friend or foe, safe or unsafe, aggressive or passive, competent or otherwise, trustworthy or untrustworthy. Or perhaps some people only process the facial information and ignore the rest. It is plausible; after all, I've seen it at work in the dark streets of Sheffield, to my personal cost.

- You cannot make an accurate judgement about another person in one-tenth of a second, on the basis of how they look, even though your unconscious mind might be telling you differently

- To read someone accurately on very first impressions, consciously try to slow your brain down

- The problem with instantaneous judgements, is that you will look for evidence to support your original judgement rather than looking out for new information to test or refute it

- Other people may well be making judgements about you very quickly on the basis of how you look

- Think carefully about how you look and the messages others may be getting from your appearance

How to find the perfect mate

I am sure at one time or another we have all sat, wondering how we could find the *perfect* partner. How do you find *the one*? We see couples, so connected, matched, blissfully and annoyingly happy and we think to ourselves, how did that happen? It turns out that if you want to find the perfect mate, here is the best single tip: start the process with an open mind about what you are actually looking for, because whatever characteristics people say they are looking for in advance of that first date do not necessarily match those that they actually use as a yard stick when they meet potential partners. If you talk at length to your friends about what you are looking for in a partner before you start the whole process, this will only make matters worse. This will constrain you even more because you then become publicly committed to seeking certain characteristics. So if someone asks you what kind of man or woman you want to go out with, just say, 'I don't know. We'll see.' This is more psychologically accurate.

Research on dating was carried out by Robert Kurzban of the University of Pennsylvania and Jason Weeden of Arizona State University, who studied mate selection on an internet dating site in a large sample of over 10,000 participants. They were interested in the relationship between the preferences that people specified in their advertisements and the choices that they actually made, when they later met their potential partners in a three-minute speed-dating situation. The researchers analysed a well-educated sample with relatively high incomes, about a third of whom had no religious affiliation. What men and women said that they were looking for in a potential partner was significantly different. Men were more likely to specify certain body types and they had clear age preferences (they basically wanted young, slim women). Women were looking for older, richer and taller men (women were five times as likely as men to specify a minimum annual income and women were more restrictive in terms of height preference than men). There were also clear preferences stated for racial or ethnic origins and less frequently, religious affiliation, and also whether the potential partner had been married before or had children.

So it would seem that people have a pretty clear idea of what they think they want in a partner. The big question is whether these consciously held preferences have any value in predicting who people actually go for in a speed-dating session? Surely these consciously held characteristics must have some value? After all, they must have thought long and hard before writing the advertisements in the first place; they probably discussed many of these features with their friends and surely, when it comes down to it, we must know what we are looking for in a potential mate?

But the results of this study demonstrated conclusively that these advertisements were, in the words of the researchers, 'of little or no predictive value in determining the features of potential matches who were chosen . . . except with regards to race'. In other words, once you get to the actual speed-dating situation, all of these stated preferences seem to go out of the window and are replaced with something more basic, more intuitive and probably a good deal more unconscious.

So how do you find the perfect mate? If you want to find the perfect mate, do not constrain your choices in advance, keep an open mind and let your unconscious instincts make the choice for you.

What is impressive about this study is the size of the sample and the counter-intuitive nature of the conclusion. We all know that attraction is a complex process, but most people would think that allowing people to specify their ideal characteristics in advance should have some influence on actual decision-making. But according to this study, it doesn't. The big question is: do people know their own minds? The results would suggest not.

- To find the perfect mate, keep an open mind about what you are looking for

- Don't discuss what you are seeking at length with your friends beforehand; it will just constrain you more

- Be prepared to be surprised by what you go for

How to laugh more effectively

I once had a friend who had the most annoying laugh I have ever heard. She thought that it was her most endearing, playful and flirtatious characteristic. It was a breathless sort of hiss – it always reminded me of a dog panting after a long run. It certainly got her attention in social groups and it was a little predictable in terms of what occasioned it. When there was an attractive man in the room, and she was being ignored, she would start to pant. Most people would look her way, including the attractive man, and this seemed to reinforce her behaviour. I always thought that she needed to do a basic rethink of how to produce a laugh. All laughs it seems are *not* equal, some are attractive to other people and to the opposite sex; some clearly are not.

Should this come as any surprise? Well, there is one school of thought (what you might term 'the misguided school') which says that all laughs are very much alike. Some would argue that laughs are signs of positive emotion (regardless of how they sound), and all laughs should have a positive emotional impact on the listener. But, according to Jo-Anne Bachorowski of Vanderbilt University and Michael Owren of Cornell University, all laughs really are not equal; some have a very positive impact on the emotional state of the listener and some don't. Bachorowski and Owren studied whether the laughs were 'voiced' or not (where the breath is pushed out through the vocal cords). They recorded laughs of a large number of people as they watched funny films and then selected a sample of voiced and unvoiced laughs which they played to participants who had to rate their interest in meeting them, thus:

Definitely Interested
Interested
Not Interested
Definitely Not Interested

Participants also had to rate their emotional response to the laughter. The study found that people were especially interested in meeting those who produced the voiced laughs and much less interested in meeting those who produced the grunt and snort-like sounds. The study also found that the voiced laughs elicited a more positive emotional response than the unvoiced laughs and that voiced laughs produced by females were rated as the most positive of all. The conclusion of the study was that the social effects of laughter depend greatly on how it is produced. Voiced laughs with their song-like character have a much more positive effect than unvoiced grunts, pants and snort-like sounds.

So in order to laugh more effectively to ensure that someone likes you, make sure your laugh is voiced and make it more song-like in character. This is something that is usually done unconsciously but you may be able to change your pattern of laughter by listening out for it in others and by practising it.

Of course, if you are being picky with this research you might like to consider whether different laughs may be appropriate in different contexts; it clearly would be interesting to determine the relative impact of different categories of laughs in different social situations. Surely unvoiced laughs must have a positive impact sometimes? Presumably grunts, pants and snorts have some clear functional significance in certain contexts. The researchers, however, don't tell us what these might be, and I am hard pushed to think of any situation in which I would enjoy my old friend's dog-like panting.

- All laughs are not equal. Some laughs have a very positive effect on other people; some do not

- Laugh more effectively by 'voicing' the laugh and making it more sing-song

- You will appear much more friendly and sexy if you 'voice' your laugh

- If you are a woman, never pant as a form of laughter (unless you really, really can't help it)

How to become more cultured

I am from a traditional working-class background that luckily put great emphasis on education. School may have successfully introduced me to Dickens and Chekhov and Tolstoy, but music lessons left me cold and awkward. Even the names of the instruments – French horn, oboe and viola – to this day make me a little anxious. At home we listened to Jim Reeves, Andy Williams and Engelbert Humperdinck, but that was about it.

Many years after I had left Belfast I was on *Nightwaves* on Radio 3 (the home of classical music), waiting to be interviewed on a book that I had written about the lives of boxers called *On the Ropes: Boxing as a Way of Life*. The other guest was Valentine Cunningham, Professor of English at Oxford, who was going to review my book. We sat in the studio waiting for the show to start, as the music from the previous programme began to fade. The interviewer, whose name I have forgotten, hurried into the studio with a pile of papers tucked messily under his arm, turned to me and asked politely, 'What are we listening to? A little bit of Shostakovich, maybe?' Professor Cunningham glanced my way. I smiled back, but I could feel a slight nausea building up inside me. I could hear the clock ticking on the studio wall, filling the deadened silence in the sound-proofed room. I cleared my throat, slowly and deliberately. I knew that the music wasn't Jim Reeves, and I was pretty certain that it was not one of Engelbert Humperdinck's early acoustic numbers. But that was more or less all that I knew. However, I had to say something; the silence demanded that. My lips eventually parted. 'I think that it's early Shostakovich,' I said into the silence, with a singular emphasis on *early*. The inter-viewer looked at me for a second more, a look of slight puzzlement held briefly. 'You're absolutely right,' he said. 'It is early Shostakovich. Well recognized. Some might have thought it was from his later period – I thought that to begin with – but well spotted.' Professor Cunningham threw me a benign but essentially connecting smile. The interview had started well.

I would love to know and to understand and to appreciate classical music, but how? Some friends have proposed an obvious solution. 'Go to the shop, buy some music, stick it on and listen to it. It's that easy. You'll grow to love it.' But it may not be that easy according to the latest psychological research (I think that I have always sensed this). It seems that if you want to become cultured and learn to love classical music, it may not be enough to just play classical music over and over again to give you a sense of familiarity with the music and to develop an emotional bond with it. Research suggests that repeated exposure to emotionally evocative music polarizes your response to the music, i.e. it makes your response to the music more extreme. An experiment was conducted by Charlotte Witvliet from Hope College, Holland (Michigan) and Scott Vrana from Virginia Commonwealth University. They played pieces of instrumental music to a set of participants a number of times who had to rate how pleasant they found the music after each listen. The researchers also took a number of physiological measures (including heart rate) and measures of non-verbal behaviour (including smiling). The researchers found that familiarity with the music did not necessarily lead to people liking it more. Instead, they found that the repetition of the music amplified the initial response of the participants, in that when people liked the music the first time they heard it, then the more they subsequently heard it the more they liked it. However, if they disliked the music the first time they heard it, the more they heard it, the more they disliked it. In other words, you cannot develop a love of all classical music simply by playing it over and over again. Repetition of the music didn't just affect psychological judgement, it also affected behaviour and the basic physiological response, in that subjects smiled more with increased repetition of the music they originally liked, and their heart rate increased.

So if you want to become cultured and develop a love for classical music, find some pieces of music that you enjoy on the first hearing, and then play these pieces over and over again. Of course, the limitations of a study like this are that the music was studied in a strict experimental situation devoid of any real social meanings. But what happens if you pair the repetition of disliked classical music with a positive social context like a family get-together? Can you increase the liking for music that you don't like to begin with using this associative process? That is a question worth further exploration.

- Familiarity does not necessarily lead to a positive emotional bond, especially when it comes to music

- To become more 'cultured', find classical music that you like at the outset and play that repeatedly

- Do not play classical music over and over again that you originally disliked. You will not come to like it; you may well just come to hate it more

2. JUDGING OTHERS

'We are better able to study our neighbours than
ourselves, and their actions than our own.'

Aristotle, *Nicomachean Ethics* (4th century BC),
9.9, tr. J. A. K. Thomson

How to tell if a story is true or false

You can tell if a story is true or false by looking out for certain critical details in the story itself which can give the game away. Things like the tense of the verb used and whether the emotions of the people in the story are spelt out in detail are, on occasion, the critical cues. When somebody is talking about an event that supposedly happened to them in the past, look out for whether the tense of the verb is present (less likely to be true) or past (more likely to be true):

PRESENT	PAST
I'm walking	I walked
I walk	I was walking
I'm talking	I was talking

Also look out for the presence of what are called **filled hesitations**; those odd sounds that people make when they are talking, like 'um' and 'ah', which are signs of extra mental activity (and more common in *true* stories). Stories that have been embellished, or are being told for effect, tend to be in the present tense. They also tend to contain lots of emotional words in which the characters' feelings are spelt out. The stories tend to be more fluent with fewer 'ums' and 'ahs' than true stories (getting a story really accurate requires more mental activity and therefore more 'ums' and 'ahs').

It seems that when people talk about what has happened to them in their lives, sometimes they try to be very accurate in their account, painfully accurate at times, but on other occasions their primary goal is quite different. Here they may be much more liberal with the facts; their goal is to entertain you, to keep you amused and interested, in effect to tell a good story. And, of course, when people are being entertaining they may change critical details of the account, and generally distort the truth, to make a better story. But how can you really tell a genuine story from one that has been changed to make it more entertaining? Nicole Dudukovic and her colleagues Elizabeth Marsh and Barbara Tversky from Stanford University analysed this by asking participants in an experiment to retell a story that they had read about a bartender's hectic life and either to make the story as accurate as possible, or to retell it to make it amusing and entertaining. In other words, they looked at how people retold a story with essentially different goals. Dudukovic and her colleagues analysed the retellings using something called the Linguistic Inquiry and Word Count Program (LIWC), which counts the number of words falling into several different linguistic, emotional and cognitive categories.

They found that the story designed to entertain and amuse contained a higher percentage of verbs in the present tense than the retellings designed to be deadly accurate. For example:

'He *starts* to serve the Martinis' – (*told to entertain*)

rather than

'He *started* to serve the Martinis' – (*accurate retelling*)

The 'entertainment' retellings had a higher proportion of words about the emotional state of the characters than the accurate retellings. For example:

'He walked out because he was angry' – (*told to entertain*)

rather than

'He walked out quickly' – (*accurate retelling*)

The 'entertainment' retellings also used more words indicating tentativeness (words like 'maybe', 'perhaps' and 'guess', as in 'I guess he is a little surprised when this happens'). The retellings with the focus on accuracy also contained more disfluencies like 'um' and 'ah'; these disfluencies reflect higher levels of mental activity (or cognitive difficulty) and show that when a speaker is trying to be as accurate as possible, this is a much more complex task than merely telling an entertaining story and requires time to access accurately the stored memory.

So the next time that someone is telling you bits of their life story and you want to know whether it is accurate, or whether it is being told in a way just to entertain and amuse you, ask yourself the following questions. Is it being told fluently (are there very few 'ums' and 'ahs' in it)? Does it have lots of emotion words in it? Is it in the present tense? And does it have lots of words indicating uncertainty? In Dudukovic and her colleagues' words, 'These are all linguistic devices to hold a reader's attention, in other words, treat it with a pinch of salt, enjoy the story but accept that they really want to entertain and amuse you rather than to tell you what really happened.'

It is, of course, not that surprising that people take a different perspective on a story when they are essentially working on it to entertain another person. They opt for the present tense and want to invite the person that they are talking to into the story by using the immediate present and by telling them about the emotional state of the characters. In other words, they may have to embellish the original story to make it more interesting by imagining what the characters were feeling. This is work that they are having to do to connect with the listener in their story-telling task and despite all of this extra work it seems much more difficult to do the opposite, to try to get the story as accurate as possible, and that is why there are more 'ums' and 'ahs' when this is the primary goal. Of course, this research does not give us such a clear indication about what to do when we are faced with the much more common problem of someone telling us about what happened to them and being accurate one moment and entertaining the next. In this case, would the tense of the verb start to change? But if it did, surely we would spot the tense changes? Will there be some contagion effects when the verb starts off in one tense? If the story starts off entertaining (in the present tense), when it gets to the part with the focus on accuracy will it stay in the present tense? And similarly with all the emotional words – once you have started being explicit about how people feel, how easy is it to change, to start ignoring the emotional state? These are much more complicated questions, and we simply don't know the answer to these yet. In the meantime, this study gives us some idea of the kinds of features that we should look out for.

- If a story about an event that took place in the past is reported in the present tense, it is more likely to be *false* than if the past tense is used

- If a story about an event that took place in the past has lots of 'ums' and 'ahs' in it, it is more likely to be *true* than one that is more fluent

- If a story about an event that took place in the past has lots of emotion words in it, then it is more likely to be *false* than one with fewer emotion words

- Many people embellish their stories to be entertaining. Don't treat them too harshly

How to tell if someone is interested in you while they are laughing

If you want to tell if someone is physically interested in you while you are chatting with them, but you are overwhelmed by the sheer number of body-language (non-verbal) and speech signals coming your way, then you need to learn to focus your attention more on some of the most relevant signals. Try to concentrate on their behaviour carefully during their periods of laughter. Laughter is an easy signal to spot, but because of its essential ambiguity – after all, we laugh both *at* and *with* others, it can be both a very bonding and a very divisive signal – it tends to be accompanied by a number of other body-language signals which can be highly revealing. These other non-verbal signals that accompany laughter essentially disambiguate it. The signals are different for men and women. Women who are sexually interested in a man tend to have more open-arm and open-leg positions during laughter, than those who are not sexually interested. Men who are sexually interested in a woman tend to show more head tilts and forward leaning during laughter, than those who are not. So the next time you are flirting with someone, focus in on their behaviours when they are laughing and look out for these particular features.

The science behind all of this starts from the assumption that laughter is a complex, but ambiguous, social signal. In different situations (and in the *same* situation at *different* times), laughter can have very different social meanings, ranging from the aggressive to the seductive. It is also a signal that is crucial to courtship, a form of interaction fraught with anxiety and nervousness (for many people) as well as a great deal of fun. So how can we tell what a particular laugh means during courtship?

A good deal has been written about the courtship rituals of men and women. Much of the signalling of sexual interest is executed with subtle and silent non-verbal signals rather than explicit verbal signals like 'I like you a lot at this point in time . . . actually I am liking you more at this precise moment . . . oh! . . . it's changing again'. Since these non-verbal signals are not explicit, any invitations signalled non-verbally can be withdrawn without causing affront. It has been suggested that in any competitive situation where males are subject to competition by other males, they use non-verbal signals that are immediate and fast (because they are in competition and they want to get their signals in first) and males often tend to go in for a degree of over-presentation of themselves. Females, on the other hand, it is argued, use more subtle non-verbal signals than men, because they want to attract interested parties in a non-explicit way. The way that this is accomplished, according to Karl Grammer, is through 'the use of composite signals in which signals of avoidance and solicitation are mixed together, as in a coy smile'. Grammer focused on the signals that accompany laughter because, in his view, laughter is especially interesting as it is hard to miss, and yet potentially extremely ambiguous. Its meaning in a sexual context can range from extreme interest ('he laughed me all the way into bed') to extreme derision ('you want me to go on a date with you? Ho! Ho! I'm out of your league').

Grammer analysed students meeting each other for the first time. He filmed them and analysed every single laugh and every bodily movement that accompanied each of these individual laughs. He also asked the students to rate their interest in their conversational partner as well as their ratings of the attractiveness of the other person.

So what did his study reveal about the not-so-silent language of laughter? It showed that females laughed significantly more than men in conversation, and that, perhaps not surprisingly, females had their legs open less frequently than men. But what was interesting was the non-verbal behaviour of the males and the females when they were interested in the other person. Grammer found that a female who is very interested in her conversational partner, 'typically turned and tilted her head away from the male. She leaned back and had her trunk turned away from the male. Both arms were open, i.e., there was a visible angle between arms and body, and her hands touched her body, usually in the region between hips and chin. Her legs were open to a visible angle.' In the case of the males who are interested in their partner, when that partner turns away, 'He leans forward and has his trunk turned toward the female. He has his elbows lifted so that his arms are in at an angle of approximately 90 degrees to his trunk and his hands folded behind his neck. At the same time, his arms are either held by the wrist or the palm, supported by his head or other hand. His hands touch his arms and his legs are crossed but open.'

Grammer carried out this very detailed description for every possible combination of interest on the part of one or both conversational partners. His general conclusions were that the more open the female posture (arms open plus legs open versus arms or legs open), the higher the level of interest in the man (but only when the woman was being watched). For men this did not hold true: there was no simple additive effect of openness in their case. He also found that women moved more during laughter than men. They made five to six movements per laughter sequence, whereas men only made four. In other words, women do much more active signalling during laughter than men. In the case of men, the two movements which most reliably reflected high interest were the 'head tilt' and the 'trunk lean forward'. Tilting the head is usually associated with a signal of submissiveness and this may be the male way of saying that they are prepared to play a less dominant role during a courtship sequence because they are sexually interested in the female. The trunk lean forward seems to be a reliable indicator of general sexual interest.

So the next time there is some laughter in a bar or restaurant, look out for the accompanying movements because it is they, rather than the laughter itself, which is crucial. Men need to look out for arm and leg openness and especially for both together. Women need to look out for the head tilt and the forward lean. These would seem to be the proven signals of genuine physical interest during the mating game.

This is an interesting and detailed study that moves beyond anecdote and example. The main limitation, however, is that it focuses exclusively on pairs of individuals when they are meeting for the first time. It therefore tells us nothing about how these signals of sexual interest change across encounters as the relationship gets more intimate. Are these signals still the main ones as the relationship develops? What is interesting about the Grammer study is that it gives those trying to decode the signals of physical interest a more manageable task. It identifies laughter as one of the main aspects of getting to know someone and it gives you hints as to what to look out for during these detectable behaviour sequences – if you are not carried away by the joke that is.

- Laughter is a very important social signal in courtship

- It is not necessarily the laughter itself that is the most revealing signal, but the non-verbal behaviours that accompany it

- Non-verbal behaviours essentially 'disambiguate' laughter

- Women who find men attractive show more arm and leg openness during their laughter

- Men who find women attractive show more head tilt (a sign of submissiveness), and forward lean, during their laughter

How to tell a fake smile from a genuine smile

Genuine smiles are signs of positive emotion and fake smiles are not. A fake smile is the commonest mask that people use in their everyday life to cover their real emotional state, which might well be negative. There are a number of distinct differences between a genuine smile and a masking smile that allow you to identify whether a smile is real or fake. In the case of genuine smiles, people smile with both their eyes and mouth; in fake smiles they smile just with their mouth. Genuine smiles are more symmetrical on both sides of the face than fake smiles and genuine smiles have a much more gradual onset and offset than fake smiles. The simplest way to tell a genuine smile from a fake smile is to watch a smile fade, to see how quickly it leaves the face. If the smile leaves the face quickly, it is almost certainly fake. People use fake smiles to cover their real emotional state, so if you want to discover what someone is really feeling when they are showing a fake smile, then pay close attention to the very brief micro-expression of emotion revealed as the fake smile abruptly leaves the face. That micro-expression will tell you all you need to know about how they are really feeling.

The basis of this advice is rooted in the underlying physiology of emotional expression. Smiles are very effective social signals. We smile in order to create bonds with other people and to make a favourable impression on those around us. True smiles reflecting positive emotions and false smiles covering negative emotions can be distinguished in a number of ways. These differences were first described by the French anatomist Duchenne de Boulogne. Duchenne (1862) described how genuine smiles involve the facial musculature around the eyes (the *orbicularis oculi*), whereas false smiles just involve the activation of the muscles around the mouth (the *zygomaticus major*). Paul Ekman and Wallace Friesen (1982) agreed with Duchenne's basic classification, and they went on to describe the differences between the two types of smile in the following terms: in genuine smiles the muscles lift the cheek upwards and push the skin towards the eyes, narrowing the eyes and causing crowsfeet wrinkles at the outer corners of the eyes. In false smiles, on the other hand, the muscles pull the lips obliquely upwards and back deepening the furrows running from the nostril to the lip corner (genuine smiles have been termed *Duchenne smiles* in honour of the work of the great French anatomist).

False smiles can be very frequent in many types of daily social interaction. We can see this perhaps most clearly when we have a video recording of interaction so that we can play the smiles back. For example, I carried out an analysis of the relative frequency of genuine and false smiles at the start of the 2002 series of reality TV show *Big Brother* for which I was the resident psychologist. As contestants entered the house full of excitement and anticipation to greet their fellow housemates who they had to live with for several months, I discovered that two-thirds of all the smiles were false. False smiles in this context were being used to mask the nervousness and uncertainty of the housemates, as well as their immediate emotional response to the people that they would be living with. The easiest way of identifying (or reading) their actual negative emotion was to look out for their very brief micro-expressions as the false smiles faded. This was very informative.

Is it important what kind of smile you show in everyday social interactions? All smiles might seem like pleasant social signals, but do they have the same impact? This is what Marc Mehu, Anthony Little and Robin Dunbar (2007) examined. They showed participants a range of male and female faces displaying either a Duchenne or a non-Duchenne smile. The participants had to rate each of the faces on ten dimensions:

'attractiveness'
'generosity'
'trustworthiness'
'competitiveness'
'health'
'agreeableness'
'conscientiousness'
'extroversion'
'neuroticism'
'openness to experience'

The analysis revealed that the type of smile had a significant impact on social judgement and particularly on judgements of *extroversion* and *generosity*. But one of the more surprising results of the study is that the type of smile did not affect judgements of *trustworthiness*. Indeed, pictures of people showing a false smile did not result in their being judged as any less trustworthy (so genuine and false smiles cannot be discriminated by people in this regard, at least from a photograph). But the two types of smiles do seem to have an impact on social judgement. Those who display genuine smiles are seen as more 'generous' and more 'extroverted', in other words, more sociable generally. Research has also shown that it is hard not to reciprocate a smile and when people show us a genuine smile, it is hard not to respond in kind. Smiling also affects our own emotional state and makes us feel good, which is why we like people with natural, genuine smiles.

It is clear that we warm to people who display genuine smiles, but the results of this study by Mehu and his colleagues seem a little inconclusive because it would intuitively seem to be the case that anyone who uses false smiles frequently might well be perceived as untrustworthy. But this study did not allow participants to see the habitual use of false smiles. They merely judged the face on one exposure and participants were asked to rate photographs rather than to rate video clips, where the full dynamic features of the smile would be apparent. The participants did not get the opportunity to take into account the abrupt onset and offset times which are the most obvious and salient features of the false smile. If the experiment were to be repeated using video clips, then we might well see that false smiles really do affect the judgement of trustworthiness as well as some of the other social judgements.

- Genuine smiles of positive emotion involve the muscles around the eyes. False smiles do not involve the muscles around the eyes

- Genuine smiles are more symmetrical on the face than false smiles

- Genuine smiles have a gradual onset and decline. False smiles start and stop very abruptly

- False smiles are used to mask negative emotion. To see underneath the mask, look out for the micro-expression when the false smile has just left the face

- People who display genuine smiles are seen as more sociable and more fun to be with

- It is hard not to reciprocate a genuine smile, and when we smile back it makes us feel good

- Our inner emotional state is affected by our outer non-verbal behaviour, so we feel happier when we smile (even if that smile is brought on as a response to somebody else's smile)

How to read touch

I have to confess that I am not a touch-feely kind of person, except with those very close to me, with whom I am very tactile (too tactile if you ask my embarrassed children who I insist on kissing in public). I am fine with handshakes and kisses on both cheeks (so beloved of celebrities and continental Europe) with colleagues and friends; in other words with the predictable touches of first greeting. But I am awkward when someone pats me on the shoulder in a more spontaneous sort of way, or rubs my arm in appreciation, or worse, when a male work colleague gives me a full bear hug ('Lovely to see you', they say, and I stand there like a wax dummy). I freeze in this situation, my hands hang limply by my side as my colleague rubs my back and

I am expected to reciprocate. This is exactly how one senior executive producer in television that I work with greets everybody on a shoot on the first night, before we get down to business. I wait my turn endlessly (it is a big shoot), watching carefully where everybody else positions their hands, but inevitably embarrassment takes over and I stand there, waiting for the moment to end. I don't know if he can sense my emotional uneasiness – it must be hard not to – but perhaps he thinks that he's reading me all wrong. After all, I am a psychologist; I must be used to hugs.

So what's my problem? Is it basic human intimacy that I'm frightened of, or the control of intimacy (the person doing the original touch is clearly exerting a form of control), or is it something about the ambiguity of touch as a social signal? Is it just too ambiguous a signal, too open to misinterpretation, too confusing for the likes of me? Does touch, in fact, reliably send any information about emotional state and can you actually learn to read touch by tuning in to it? We know that behaviours like facial expression can send reliable information about emotional state and we know that there are deep-seated and hard-wired cross-cultural similarities in how facial expression communicates emotional information. But what about touch? How does touch actually work?

Humans touch frequently. Touch is a mode of communication absolutely central to humans and is the most developed of our senses at birth. It is used extensively by non-human primates for a whole variety of functions. But how effective is it? And what kinds of emotions are communicated best by touch? Can we learn to read touch and interpret different emotional messages from the way another person touches us? Matthew Hertenstein and his colleagues of DePauw University carried out a series of studies in which they asked participants (deliberately and consciously) to communicate a variety of emotions through touch. These included the six core emotions which we know can be reliably communicated by facial expression, namely:

> *'anger'*
> *'fear'*
> *'happiness'*
> *'sadness'*
> *'disgust'*
> *'surprise'*

As well as three pro-social emotions connected with cooperation and altruism:

> *'love'*
> *'gratitude'*
> *'sympathy'*

Plus three self-focused emotions:

> *'embarrassment'*
> *'pride'*
> *'envy'*

The researchers asked the person doing the touching (the sender) to consider how they wanted to communicate each particular emotion and then to touch the other participant's (the receiver's) bare arm 'from the elbow to the end of the hand to signal each emotion, using any form of touch he or she deemed appropriate'. The two participants were separated by a black curtain and the receiver could not see their arm being touched, nor could they see the person doing the touching; they were also unaware of the sex of the sender. The participant who was being touched was then given a response sheet with thirteen basic options:

'anger'
'disgust'
'fear'
'happiness'
'sadness'
'surprise'
'sympathy'
'embarrassment'
'love'
'envy'
'pride'
'gratitude'
'none of these terms are correct'

The first analysis revealed that neither the sex of the person doing the touching nor the sex of the person being touched affected their ability either to send or receive touch information. Moreover, contrary to what is normally found in the communication of emotion, women were not significantly better at sending information through touch, or significantly better at reading the touch information.

The researchers also found that the emotions that were reliably transmitted through touch were *disgust* (which was the highest at 63% accuracy), followed by *anger* and *sympathy* (57%), then *gratitude* (55%) and finally *fear* and *love* (51%). *Happiness* and *surprise* (two of the core emotions), along with *embarrassment*, *envy* and *pride* (the three 'self-social' emotions) were not reliably sent via touch.

The researchers also filmed all of the types of touch and found that each of the emotions were associated with a different pattern of movement.

EMOTION	ASSOCIATED MOVEMENT
Disgust	Pushing
	Lifting
	Tapping
Anger	Hitting
	Squeezing
	Trembling
Sympathy	Patting
	Stroking
	Rubbing
Gratitude	Shaking
	Lifting
	Squeezing
Love	Stroking
	Finger interlocking
	Rubbing
Fear	Trembling
	Squeezing
	Shaking
Sadness	Stroking
	Squeezing
	Lifting

Some of these patterns were very similar. For example, *anger* and *fear* had two elements in common ('trembling' and 'squeezing') and only differed in the way that *anger* contained a 'hitting' element, whereas *fear* contained 'shaking'. The researchers found that *sadness* was often misinterpreted as *sympathy*. The average duration of the touch signalling *anger* was 4.5 seconds whereas *fear* tended to be longer at 6.5 seconds. The longest touch of all seemed to be associated with *love* at 9.5 seconds and the shortest was *disgust* at 3.8 seconds. This all intuitively makes some sense – when you are signalling love, you are signalling that you want to be with someone, and when you are signalling disgust you want to be away from the object of disgust as quickly as possible. The emotion associated with the most intense behaviours was *anger* with 54.5% of the movements being of strong intensity, followed by *fear* with 40.1%. The emotion associated with the lightest of touches was *sadness* with 18% of the movements having a light touch.

This study thus seemed to show that we can communicate several different types of emotional state through touch and that touch does much more than simply communicate whether one's feelings are positive or negative. The accuracy rates for sending and receiving emotional information through touch are quite similar to those that have been observed with facial expression and this suggests that touch is a channel of communication which is well adapted to be a strong emotional signal. It is often thought that touch is one of the more ambiguous channels of communication, but this study suggests that by considering the type of movement, the duration of the movement and the intensity of the movement, we can reliably interpret what emotional state someone wishes to convey. In terms of the core emotions, anger, fear, disgust and sadness can be communicated via touch, but happiness, sadness and surprise are much harder to send. Pro-social emotions like love, gratitude and sympathy can also be reliably transmitted, whereas self-focused emotions like embarrassment, envy and gratitude cannot.

This is novel research into how touch communicates, but which also has its limitations. The study only considered people intentionally trying to communicate an emotion through touch; it wasn't concerned with the spontaneous display of emotions as they are actually felt. In comparable studies of facial expression, intentional communication can lead to the exaggeration of the display. Would the emotional states have been communicated so reliably if the intention to communicate had been removed? In the experiment the receivers were given a checklist of possible emotions. So, for example, when they had to identify *love*, they simply had to distinguish it from other possible emotions like *sympathy*, which also involved stroking and rubbing. But of course they didn't have to distinguish it from 'lust' or 'sexual attraction'. In other words, if the questions asked had been more open-ended some of these results might well have changed. So touch might not be such a reliable signal after all. These are major issues and I still think that it is why some people (including myself) like to avoid it at all costs in many situations.

- Touch can communicate *some* core emotions, when the touch is consciously being used to send the emotional message

- Neither the sex of the person doing the touching, nor the sex of the person being touched, affects the ability to either send or receive the information in touch

- Some core emotions ('disgust', 'anger', 'fear', 'sadness') can be reliably sent through touch, when touch is consciously being used to send the emotional message

- Some core emotions (like 'happiness' and 'surprise') cannot be reliably sent through touch, even when the touch message is consciously being sent

- Self-focused emotions (like 'embarrassment', 'pride' and 'envy') cannot be sent reliably through touch

- Pro-social emotion (like 'love', 'gratitude' and 'sympathy') can be sent reliably through consciously directed touch

- When it comes to touch, many different emotions show similar behavioural features

- The *spontaneous* communication of emotion by touch (i.e. communication without conscious intent) might be much more ambiguous, and much less reliable, than the kinds of touch so far studied

How to use your gut instinct

The most effective way of using your gut instinct is to remember one very simple thing about how we use it. We are more prone to rely on gut feeling when we are in a happy mood than when we are in a sad mood (and we are more likely to use slower, more rational, decision-making when we are sad than when we are happy). In other words, never be persuaded that gut instinct is somehow always better than slower, more rational, decision-making just because it feels 'right'. It's more likely to feel 'right' when you're in a certain type of mood. When people are happy they are more likely to make a judgement about something based on their gut reaction and nothing more. When they are sad they are more likely to think carefully about the pros and cons of each option and weigh things up slowly and deliberately. When people are in a happy mood, if you force them to use the slow deliberate strategy they like the outcome less than when they are allowed to rely on their gut feelings. And when people are in a sad mood, if you force them to use gut feelings, they also like the outcome less. This is clearly a worrying tendency because mood is affected by a whole series of things which may not be connected with the decision itself, like what you had for breakfast, what your partner said to you and whether your computer is or isn't working.

So how can you make the best decision using your gut instincts? The answer is that you need to be aware that this is something that is naturally affected by mood state. So when you are trying to make a decision always be mindful of mood, and reflect that the type of decision strategy you use needs to be determined more by the problem in hand than by the way you feel. If you don't consciously override your psychological state, then you may make decisions based on an erroneous strategy and this could lead to the wrong conclusion.

De Vries and her colleagues at Radboud University in Nijmegen asked what happens if you break this connection between mood state and decision-making strategy. How would people feel about the decisions they had made? They changed people's mood state by asking them to watch either a happy or sad film and then participants were instructed to decide between two objects either deliberately ('think of the pros and cons . . . take your time') or quickly ('based on your first feelings, please indicate which you prefer'). After they did this they had to rate how valuable they thought the object was. What the researchers found was that when mood state matched the decision strategy, the estimated price was judged to be significantly higher than when mood state did not fit with the decision strategy. In other words, if you make a choice based upon your gut feelings when you are in a happy mood, or after slowly and carefully thinking of the pros and cons when you are in a sad mood, this leads you to estimate the value to be higher for the object that you have chosen. So the degree of congruence between your mood and the type of decision-making that you have used has implications for how you judge the outcome of the whole process. This in some ways is a worrying tendency which shows that there is not just a relationship between mood state and the type of decision you make but if you are explicitly forced to break the relationship, this affects what you think about the outcome of the decision. This is a result with implications for how we should conduct our lives, in that we clearly shouldn't allow mood state to have an impact on the kind of decisions we make in this way. The major shortcoming of this study is that it just used the one domain, i.e. the choice between different objects. Clearly it would be very useful to know how general or widespread this result is.

- Our mood state affects the kinds of decision-making strategies that we like to use

- People are more inclined to make a gut response to something when they are in a happy mood

- People are more prone to careful decision-making, and weighing up the pros and cons of a course of action, when they are in a sad mood

- We like the outcome of any decision less when we are forced to use the decision-making strategy which does not align itself naturally with our mood state

- Be aware of your mood when you have an important decision to make

- A 'gut response' isn't always the correct one, but it may well feel right in many situations (i.e. happy ones)

How to spot the Pinocchio effect

Carlo Collodi may really have had something when he penned *The Adventures of Pinocchio*. Research has now demonstrated that your nose does actually grow longer when you tell an intentional lie. The mechanism is based on the biochemistry of the brain; when you lie, chemicals known as catecholamines are released in the brain, causing tissue inside the nose to swell and blood pressure to increase. This increased blood pressure inflates the nose ever so slightly but very importantly it causes the nerve endings in the nose to tingle. The slight increase in the size of the nose through swelling could never be detected without specialist apparatus, but people's overt behaviour is much more obvious. People will sometimes scratch their nose briskly (although there may be other more reliable behavioural cues, as we will see) when they are lying. The reason they are doing this is to relieve the tingling sensation caused by the engorging of the nasal tissue. So the next time someone rubs their nose briskly when having a conversation with you, you should be on your guard. Just think 'Pinocchio'.

- Tissue in the nose can swell when we tell a lie, as a result of the release of catecholamines in the brain

- Sometimes rubbing the nose, in order to relieve the tingling sensation, can be an indication of deceit

- 'The Pinocchio effect' is, at best, an extremely subtle cue and should never be relied on too much (except maybe for fun)

How to read a mind

You can read someone's mind by examining the spontaneous hand movements they make when they talk. These movements are generated unconsciously and they are not under the same control that speech is under. So they can provide a genuine insight into what someone is thinking. For example, if your partner is telling you how close they are feeling to you, notice how far apart their hands are while they are talking about the two of you. If they are spontaneously gesturing, they will almost certainly use one hand to represent themselves and the other to represent you in the gestural space in front of the body. 'You and I get on so well.' Watch for the gestures. 'We were made for each other.' 'I feel really close to you.' Keep watching the accompanying gestural movements. The critical clue here is the distance between the hands signalling 'you' and 'I'. The closer the hands are together in that gestural space, the better a sign it is for the intimacy of the relationship. The greater the distance between the hands then the less close your partner feels to you, regardless of what they actually say in their speech. So if they are saying that they feel really close to you at the present time, but their gesturing hands are actually quite a distance apart, what they are saying is almost certainly not true and what you have just observed is a gesture–speech mismatch. This particular type of gesture is called a 'metaphoric' gesture because it is being used to represent an abstract concept, namely psycho-logical intimacy. When you spot a mismatch like this, focus on the spontaneous unconscious gesture, not on the speech itself. The gestures reveal what the speaker is really thinking. However, never make a rash decision about the future of a relationship based upon just one gesture, or even a few gestures in quick succession. Just bear in mind the information contained within those unconsciously generated movements, as you talk about the quality and depth (or otherwise) of your relationship and its possible long-term future (or imminent demise).

- Spontaneous hand gestures are largely unconscious, and can act as a window on the human mind

- Try to notice when these movements do not match the speech that they are accompanying. These are 'gesture–speech' mismatches and they can be highly revealing

- The hands don't lie to nearly the same extent as we do when we speak

How to interpret the language of the feet

A number of psychologists have argued that the feet are one of the most revealing channels of non-verbal communication. The feet can reveal a great deal about the personality of an individual. They can tell us about the relationship of the individual with the person they are talking to and they can even indicate the individual's underlying emotional and psychological state.

One reason why the feet are so informative is that they are the part of the human body from which we have the least internal feedback. In other words, people may know what their facial expression is (I know, for example, that I am smiling slightly as I write this). People will often be aware that their hands are moving (although they may not know what complex images their hands are mapping out), but they will often have no idea as to whether their feet are even moving or not (and if they are moving in particular ways).

The movements of the feet were studied in detail thirty years ago by Susan Frances who was then at the University of Chicago.

She has studied many forms of non-verbal behaviour, including the foot movements of people who were just getting to know one another. She discovered that men and women moved their feet differently in response to social situations. She took a large number of measures, including the time spent moving the feet, the average duration of foot movements and the duration of the longest foot movements. She found that for men, all of these measures decreased as they became more familiar with a social situation, whereas for women, they significantly increased. In other words, when men are put in a situation where they have to talk to someone for the first time, they display their nervousness and anxiety through their foot movements. They control those areas of non-verbal behaviour over which they have most control, like their facial expression but, since they have less feedback on what their feet are doing, they allow their feet to display their nervousness. Women, on the other hand, despite the basic neurobiology of the feedback from the feet, inhibit the movement from their feet in the nervous first encounter; only when they become more comfortable in a situation do they allow the feet 'to discharge accrued nervous energy through body activity'.

Forty years ago, Paul Ekman, one of the leading American psychologists of deception, suggested that foot movement could potentially be an important indicator of the anxiety associated with telling a lie on the basis that foot movement is sometimes hard to control. But numerous studies since have suggested just the opposite. As with hand movement, foot movement actually decreases when people are lying; the reason for this is that people seem unconsciously to attempt to control any parts of the body which may reflect nervousness or anxiety while they are lying.

There seems to be a general dampening down of behaviours. Aldert Vrij and Gün Semin analysed beliefs about behavioural clues to deception in several samples of ordinary people as well as professional groups who might be thought to have special skills and experience in this area (police officers, prison guards and customs officers). They also included a sample of prisoners in the study who the psychologist thought might be particularly skilled at both telling lies and reading lies. The researchers found that, as in previous research, both the professionals and non-professionals associated lying with an increase of general bodily movement, including foot movement. Interestingly the prisoners had the highest accuracy rating among all of the groups (customs officers and police detectives came out joint bottom, even lower than the student group).

So if you want to tell if someone is lying by the language of their feet, watch them moving their feet and then monitor their movements carefully during the critical phase to look for signs of behavioural inhibition.

The question of the relationship between bodily behaviour, including leg movement, and personality was examined in detail by Robert Gifford from the University of Victoria in British Columbia. He used a number of different personality attributes (dominance, warmth, extroversion and arrogance) and analysed how a whole range of behaviours connected to these attributes, including head orientation, nods, object manipulation, leg lean and leg movement. What was especially interesting was that there appeared to be a significant set of relationships between the frequency of the leg movements and the underlying personality, such that the main personality factors that seem to affect frequency of leg movements are extroversion and introversion. Extroverts are essentially social creatures who need the company of others to be at their best, whereas introverts prefer to be on their own. Introverts showed a much higher frequency of leg movement than extroverts and aloof extroverts showed the highest frequency. The second personality group that showed a very low frequency of leg movements were the ambitious dominant group. The gregarious extrovert group showed very low levels of leg movement because they were very comfortable in interaction and felt no need to control or inhibit this small bodily motion. The ambitious dominant group had a low level of frequency for quite a different reason; these were people who liked to dominate a conversation, and part of that controlling strategy was to control the signals they send. They inhibit foot movement because it gives too much information away when they are trying to take control of a conversation.

The role of non-verbal signals including the movement of the feet and legs in flirting was studied by Karl Grammer from the Max Planck Institute in Germany (we have heard about Grammer's work already). He studied the non-verbal behaviours that accompany laughter between couples who are trying to get to know each other. He focused on laughter because some people take it as an obvious sign that things are going well, but it is no such thing as we have already seen. It is a highly ambiguous signal with a range of meanings, from intense interest to intense disinterest (and derision). Grammer argued that it is not laughter itself that is the powerful signal; it is the behaviours that accompany it. So he filmed a large group of couples getting to know each other and he analysed their behaviour and they scored their sexual interest in the other person. For women, the most obvious and reliable sign that they were sexually interested in their partner while they were laughing was their open-leg posture (and their foot movement away from their body). Indeed for women, the more open their posture (legs open and arms open) the more sexually interested they were. For men it simply didn't work like this. Men's sexual interest was indicated by two signals, neither of which involved the feet, namely the head tilt (which is normally a sign of submission) and by the male leaning forward. It is almost as if men are prepared to present themselves as submissive in order to get a woman to like them when there is strong sexual interest on their part.

The silent language of the feet is a fascinating topic because the feet can be so revealing. They can reveal our inner anxieties and when we lie we learn, probably from an early age, to inhibit their telltale messages. Although extraordinarily, both college students and experienced lie detectors consistently look for an increased frequency as a reliable factor of lying, when what they should be looking for is exactly the opposite. The foot movements also appear to be linked to underlying personality in that extroverts and dominant individuals (for quite different reasons) show fewer foot movements in interaction. When it comes to sexual relations, foot movements seem to be particularly important for women and the feet and legs, in subtle ways, spell out their messages when they are sexually interested in a male partner. The feet appear to do this subtly and unconsciously in the interactions of everyday life.

- Generally speaking, we have little internal feedback about what our feet are doing in social interaction

- People tend to inhibit their foot movements when they lie

- Men display their nervousness through their foot movement when meeting someone new

- Women tend to use foot movement to get rid of nervous energy only when they know someone a little better

- Foot movements are also affected by personality characteristics

- Introverts move their feet more than extroverts

- Dominant people show lower levels of foot movement in conversation than less dominant individuals

3. MOOD: UPPERS AND DOWNERS

'The secret of life is never to have an emotion
that is unbecoming.'

Oscar Wilde, *A Woman of No Importance* (1893)

How to get yourself out of a bad mood

My mother was sometimes prone to dark moods and she was hard to shift out of them. My father had died in his early fifties and she was alone and widowed in her forties. 'How do you expect me to be?' she would say, rationalizing her demeanour. She didn't seem to have any successful mechanism or strategy to change her mood. There would be a blackness in the small, claustrophobic family home that was almost unbearable. It could last for days.

It seems that when people are in a bad mood, they tend, quite naturally and instinctively, to use a variety of strategies to get themselves out of this bad mood (things that they have used in the past often without much thought or analysis). The problem is that, according to the latest psychological research, many of these tactics simply don't work. Some involve the individuals actually going out and doing something; others involve the person concerned doing very little. Some are primarily about the individual trying to distract themselves from their current situation; while others involve trying to redirect their thoughts. Some are really quite basic and straightforward, and you can see the obvious reasoning behind them; things like 'going out for a drink', 'having sex' or even 'going shopping', all mildly distracting in their own way, but how effective are they in actually changing mood state? It seems that people will try all sorts of things to get out of a bad mood, particularly things that they quite enjoy anyway. The problem here is that most people have strategies that they typically rely upon without ever evaluating what works and what doesn't.

So what does actually work when you are in a bad mood? It turns out that the best strategy is one that works simultaneously on your body and on your mind, allows you to relax and helps reduce your stress, but, in addition, also allows you to step back and think about the situation in a new way. The most effective strategy is also one that allows you to put your feelings into perspective. Therefore, it's quite simple – all you need to do is to find a form of behaviour that allows you to do all of this at the same time.

Research was conducted by Robert Thayer, Robert Newman and Tracey McClain of California State University, who identified thirty-five different behaviours that people typically engage in to get themselves out of a bad mood. These thirty-five behaviours fall into six different groups, as follows:

Active Mood Management
- Various relaxation techniques
- Stress-management activities
- Putting one's feelings into perspective
- Evaluating or analysing the situation
- Exercise
- Taking a shower
- Having a bath or just splashing water over yourself
- Controlling one's thoughts
- Having sex
- The use of humour
- Engaging in self-gratification

Seeking Pleasurable
Activities and Distraction
{
Engaging in alternative pleasant activities
Using humour (again)
Spending time on a hobby
Listening to music
Changing location
Avoiding a thing or person
Controlling one's thoughts

Passive Mood
Management
{
Watching TV
Drinking coffee
Having something to eat
Having a rest
Having a nap or going to sleep
Going shopping

Social Support,
Ventilation and
Gratification
{
Telephoning a friend
Talking to someone or being with someone
Engaging in emotional activity, for example
    crying or screaming
Smoking
Eating
Avoiding a thing or a person

Direct Tension Reduction
{
Using drugs, including alcohol,
    smoking or drinking coffee
Having sex (which clearly falls into several of the
categories)

Withdrawal–Avoidance
{
Trying to be alone
Avoiding a thing or a person
Engaging in emotional activity,
    for example crying or screaming

These six factors differ in a number of critical ways. *Active Mood Management* is an attempt to control the bad mood, and includes behaviours designed to reduce tension by engaging in various relaxation behaviours and stress-management techniques. It is also designed to enhance energy levels by, for example, engaging in exercise. But importantly this factor also contains behaviours designed to produce changes in the pattern of thinking (e.g. by putting one's feelings into perspective and by evaluating or analysing the situation). *Seeking Pleasurable Activities and Distraction* is all about engaging in behaviours that may distract the person from the bad mood. *Passive Mood Management* involves fairly passive activities like watching TV, drinking coffee and eating. The only non-passive behaviour within this group might appear to be 'going shopping', which might *seem* like a more active process. But Thayer says that this is illusory: 'Regarding the assumed passive nature of shopping, analyses of the item grouping may provide an important observation about the motivation underlying this behaviour. The factor grouping suggests that the motivation is the same as that involved with watching TV, resting, or eating.' *Social Support, Ventilation and Gratification* is concerned with attempts to elicit social support, but can also be a device for letting off steam and 'ventilating' emotion. *Direct Tension Reduction* is solely concerned with dealing with the tension aspect of the bad mood. *Withdrawal–Avoidance* is about being alone and avoiding people and crying or screaming while alone.

Thayer and his colleagues analysed each of these techniques by getting the participants themselves to rate the effectiveness of each of the strategies. The researchers found that *Active Mood Management* was the most effective set of techniques, and that men tended to use this strategy more frequently than women. Interestingly, the professional women in their sample used this strategy more than any other group (professional people generally tended to use this strategy more than other occupational or social groups). The second most effective set of behaviours was *Seeking Pleasurable Activities and Distraction* and again men used this strategy more than women (and again professionals more than other groups). The least successful strategy in terms of the self-ratings was *Direct Tension Reduction* (using drugs, alcohol or having sex to get out of a bad mood). Men were more likely to do this than women, but it was only half as effective as the *Active Mood Management* strategy.

Throughout the analyses there were striking differences in the strategies employed by men and women to elevate their mood. Women were more likely to cry or scream in order to feel better. They were also more likely to eat, go shopping or talk to someone. Men were more likely to get heavily involved in their own particular hobby, use humour, have sex or attempt to control their thoughts. Professional people were more likely to use humour or have sex to elevate their mood. Few in the sample of professional people just cried or screamed to lift them out of their bad mood. Extroverts were more likely to go shopping; introverts were more likely to try to be alone.

The researchers also asked a sample of psychotherapists to evaluate the mood-change strategies that people used in their everyday life. The psychotherapists concluded that the *Active Mood Management* and *Seeking Pleasurable Activities and Distraction* were the two most effective strategies and *Direct Tension Reduction* the least successful, thus essentially mirroring the results of the respondents themselves.

The researchers also focused on individual behaviours contained within the six categories, to determine which was the single most effective behaviour to get people out of a bad mood. Their conclusion was that the single most effective behaviour to alleviate a bad mood is exercise. The second most effective single behaviour for elevating your mood is listening to music, which is a little bit counter-intuitive because you might think that talking to friends might work best. The things to avoid when in a bad mood are trying to be alone and simply avoiding the person or thing that was responsible for the bad mood. Similarly, eating and watching TV are not good options. So the next time that you are in a bad mood and you want to do something about it, get your iPod on and go for a run.

However, what is always surprising with a study like this is the range of different things that people do when confronted by the same psychological event, in this case being in a bad mood. This study suggests that some things work and some things don't, although it doesn't seem to stop people doing them. The answer is perhaps very simple. Exercise works well because it produces natural endorphins, which give you a natural high that can be repeated as often as you like because it doesn't have the same kind of harmful biological effect as other things, like drugs. But exercise doesn't just make you feel good inside, it also makes you feel good about yourself because you have achieved something. It is good for your self-esteem. It also requires a degree of focus and this is a good way of redirecting and changing your thinking away from the thing that has put you in the bad mood in the first place. Music works because carefully selected music can prime positive memories; it brings happy memories to the fore.

Of course, the one problem with Thayer's research is that it asks people to rate the relative success of the behaviours they actually use in their everyday lives. There is always the possibility that they would have found other behaviours to be even more effective if they had used them instead. And what happens if exercise doesn't work for you, no matter how much you persevere? The problem with studies like this is it tends to give you the average effectiveness of different behaviours for elevating mood. There must be some significant trends contained within the overall picture linked to personality differences. But in the meantime, try exercise; it works best for most people.

This is the strategy that I use. Of course, if I had suggested to my mother that she should also go for a run to help get herself out of a bad mood, she would have looked at me as if I had gone nuts. My compulsive running, which started when I was about thirteen, was a major issue between us, and, I have to say, the cause of many arguments. Her fundamental belief, so readily expressed, was that 'all that sweating can't be good for you'. 'It's not natural,' she would say, 'just not natural. Look at all that sweat.' I disagreed vehemently, of course. I saw it as the most natural thing in the world, something deep from our evolutionary past and something that made me feel almost high at times. She did find other ways to relax and cheer herself up. She would sit with one of her girlfriends beside the fire and have 'a wee smoke and a wee drink' (that's how she liked to put it).

Smoking and drinking are of more limited use psychologically (and they can end up killing you, which again is a little depressing). How you actually persuade certain people to take up running, however, can be a more complicated issue.

70

- To get themselves out of a bad mood, many people use strategies that simply don't work

- Women are more likely to cry or scream in order to feel better. They are also more likely to eat, go shopping or talk to a friend

- Men are more likely to get heavily involved in their hobby, use humour, have sex or simply attempt to control their thoughts

- To get yourself out of a bad mood effectively you need to both relax and to change your perspective on the problem

- To get yourself out of a bad mood, either do some exercise or put on some music. Both work well

How to stay happy

The best way of staying happy, according to US research (and the fact that it is *American* research may be important to the overall conclusions), is basically never to give up on your dream; keep imagining life for you getting better and better. Consciously and deliberately think about yourself in the future when everything has turned out very well for you. Set aside twenty minutes a day, find a quiet space and think about this carefully. Think of all the good things that you want in life and how things could be for you. This helps you clarify your priorities, your motivations and your values. In addition, you are channelling both your thoughts and your emotions in a particular direction, and this can act as an effective buffer against negative emotions. It will keep you in a happier state.

It turns out that psychologists have made quite a number of recommendations in the past few years about how to enhance mood state, and about how to stay happy. Some of these are activities that can be carried out on a daily basis, like counting one's blessings, carrying out small acts of kindness for other people, imagining oneself at one's best and focusing on personal goals. Kennon Sheldon of the University of Missouri – Columbia and Sonja Lyubomirsky of the University of California selected two mental exercises which they saw as especially promising in this regard: expressing gratitude and visualizing best possible selves. Their theory is that expressing gratitude is likely to work because it involves a range of distinct psychological processes. Firstly, if you habitually express gratitude for what you have got, then you are more likely to appreciate and savour the positive experiences of everyday life. Secondly, by expressing gratitude in this way, you can prevent yourself from taking too many of the good things in life for granted. The third thing is essentially social; by expressing gratitude you are building social bonds with other people. The final thing is that by expressing gratitude you may actually inhibit feelings of envy, bitterness or greed.

The second mental exercise studied was one in which participants were asked consciously to visualize and then write about their 'best possible selves'. The reason that this may work, according to the researchers, is that it allows an individual to 're-structure one's priorities, and to gain better insight into one's motives and emotions'. It also allows the person concerned to clarify their priorities, motivations and values.

In the case of expressing gratitude, what the participants had to do in this study was to 'write about the many things in [their] life, both large and small, that [they] had to be grateful about. These might include particular supportive relationships, sacrifices or contributions that others have made for you, facts about your life such as your advantages and opportunities, or even gratitude for life itself and the world that we live in. In all of these cases you are identifying previously unappreciated aspects of your life, for which you can be thankful.'

In the case of the best possible selves exercise, participants were asked by Sheldon and Lyubomirsky to imagine themselves 'in the future, after everything has gone as well as it possibly could. You have worked hard and succeeded at accomplishing all of your life goals. Think of this as a realization of your life dreams, and of your own best potentials. In all of these cases you are identifying the best possible way that things might turn out in your life, in order to help guide your decisions now'.

It turned out that both of these exercises did produce immediate reductions in negative emotion. In other words, they both worked, but only the 'best possible selves' exercise produced an additional significant increase in positive emotion. Furthermore, those participants who continued with the exercise after the initial session produced the most significant longer-term changes in positive emotion. In respect of these longer-term changes, it was not that the participants became progressively happier, but that their positive emotion didn't drop after the initial exercise, unlike the rest of the sample. In the words of Sheldon and Lyubomirsky, 'exercises such as ours may function more as buffers or sources of resilience than as means of becoming even happier.'

So what is the best way of staying happy over a period of time? The most effective way is to think about yourself in the future when everything has turned out really well for you. You have achieved your goals, you have really succeeded; everything is great. Spend twenty minutes a day for a week doing this and let this simple exercise focus your mind and modify your emotional state. It won't necessarily make you significantly happier over time, but it will stop your level of happiness from declining over time, which itself is a real plus.

It may, of course, seem a little odd to think that simple and deliberate mental exercises can affect our emotional state, and in particular our experience of positive and negative emotion, but this is exactly what can occur. There is a large body of evidence now to suggest that our patterns of thinking have a major influence on our emotional state. (This is not, of course, to deny that the opposite can also occur. Our emotional state can also have a big effect on our thoughts, including how we process and remember information.) Sometimes simple exercises can change the way we feel and that is what this study shows. It analysed the experience of positive and negative emotion separately and showed that both exercises reduced negative emotion, but only one (visualizing best possible selves) improved positive emotion. (It's always odd, by the way, not to think of positive and negative emotion as simply opposite poles on the same continuum. Sometimes an intervention can affect one but not the other, and that is exactly what happened here.) This exercise also keeps happiness levels up over the longer term, acting as a buffer against all those things that can bring us down. One day, these kinds of exercises might be as common as brushing your teeth to protect against tooth decay. Last thing at night, you might brush your teeth and then visualize best possible selves as a sort of physical and mental routine. Both activities are designed to prevent bad things happening. It might seem like an odd idea, but it could just be an odd idea that works.

- Our everyday, mundane thoughts affect our emotional state

- We can work on our everyday thoughts to make ourselves happier

- Keep yourself happy by imagining yourself in the future when everything has gone really well for you

- Remember to express gratitude for all the good things in your life

- After you brush your teeth last thing at night think about all the good things that have happened to you that day. Don't focus, last thing at night, on all the bad things that have happened to you. 'Prime' your positive memories, and you will wake up in the morning feeling happier

How to recall happy childhood memories

I have always found it difficult to recall my happy childhood memories, although I have little trouble recalling many of the very sad ones. Perhaps I come from a particularly sad family in which the balance between happy and sad experiences was not quite right. My father and brother both died suddenly and without any proper goodbyes, and perhaps that was a major part of the problem with what remained of my family and the grief that clung to my mother. My brother died in a climbing accident in the Himalayas when he was barely thirty. My father was fifty-one when he died, twelve and a half years before my brother. He had gone into the Royal Victoria Hospital in Belfast for routine observations. At least that's what he told the family; he didn't even tell us that he was going into hospital until the day before; he didn't want to worry us. My mother and my brother and I visited him the night before his operation. In my last conversation with him, on the Sunday night, I told him that one of my guinea pigs had died. I just blurted it out, as a bit of a joke; maybe something to say to break the emotional tension that I could feel in the ward that night. He looked really saddened; he sat up in bed in his blue striped pyjamas, his glasses moved on his face, falling forward. I couldn't bear it. 'No, I'm only kidding you, Da,' I said laughing, 'I'm only joking, Da. It's only a wee joke.' It was part of my strange repertoire at the time to help people; I would tell someone made-up bad news and then explain to them that it was only a joke, so that I could be responsible for bringing good news their way. The good news was, of course, only good news because of the made-up bad news that had preceded it. After all, telling your father that a guinea pig is still alive is hardly great news in itself. But my father smiled with such relief when I told him; he was so pleased that I wouldn't be upset by any loss. He knew how attached I was to my guinea pigs. The next day he never regained consciousness. He lay in a coma for a week and died the following Sunday. Every day on the way home from school during that fateful week, as the bus made its sharp left at the 'turn-of-the-road', I would glance nervously at my house to see if the blinds were down, my stomach in my mouth. The words I uttered about my Albino guinea pig were the last I ever said to my father.

My mother liked to talk about my father whenever I was home. Her stories about him always began in exactly the same way. 'Do you remember?' she would ask. I would nod in a non-committal sort of way, because the truth was that I no longer really remember many important details about him, but I was too embarrassed and ashamed to say. I think that it was a sort of defensive forgetfulness, a form of repression to ease the pain. But I had heard the stories many times and my father was reborn in them.

But I have mental images of him as well, somewhat disconnected images that don't really add up to a whole, complete person. I remember the way he smiled (but then again I have photographs to remind me), and the way his glasses sat on the end of his nose when he was reading. I remember how he stretched his arms out to put his coat on and how he tugged his cap down on his forehead. I recall the way that he read the paper, the way that he held it, but funnily enough I don't remember what paper he read. After he died we didn't buy a daily paper any more. We were just given papers at the end of the week by a neighbour.

I can, of course, recall vividly the night of his death (too vividly really for my own comfort), and my aunt Agnes being annoyed that nobody had come to pick us up to take us to the hospital to see him. Although I wouldn't have been allowed to see him anyway, as he lay there without sense or feeling (although my mother always said that he knew that she was there beside him, because he used to play with her wedding ring;

she clung on to this idea for many years). I can recall the expression on my aunt's face from that night (even now), and the face of my uncle Terence, who stopped us going into the hospital. I remember the rain that night, and the puddles in the hospital car park. I remember my father resting in his coffin in the front room for the days in which 'he was home', and how ridiculously well he looked, on that white shiny satin, with (I was told) some powder on his face, in the glow of the pink lampshade that seemed to light him up. 'Those colours bring out the best in your da,' my aunt Agnes said to me when they brought him home. 'It's just like he's had a good walk in the fresh air up to the wee shop and down the Ligoniel Road. He loved that walk. He's a handsome man, your father, he always has been.' My mother always said that he looked so good as a corpse because he had died in good health. 'He just had an operation, and didn't come out of it,' she explained. It made quite a lot of sense then; it still does.

I remember certain things about my father, but his voice has faded in my memory. I watched a TV programme the other night in which a hypnotist said that human memory is a bit like a video-recording of life, with all the events stored on some kind of biological spool, waiting to be played over and over again, if you just have the key to unlock it. But I have always thought that this wasn't quite true because no matter how hard I tried I just ended up with fragments of images and events involving my father. I remember an afternoon up the Hightown Road, with me kicking the rugby ball about, him lying there reading his paper, his glasses over the end of his nose, and the smell of the air. I can remember kicking the ball up into the air and chasing it over the ground covered in prickly yellow gorse and loose, sharp brick. I remember feeling the sharp brick through the soles of my thin trainers and then stumbling on a shard of broken glass, which somehow managed to pierce the side of my ankle. My father had to carry me back to the car. I don't remember how his voice sounded or what we talked about that day. I just remember him struggling under my weight, and wheezing with the effort, as he had a bad chest sometimes. I remember that his glasses dropped off on the way back, and that he had to put me down on the wet grass while he picked them up. His glasses fell off a lot, as the frames were loose.

I remember smells from him. I can recall the smell of engine oil, engine oil that's been on the road and seeped into old overalls. His nickname was 'Half-shaft' because he worked as a motor mechanic for the Belfast Corporation at the Falls Road depot. He worked with bus engines and smelt of the oil that they put into buses, even on his days off. I can always remember the smell of those old overalls, weeks between washes. It wasn't unpleasant in any way. For years I liked to pick up oily rags and hold them right up to my nose and to breathe deeply, to breathe him back to life. As Proust knew, smells can be so evocative, like nothing else for recapturing what has been lost. I was caught once by a woman in our street, sniffing an oily rag some time after he died. She thought I was trying to get high on something or other, and she vowed to tell my mother. 'Run away off home,' she said. 'You shouldn't be doing that, that'll get into your lungs, that'll kill you.' After his death, I wanted to keep his clothes as another way of connecting to him. But my mother gave them all away to his brother Jim. Jim had been drinking the day he came to collect them. You could smell the alcohol on him, and he wouldn't come into our house. He waited on the street, too shy or awkward to come in (perhaps shyness was a family trait). He just stood there, red-eyed, waiting for an armful of my father's clothes to be carried out to him.

I wanted to keep something of my father's. I scoured the cupboard above the TV, and found his glasses case in the bottom of a little wicker basket where my mother kept her sewing. The glasses had gone, so I was left with the case. It didn't smell of him, it just smelt of old plastic; and the spring had broken so the case didn't snap shut the way it should have done. I used to just lie on the bed and look at it, trying to conjure up some missing parts of him, but it didn't work. My memories weren't under voluntary control, some bits came back on their own but most stayed hidden, and many were lost.

I can remember Colin, my best friend at the time, shuffling up beside me on the day of the funeral, saying that he was sorry. He had lost his father a few months before so it meant something. Many of us had lost our fathers; maybe that was the source of my prejudice against smoking. I remember Colin telling me afterwards that I never once looked him in the eye on the day of the funeral, or anybody else for that matter. I just kept my eyes on the ground the whole time. I walked behind the coffin without ever looking up. I didn't know what might happen if I let go, even a little. I was a thirteen-year-old boy trying to stay in control of himself.

I can't remember how my father talked or laughed or cried or shouted or cursed – the sounds I mean, the tone and timbre of his voice. But I can see a woman with long tangled hair, an old alcoholic that we boys used to torment, getting into our house the night before the funeral and trying to kiss him in the coffin. I can even recall the way she did this, like a film slowed down. I saw it coming, I could read her intentions. Nobody else seemed to realize what she was doing there at first. 'It's terrible what drink can do to you,' they were all saying, but I knew that she liked my father. She was saying that my father was a good man, too good for round here. And then I can visualize her leaning over the coffin. I remember somebody shouting that she shouldn't be allowed to slobber all over him like that. That was the word they used, 'slobber'. I can remember how *she* sounded, that's the awful thing, as Uncle Terence tried to pull her away and get her out the door. There was some sort of terrible scuffle, my mother was crying, my brother Bill and I looked at each other in embarrassment and indecision. I remember the sound of the old woman sobbing on the street outside, the big door – that's what we called it although it wasn't very big – being slammed, her banging the door to be let back in, and then her crying getting fainter as she made her way home. Everybody in the room paused to listen, all the talk and all the tears stopping for a few moments as we waited for this clamour to pass.

But I also have another image from that time. An image that has never faded or been diminished by time, slightly disconnected, it stands out on its own, but it is an image that has haunted me for a lifetime. On the night of my father's funeral, we were in my aunt's house for the sandwiches and tea, because our own house wasn't big enough for the friends and family. Everyone was there, drinking quietly, the gentle and sporadic sobbing made worse by the memory of the coffin juddering down into its final position. Everyone except my beautiful cousin Myrna, that is, who inexplicably had gone to work that day. Nobody had explained why. Life at the time seemed to be full of things that were never properly explained, at least to a thirteen-year-old boy like me. Myrna walked in right in the middle of our wake. She seemed to cling to the doorframe, not entering but just standing there, staring at us all, and I can picture her now, an image etched on my mind for ever, an emaciated grey ghost, already dead in the eyes and the mouth.

I had heard, overheard to be more accurate, that she had got an eating disorder, anorexia nervosa, 'slimmer's disease', my mother called it, but I hadn't seen her for months, as the slimmer's disease took hold. She avoided seeing relatives. But there she stood in the silence and the sadness, and everyone looked at her and nobody said a thing, as if she looked normal and healthy and was just late for the funeral.

She died a couple of weeks later of pneumonia and was buried in the row opposite my father. Her mother, my aunt May, a sweet, lovely woman with a giggly, girlish voice, always said that what triggered the anorexia was a chance remark from a doctor during a routine medical examination. The remark was allegedly that she was a little overweight. From that day on, my aunt always said, Myrna never ate properly again.

It sounds almost ridiculous that such a life-threatening disorder could be triggered in this way but many years later I supervised a postgraduate student who analysed anorexia nervosa in the families of sufferers and it was extraordinary the number of interviewees who pointed to a similar 'chance remark' as the cause of the whole thing. Anorexia is a complex psychological disorder with cultural, personality and biological factors all linked in its development, but people like to identify a single cause that they can pick out and say 'if only that hadn't happened . . .' This single cause is usually something fairly random (so that any normal family could potentially be affected) and external to the family itself (so that no blame could ever be attached to the family). The PE teacher who commented that Tracy was too fat to be any good at games, the boyfriend who said that Jane's bum was too big for her skinny jeans, the doctor who quipped that his patient could do with losing a little weight. It was always things like that. It reminded me of what Friedrich Nietzsche wrote: 'To trace something unknown back to something known is alleviating, soothing, gratifying, and gives moreover a feeling of power. Danger, disquiet, anxiety attend the unknown, and the first instinct is to eliminate these distressing states. First principle: any explanation is better than none.'

My family, and many other families, had found an explanation, one which stressed the power of the chance remark (and I suppose by implication, the dangerous power of the carelessly chosen words of those in authority). Nobody ever disputed my aunt's account, and it became the truth of what had become of my beautiful cousin. In that awful year of my life I sometimes think that my prejudices towards my own weight, and other people's, were probably laid down for ever. I run every day to keep myself looking lean, and this is both a rare blessing and an absolute curse, for someone as busy as myself, running along the Pacific Coast Highway in the dark, having arrived at LAX airport late at night, lest I miss a single day of training. (Knowing this, you can imagine some of the scenarios that have formed the basis for my life.)

I have one other brief image of Myrna, however, which is a positive image. Here several of us, as children, were sitting and playing in a sloping field with a slight dip in the middle. It's funny that I can recall the dip so vividly, but we were all sitting on or around it, playing some sort of game. This was a meadow

GET THE EDGE

full of flowers, a carpet of bright, shimmering, yellow butter-cups, and I have a vague recollection of the way Myrna sat and laughed that day; it was a very girlish laugh just like her mother's. I think I remember the sound. But this is really just a fragment of an image with no real narrative, with no beginning or end. I don't know how we got to the meadow or what we were doing there. I think we were playing games but I don't remember what games we were playing, or whether Bill was there or not. I don't remember whether I picked some of the flowers to take home to my mother, which I often did. Nor do I remember where the meadow was. This is, it would seem, a very limited and very transient image, not sharp and clear, not like the other image of Myrna in the doorway, which has stuck firmly in my mind; that grey look and the deadness in her eyes on the day of my father's funeral, is permanently etched on my imagination. This darker memory, unfortunately, is crystal clear and shows no evidence of ever fading.

These are some of the things that I remember from my child-hood but on many occasions I wish that it was very different. I wish that I could be more in control of my memories, so that I could balance them out a bit more. I wish that I could recall the good and the bad with equal clarity. But sometimes, no matter how hard I try, it is only the bad memories that spring somewhat uncontrollably to mind and torment me with their presence and their detail. But, according to a number of psychologists, there are steps that you can take to facilitate the retrieval of autobio-graphical memories, including the good ones, and some of these steps may seem a little surprising. One technique to aide more detailed and more accurate recall of childhood memories is to try to recall the memories while displaying the same bodily

84

behaviours that would have accompanied the formation of the original memory.

For nearly forty years we have known that the retrieval of memories is better if the conditions under which the memory is being retrieved match the conditions in which the memory was first established. So if you were under the influence of alcohol when a particular event happened, it is easier to retrieve the memory in the future when you are again under the influence (that is why sometimes memories flood back to you involuntarily when you have been drinking alcohol). But recent research (Riskind, 1983) suggests that mental processes like memory are not separate from bodily experiences, but rather are an integral part of human beings' sensory and motor environment. One study asked people to stand upright with a smile on their face while they recalled either pleasant experiences or alternatively unpleasant things that had happened to them. Others were asked to stand with their bodies slumped with their head and neck bowed, and with a downcast expression on their face, and again they were asked to recall pleasant or unpleasant experiences. The researchers found that pleasant life experiences were better recalled when people were smiling and in an upright position and unpleasant experiences were recalled better when the body was slumped with the head and neck bowed and people wore a downcast expression. In other words, both bodily posture and facial expression seems to have a significant effect on the recall of information from autobiographical memory – when these behaviours match the original behaviours shown in the context in which the memory was being stored, memory is improved.

Katinka Dijkstra, Michael Kaschak and Ralf Zwaan of Florida State University tested this theory further by asking people to retrieve memories from specific events in their past in different bodily positions. The participants had to recall eight different memories which included things like going to the dentist, playing sport, opening a door for someone, clapping their hands at a concert, waving at someone and placing their hand on their heart. The participants were asked to do this in one of two conditions. In one condition (the congruent condition), the bodily position was 'consistent' with the original bodily position when the memory was stored, for example lying on one's back in a dentist's chair in recalling the visit to the dentist. In the second position (the incongruent condition), the bodily position was not consistent with the original bodily position, for example, standing up with your hands on hips while recalling a visit to the dentist (few people have their teeth extracted while standing up in this manner). Then the experimenters asked the participants to come back two weeks later and recall for the second time the memories that they had retrieved in either the body congruent or body incongruent condition. The researchers found that the time taken to access the memories was significantly lower in the body congruent position and that after two weeks participants remembered a higher proportion of the autobiographical material they originally recalled when they were in the body congruent position. The researchers also found this effect with both younger (mean age 22) and older (mean age 70) adults. In the words of Dijkstra *et al.*, 'Physically assuming an elaborate body position plays a major role in access to autobiographical memories and their subsequent recall. Assuming a memory-congruent body position helps both younger and older adults to gain access to their memories. This demonstrates encoding specificity in an autobiographical memory domain with the same body position during retrieval and the original experience facilitating access to that experience.'

The reason why this works is that the brain stores information in a way that links the meaning of things or events with records of our interaction with them. In the words of Antonio Damasio (1999), 'The brain forms memories in a highly distributed manner. Take, for instance, the memory of a hammer. There is no single place in our brain where we will find an entry with the word "hammer" followed by a dictionary definition of what a hammer is. Instead . . . there are a number of records in our brain that correspond to different aspects of our past interaction with hammers: their shape, the typical movement with which we use them, the hand shape and hand motion required to manipulate the hammer, the result of the action, the word that designates it in whatever many languages we know.'

You can thus use the basic structure and functional aspects of the brain to facilitate your autobiographical memory. So, for example, if you are trying to recall a happy memory from childhood, don't try to do this in a downcast position with a serious or unhappy face (as you might naturally try to do, on the assumption that this is going to be a hard and a serious affair), instead put on a happy face and adopt a much happier bodily posture. If you are trying to recall a sad memory, on the other hand, make sure that your posture and expression are sad and downcast. By manipulating your posture and facial expression as an aid to recall you are essentially using the structural properties of the brain to help you access your memories. If you want to recall how happy you were as a child back in primary school, sitting on the floor cross-legged listening to the teacher's story, being praised for your contribution, sit in that very same way, with an expectant look on your face, fidget like a child, and then try to recall the memory.

If you want to recall your first day at primary school and your first sight of the school, assume the position with your hand stretched up holding your parent's hand as you are led to the school gate. When you want to recall the joys of getting some exam results, stand and open an imaginary envelope. When you want to recall being a young child, and the joy of seeing your parents after they have been away for a few hours, think about the position you may have been in, kneeling on the settee looking out of the window, smiling as they approach. The congruent bold position should facilitate recall. If you try to recall these precious memories in a serious and focused way, as we usually do, sitting at a desk without a smile and without trying to adapt the congruent position, it will be that much harder. It may all look a bit strange but it appears to be effective.

I need to point out though that the way that these researchers tried to measure the accuracy of recall was by asking their participants to recall the memory twice and by looking at the amount of material recalled on the second occasion compared to the first. The research couldn't compare the first recall with the actual event because it didn't have any video evidence of the event rooted in the participants' past. This would, however, be easy to do with the amount of video material that now exists. It is clearly an interesting idea that could easily be extended. I aim to try this one day, but for the moment I'm slightly worried about what might come back. It could be like opening the floodgates in so many ways. You might be a lot braver.

- Our autobiographical memories are highly selective

- The retrieval of memories is better if the conditions under which the memory is being retrieved are similar to, or match, the conditions in which the memory was first established

- If you want to recall memories from childhood, adopt a congruent body position to that which you might have been showing at the time

- If you want to recall happy memories, act happy

- If you want to recall sad memories, act sad

How to bite your tongue without blowing your top

The best way to stop yourself from blowing your top is basically not to consciously try to control your anger at all, but to learn to do this *unconsciously*, which, of course, is a lot harder. In other words, it is better if you can change how you think at a deep level about expressions of anger. But the good news is that we know from other areas of research that unconscious attitudes like this can be changed. One way of doing this is by being exposed to positive role models with characteristics different from ourselves. If you have an aggressive temperament, and are prone to angry outbursts, some of this attitude may be influenced by a poor role model – your boss, for example – who is also prone to violent outbursts. This is reinforcing your implicit (or unconscious) beliefs about the role of anger in stressful situations. This may be implicitly teaching you that the experience and expression of anger is essentially a good thing because successful people do it. You need to look out for alternative role models, people who stay calm in the vast majority of situations. Reflect on these new role models and how well they cope with the trials of life. Alternatively, watch a film with a cool, calm and collected hero. Do this every night if you have to because you need to work on your implicit beliefs.

The science works something like this. Blowing your top when you are feeling extremely angry may well feel wonderful for a few seconds (but in my experience and the experience of most others, it often lasts only a few seconds), but outbursts of temper like this do not have a lasting positive psychological impact because they usually leave you feeling much more stressed afterwards, and often unable to think clearly for moments or even hours after the outburst. But trying to bottle it up inside can be equally damaging (or that's the way it often feels). Iris Mauss and her colleagues of the University of Denver researched whether there was any way around this 'damned-if-you-do and damned-if-you-don't dilemma of emotion regulation'. These researchers argued that previous studies which tried to do something about people blowing their top have concentrated on conscious and deliberate attempts by people to regulate their emotional state. They argued that the negative aspects of attempting to suppress anger may well result from the conscious effort that is necessary to do this. But they suggested there may well be an alternative strategy. There is the possibility that less deliberate and conscious emotional regulatory processes might allow people to regulate their negative emotions, including anger, without the obvious costs involved in their conscious and deliberate attempts. In other words, the researchers asked, can we harness automatic processes to deal with anger?

The first interesting issue posed by this research was to try to get at these automatic processes. These are, by definition, processes that occur outside the conscious awareness of participants, so you can't hope to eliminate them by merely asking people about the processes or using any kind of self-report. The way that Mauss and her colleagues approached this topic was to use the Implicit Association Test (IAT) developed by Anthony Greenwald and his colleagues. The IAT is essentially a reaction-time task that measures the implicit evaluation of categories. It is based on the idea that the more closely two categories are associated in the unconscious mind of an individual, the quicker that person will be at deciding that they belong together – and they will make fewer errors in creating that association. In a recent study I used the IAT to measure unconscious attitudes towards the environment and specifically to measure unconscious attitudes to high- and low-carbon-footprint products. We found that people were quicker in this experiment at associating low-carbon-footprint products with the evaluative category 'good' compared with high-carbon-footprint products. In other words, people have an implicit positive attitude to low-carbon-footprint products – though why they don't therefore buy more low-carbon-footprint products becomes an interesting and pressing question! In their study, Mauss and her colleagues used words associated with strong emotional *regulation* (such as 'controlled', 'cool', 'hide', 'contained', 'suppress'); words associated with strong emotional *expression* (like 'expressive', 'emotional', 'reveal', 'disclose', 'discharge'); a series of positive words (for example 'pleasant', 'good', 'gold', 'honour', 'lucky'), and negative words ('negative', 'bad', 'gloom', 'filth', 'rotten').

REGULATION WORDS	EMOTIONAL EXPRESSION WORDS	POSITIVE WORDS	NEGATIVE WORDS
Controlled	Expressive	Pleasant	Negative
Cool	Emotional	Good	Bad
Hide	Reveal	Gold	Gloom
Contained	Disclose	Honour	Filth
Suppress	Discharge	Lucky	Rotten

The IAT measures how quickly each of their participants unconsciously associates the emotion regulation words and emotion expression words with the categories positive and negative, thereby revealing what the participants' unconscious attitudes are to the regulation or expression of emotion.

In the second part of the study, Mauss and her colleagues measured the actual behaviour of the participants in a series of tasks designed to induce anger. In one task, participants had to count as quickly as possible a series of letters that looked very similar in extremely blurry copy, while the experimenter constantly interrupted them and told them 'to speak more loudly'. The experimenter also implied that they were not doing very well on the task. The question these psychologists were trying to answer was what effects did the implicit unconscious attitude to emotional regulation of expression have on their actual emotional responses to the task? A whole series of behaviours were looked at including facial displays of anger, verbal outbursts, angry thoughts, cardiovascular response and also what individuals were consciously trying to do to control themselves in this situation. The researchers found that those participants with the most positive implicit attitudes to emotional regulation had fewer angry outbursts and were more relaxed during and after the tasks and had fewer negative thoughts and behaviours. In other words, the Implicit Association Test can reveal people's unconscious attitudes to emotional regulation of expression and from this we can predict how they respond automatically and unconsciously in a situation likely to provoke anger. In the words of the researchers, 'some people seem to be capable – without conscious effort – of remaining calm, cool and collected in a powerfully negative situation.' The downside of this of course is that some people are not capable of this without conscious effort and what they need to do is to use some deliberate strategies to change their response. What this research does highlight is the role of automatic processes in the regulation of emotion. For many years, psychologists have believed that thoughts, and their conscious interpretation, played a crucial role in what it is to feel a particular emotion, but this research tells us a good deal goes on beyond the scope of conscious reflection.

So how do you stop yourself from blowing your top? The answer according to these researchers would be that you need to change your unconscious attitude to the concept of emotional regulation. We know that unconscious attitudes can be changed because unconscious attitudes to the category of black and white changed significantly after Barack Obama became President of the United States. Using the same logic here, you can imagine bombarding yourself with exerts from films or TV series showing how a main character can remain cool, calm and collected in any situation. If you watch enough films showing how people can regulate their emotions in a positive way, this should impact on your implicit and unconscious attitude to emotional regulation. Once this happens the rest is easy. The next time you are in an anger-provoking situation, your unconscious regulatory processes will take over and stop you from blowing your top without any nasty consequences. In the meantime, just count to ten.

- Our unconscious attitude impacts directly on our behaviour
- Stop yourself getting annoyed by changing your unconscious attitude towards anger
- Watch films with calm and collected heroes, who get results but never lose their cool
- Remember that outbursts of anger make you feel stupid and make others want to avoid you

How to enjoy the moment more

How many times have you let a moment in life slip by without really savouring it? Looking back at your life, how many regrets do you have about not enjoying more particular moments and occasions? It turns out that you can learn to savour the present moment more by consciously focusing on the fact that your current experiences will soon end. If you want to enjoy a really intense holiday experience, remind yourself that you only have a certain number of days left. If you want to enjoy your work more intensely, remind yourself that you will not always be engaged on that particular task. We know that the ability to savour the moment is linked to psychological well-being, but many people do not live in the moment, they let the moment pass, sometimes hardly even noticing it. They take their day to day existence, including the everyday pleasures in life, for granted. To savour the moment, you to need fight against this pervasive bias by reminding yourself, consciously and deliberately, that all things really do pass. We all need to do this. I, for one, allowed the time with my children to pass without really noticing it in the way that I should have. I was somehow fooled into believing that it would last for ever. It didn't, and now it has gone forever.

Jaime Kurtz of Pomona College in Claremont, California investigated how to get people to derive enjoyment from the moment, from the here and now, from the pleasant things happening in one's life at the present time. She points out that although many psychologists argue that the ability to savour the moment is connected to psychological well-being, sometimes it can be hard to do. Kurtz argues that by reminding oneself that a pleasurable activity will soon end, it focuses your mind on all of the positive aspects of the experience and, in addition to that, you become more motivated to make the very best of the moment.

The way that Kurtz conducted her research was to ask a

group of students who were about to graduate in six weeks' time, to write about their college experience. They had to write about 'your friends at college', 'the campus', 'the activities you participated in here', and 'your overall college experience'. Each of these topics was preceded by a qualifying instruction such as, 'given how little time you have left' or alternatively, 'given that you have lots of time left at the University of Virginia, write how you feel about . . .'. These instructions thus cued one group to focus on the fact that there wasn't much time remaining, and the other group to focus on the fact that they still had quite a lot of time to enjoy their college experience. On the evening on which the participants did this task, they were e-mailed a link to an online questionnaire in which they had to report their mood and report whether or not they had participated in a number of college-related activities. Over the next fortnight, the participants were e-mailed links to four similar questionnaires; the final questionnaire also included measures of subjective happiness which were used by Kurtz to examine the changes in the level of happiness across the experiment as a whole.

The analyses revealed that participants in the condition in which they were made to reflect on the fact that their college experience would soon end showed the largest increase in subjective well-being during this final period. In addition to this, those participants who were reminded that their college experience would soon come to an end also engaged in more college-related activities during this time. So what this study demonstrated was that by focusing people's minds on the fact that a positive experience is limited in duration, you increase their feelings of happiness and also you influence how they actually spend their time. When you remind people that the experience is coming to an end it does not necessarily elevate mood immediately, rather it produces an accumulated effect over time. So if you want people to enjoy the moment more, you need to remind them (or you need to remind yourself) that nothing lasts for ever.

This exercise illustrates a very simple principle, but one with obvious intuitive appeal. The problem with life is that we often do not appreciate it when it is happening, and it is only when it is gone that we understand the real pleasure we were getting from something. This experiment demonstrates quite simply and quite powerfully, that by forcing people to think in a particular way, we can increase the value of the present. However, it was concerned with only one particular experience – the end of college life – which does tend to have a clear and non-contestable end-point. Would this experiment work in the same way with things like relationships, which may end at some ill-defined and uncertain end-point in the future (or may potentially, although, statistically less likely, go on for ever)? How do you get people to savour the moment in relationships with a vague notion that in the future the relationship might be over? Can we get ourselves to focus on the fact that all things pass, even the very best of relationships and therefore enjoy the succession of moments more? In some domains savouring the moment might be much trickier to apply than in this particular study.

- The ability to savour the moment is linked to psychological well-being

- Many people fail to savour the moment, and then suddenly life has passed them by

- Train yourself to savour the moment by reminding yourself that one day this phase of your life will end. This may seem painful but it can be very useful

How to elicit sympathy

If you want to get a sympathetic response from a listener when you are telling them about aspects of your life, you need to get them to show appropriate expressive behaviour, for example, a head shake while they are listening. That way they will feel more sympathetic. Why? Because our non-verbal behaviour amplifies how we feel inside. If they are shaking their head (for whatever reason) they will feel more sympathy. But how do you get them to shake their head (sympathetically) while you are talking to them? Before you start talking about important aspects of your life, ask them a number of things in which you can anticipate the answer being 'no' and watch them shake their head. Then ask them if you can talk about some things that have happened to you – they may well still be shaking their head as you start the story. Head shaking is a non-verbal cue associated with sympathy and people gauge their internal psychological state partly as a function of the non-verbal cues they display. In other words, if you can get them shaking their head while they listen to your story they will feel more sympathy and it will essentially intensify their emotions. Even explicitly asking them to shake their head while they listen seems to do the trick in an experimental situation (although this would be a very odd request in everyday life). This may seem like very odd science, but there appears to be something in it.

According to Maya Tamir and her colleagues of the University of Illinois at Urbana-Champaign, the unconscious expressive signals that we send out can have a major influence on our inner psychological state. This is not a new idea. William James (1890) thought that the perception of our own facial expression was an important cue to our own subjective experience. In other words, the fact that you are smiling and you know that you are smiling, leads to your internal perception that you are feeling happy. One implication of this idea is that if you can get people to behave in certain ways then you can change and manipulate their internal psychological state. One intriguing study by Wells and Petty (1980) showed that if people are nodding their head while listening to a persuasive message (rather than shaking their head), they tend to have a more positive response to the message. And this occurs even if you ask people to engage in the behaviour explicitly. But the question Tamir posed is whether the *form* of the behaviour always has the same effect on emotion, because the *meaning* of the behaviour can be different in different situations. Say, for example, you are watching a film about someone talking about their drug addiction and in it they explain how bad their life is. In a situation like this any head shaking on your part means something like 'oh, what a terrible situation'; this is a non-verbal signal of sympathy. On the other hand, imagine you are listening to a schizophrenic ex-prisoner talking about tormenting and killing one of his neighbours. Thirty years later he is now released from prison and says that he just wants a normal life. In the film, he is telling you that he is now psychologically much better and 'deserves to live free from the scrutiny of concerned neighbours'. In this particular context, Tamir and her colleagues say that head shaking has a completely different meaning, it means something like 'oh, what a terrible person'. In other words, what Tamir and her colleagues were investigating was whether the non-verbal response – head shaking versus head nodding – has an impact on our internal psychological state and whether the impact varies depending upon the specific context. In this study participants were told that the researchers were looking at the effects of bodily movements on memory. The participants were explicitly asked to perform one of two basic movements: either they had to move their head up and down (head nodding) or side to side (head shaking) at the rate of about one movement per second. The experiment was designed so that participants shook their head to one film clip and nodded their head to the other clip. After they had watched the clip their emotional response to the person played in the clip was measured on 13 dimensions on a 5-point scale from 'I felt none of this feeling' to 'I felt this feeling strongly':

'sympathy'
'caring'
'understanding'
'pity'
'compassion'
'empathy'

'irritation'
'annoyance'
'impatience'
'anger'
'disgust'
'contempt'
'hostility'

These emotional responses were thought of as 'pro-social feelings' by the experimenters. The researchers found that when listening to the ex-addict talking, head shaking generated more pro-social feelings towards the person in the film than head nodding. On the other hand, when listening to the schizophrenic ex-prisoner, head shaking generated less emotional sympathy to the person than did head nodding. In other words, when the participants were shaking their head and listening to the drug addict talking about how bad her life was they were much more sympathetic towards her than when they engaged in other types of head movements. The head shaking essentially intensified the feelings of sympathy. The opposite effect was found with the ex-prisoner. This time the shaking of the head while listening to the film meant that they judged the character less sympathetically.

What these researchers managed to do was to demonstrate the power of unconscious expressive movements on internal emotional state. The particular effects, however, are not solely attributable to the behaviour itself because, after all, the same behaviour led to different consequences in the case of the two films. Rather, the effects also depend upon the meaning of the situation. The same behaviour can either amplify pro-social emotions or decrease pro-social emotions depending upon the context. But what this experiment tells us is that unconscious expressive movements have a big impact on how you feel inside.

So if you want someone to feel more sympathy for you when you are telling them a story about how hard your life has been, you need to get them to display head shakes while they are listening. This might all sound faintly ridiculous but it is exactly what Tamir and her colleagues did by asking people to shake their head explicitly and deliberately. How could you elicit head shakes without the specific request? Perhaps you could ask them if they would like to do something that you know they unfortunately can't. Would they like to go to the cinema when you know they have to work late? Would they like to go for a surprise holiday when it is impossible for them? Have they got time to listen to how tough your upbringing was? There could be a lot of sympathetic head shaking as you begin the story and extraordinarily, these proprioceptive cues will feed back to their brain and intensify their sympathetic response.

This is one of those extraordinary counter-intuitive experiments, counter-intuitive in this sense: how can you really get statistically reliable effects by manipulating bodily movement in this direct way? The one major limitation in the study, which the authors are aware of, is that there was no neutral control group to compare each of the two conditions with. So we know that the conditions were significantly different from each other, but we do not know how each of them would have been different from the missing control.

- People judge their psychological state partly as a result of the non-verbal signals they send

- If people nod their head while listening to a persuasive message (because they have been required to do this), they will feel that the message is more persuasive

- If people shake their head when they are listening to a sad story (because they have been asked to), they will feel more sympathetic to the story and to the person telling it

- Get people to feel more sympathy for you by working on their non-verbal responses, by getting them to shake their head

How to stop your brain from getting angry

When I was young, I was sometimes prone to outbursts of anger. It was a frustrated sort of rage, as if others didn't understand that I had important things to do, or as if they didn't see what pressure I was under. But I would suddenly erupt, ranting and raving until this wild tide wore itself out. My mother would say, 'There he goes, losing the old head again.' Her comments didn't help. They contributed negatively in ways that I didn't understand. It was part of the inarticulate frustration on my part. After the outburst had subsided I was left feeling foolish.

Psychology has quite specific advice to give about preventing this from happening, at least in certain contexts. To stop your brain from getting angry when you have just received some negative feedback or bad news – if you have not managed to change your unconscious attitude to anger – make sure that you are reclining! Here's why.

Changing your bodily position to affect the neural response to an anger-inducing situation has been studied by Eddie Harmon-Jones and Carly Peterson of Texas A&M University. Their study is based on the observation that when someone is angry there is increased activation in certain parts of the brain. In particular, the left prefrontal cortex is more activated than the right prefrontal cortex during anger and particularly with the type of anger in which someone might actually do something. But the question they asked was how bodily position can influence this process because we know from other research that bodily movements do affect emotional processes and other internal experiences. So in their experiment they had their participants write an essay which was apparently to be evaluated by a judge. They attached sensors to the scalp to measure the brain's electrical activity; half the participants were given their feedback in a seated and upright position and the other half while they were reclining in a chair. The feedback they received was fixed so that half of the participants got positive feedback and the other half got negative feedback. The feedback was not just about the essay but about their own personalities as well (which can be a particularly negative experience for many people). The experimenters measured the brain activity of the participants and also asked them to complete a mood questionnaire.

What the researchers found was that there was a higher level of left lateral frontal brain activity in the condition where they were given negative feedback and sitting upright than in the condition where they were given negative feedback but reclining. In other words, the neural or brain activity associated with anger was reduced when the participants received the negative feedback while they were reclining. Their actual mood was also slightly lower when they were reclining but this was not particularly reliable.

Our brain is much more likely to fire in angry mode when it is upright than when it is reclining. So, it follows, if you want your brain to feel less angry, when you get some news that you know is sure to make you angry, make sure you are in a reclining position.

My main issue with this research is that the mood-state experience did not match the neural response, such that the reported mood state of the participants did not correlate well with the changes in the brain's activity pattern. Researchers were not able to explain why this was so. Thus it seems we have only really got half the story so far. If you want to stop your brain from getting angry, make sure that you are reclining when you get the news. How you stop your inner self from getting angry needs further investigation.

- Anger is associated with greater activity in the left prefrontal cortex, compared to the right prefrontal cortex, but this pattern of brain activity is reduced when you get the anger-provoking news in a reclining position

- Stop your brain from getting angry by making sure that when you receive any information that you know will make you angry, you are in a reclining position

How to make time last forever

If you want to make time last forever, what you must do is to break your daily routines of life, and do new things every day. Routine, boring activities may seem to last for a very long time while they are taking place. However, when you look back at those days where you have just done routine things, then you will recall very little that is worthwhile. If days are broken up by non-routine activities, where you have to plan and think about what you are going to do, then when you look back, these times seem to last much longer. This is why many people say that time seems to get shorter as they get older because many aspects of their later life are routine in nature. Looking back at these routines of their everyday life seems to affect their perceptions of time. It turns out that even on holiday after the first few days we fall into routines and that is why the first few days of the holiday seem longer than the rest of the holiday, and time seems to speed up towards the end of the holiday as the routines are established. So if you want time to last for ever you must avoid routine at all costs.

Our experience of the passages of time depends not just on the actual duration of time but on a number of psychological factors. This has been commented on for over a hundred years. In 1890 the psychologist William James wrote that, 'The same space of time seems shorter as we grow older . . . In youth we may have an absolutely new experience, subjective or objective, every hour of the day. Apprehension is vivid, retentiveness strong, and our recollections of that time, like those of a time spent in rapid and interesting travel, are of something intricate, multitudinous, and long-drawn-out. But as each passing year converts some of this experience into automatic routine which we hardly note at all, the days and the weeks smooth themselves out in recollection to contentless units, and the years grow hollow and collapse.'

This idea was taken up by Dinah Avni-Babad and Ilana Ritov of the Hebrew University of Jerusalem, who wanted to understand a little bit more about how 'automatic routine may affect the perception of time'. They looked at the effects of getting people to engage in either routine or non-routine activities, firstly in an experimental way and then in a number of field studies. They began with experiments in which people had to estimate the duration of a recording in which there were a number of names arranged in different intervals. In one condition the names were spread out evenly and routinely but in another tape the names were spread out in a non-routine, irregular manner. What the researchers found was that when the tape was highly but routinely segmented the duration was perceived as shorter than in the other conditions. In other words, routine patterning leads to a reduction in the estimated length of the duration of the interval.

This is in many ways an odd result because sometimes people complain that routine tasks seem to go on for ever. But what the psychologists were investigating here were people's *recollection* of duration. The researchers also used a variety of field studies to investigate this phenomenon, which included looking at people's perception of time on holiday. Their prediction was that we should all perceive the days at the start of the holiday as being the longest because they are non-routine in nature, and they represent a break from what has gone on before. However, once the holiday routine is established, the time duration should get shorter and people should estimate time passing most quickly towards the end of the holiday. This is exactly what they found. Their explanation was that routine activities do not require much original thinking but non-routine activities do and it is the presence of all of this additional mental activity that causes us to estimate those time durations as longer.

So if you want to make time last forever, then the secret is to get out of a routine and do new things which require thinking and planning. This will significantly affect your perception of the passage of time.

- Our perception of time is affected by how routine our day is

- In retrospect, days with familiar patterns pass very quickly

- To make time last for ever do something new every day

How to make someone feel happy in five seconds

Imagine your partner has just failed at something, for example an interview, and they are feeling very unhappy as a result. What can you do to cheer them up? Our level of happiness is determined chiefly by how we make what psychologists call 'attributions' (or momentary explanations) for negative events. If your partner thinks that the interview went badly because of:

Internal characteristics – 'It's all down to *me*'

Stable characteristics – 'I'm just *not clever* enough'

Global characteristics – 'There are *loads of things* I'm not very good at'

then they will be feeling particularly unhappy. The single most effective response that you can use is one that will challenge these basic spontaneous assumptions. Say something like, 'Nobody ever does well with that interview panel, they are well known for creating an intimidating atmosphere.' Say this forcefully and with conviction. This is essentially an attribution that runs counter to your partner's natural style of making attributions and may get them to change their own attribution slightly. A small change here is sometimes all that is required.

- People get low because of how they routinely think about things

- Cheer people up by challenging their explanations for the things that have gone wrong in their life

- When they say, 'I failed the test, I am stupid,' say, 'No you're not, it was really difficult.'

- Do this repeatedly, until they realize that you are sincere, and they get the point

4. PICK YOURSELF UP/ DUST YOURSELF DOWN

'Certainly there are good and bad times, but our mood changes more often than our fortune.'

Jules Renard, *Journal*, January 1905

How to mend a broken heart

The best way of mending a broken heart is not to drown your sorrows (in fact, it's *definitely* not to drown your sorrows). It is also best not to wait around for time to eventually pass. Rather it is much better to write about it, focusing on particular things. Write about the relationship for twenty minutes a day for three consecutive days. Write about your emotions and what the relationship meant to you, thus:

On day one }	Write about the relationship before the split.
On day two }	Write about the relationship as the split was looming.
On day three }	Write about the aftermath of the split and what it meant to you, and how the whole thing felt.

By writing down your reflections in this way, you are exposing yourself to (sometimes very) painful thoughts and thereby decreasing the impact of these thoughts across time (it is, in effect, a form of systematic desensitization). You are also coming to terms with these thoughts and making sense of them through language. If you use this technique, it turns out, that you will become both psychologically and physically stronger.

The scientific reasoning works something like this. Sometimes when your heart is broken the hardest thing to do is talk about the relationship, especially to your friends who may well know both parties. The problem then is that thoughts and feelings become jumbled up inside your head, and you can't stop thinking about the break-up. Your waking life is characterized by intrusive (and often incomplete) thoughts, and you simply can't focus on other things. So how do you mend a broken heart from a psychological point of view? One proven way is to write about it. This is sometimes called a 'non-social motor expression' because it is using language not to communicate to another person, but to articulate your unresolved feelings and thoughts. There is considerable evidence, which has accumulated over the past twenty years, that allowing people to write about their innermost thoughts and feelings associated with personal events is both physically and psychologically beneficial.

Research demonstrates that writing allows a physiological and psychological release which reduces stress and helps people function better. Writing is beneficial because it allows you to give meaning to what has happened and it allows you to understand it and assimilate it better. When you lay things out on paper, you can develop new insights into what has actually occurred and it allows you to put everything into perspective. Stephen Lepore and Melanie Greenberg of Columbia University researched the impact of instructing people to write about their romantic break-ups on their physical and psychological health. They used the standard Pennebaker procedure in which participants are asked to write a twenty-minute essay on each of three consecutive days in a private and quiet place. The reason for doing this over three consecutive days is to allow the development of ideas across time. Participants are instructed, in the words of Lepore and Greenberg, to 'write about your thoughts and feelings regarding the relationship, how the relationship affected your life when you were in it, or the effect of the relationship on your life in the present. The important thing is that you dig down into your deepest emotions and explore them in your writing'. The researchers wanted to assist their participants to form a coherent account of the break-up so they were told on day one that they should focus on what the relationship was like before the split, on day two they should focus on what the relationship was like as the split was occurring, and on day three to focus on the aftermath of the split. A control group were simply asked to write about relationships in general. Lepore and Greenberg assessed the physical and psychological health of the participants in a number of ways and measured the physical symptoms of illness using something they called the 'Upper Respiratory System Scale', in which participants had to rate over a week the severity of symptoms like sore throats and sneezing. They also measured psychological mood including levels of depression, tension, anger, fatigue and also the frequency of intrusive thoughts about the break-up. As well as all this, the researchers measured how participants felt about their ex-partner including whether they still cared about their ex-partner, whether they felt anger or resentment towards their ex-partner and whether they felt any guilt over the break-up.

Lepore and Greenberg found that asking people to write about the break-up of the relationship helped to protect the participants against any physical illness in that the control participants who focused on more impersonal topics had more respiratory symptoms and suffered more from tension and fatigue over time. The experimental participants who wrote about the break-up reported no increases in upper respiratory symptoms and did not suffer unduly from tension or fatigue. Furthermore, asking people to write about the end of a relationship meant that they held less resentment towards their ex-partners, they had less guilt about the break-up and had fewer intrusive thoughts and engaged in fewer avoidance behaviours. There was also a slight trend such that participants were more likely to go back to a relationship with their ex-partner than did the control group.

So why is writing about a romantic break-up so beneficial? There seems to be a number of different processes at work here. The first is to do with 'habituation'. By writing essays, individuals are exposed again and again to the painful thoughts that they might otherwise keep bottled up inside. It is essentially a form of 'exposure therapy' in which the negative emotional response to the events gradually diminishes. But, in addition, by writing about and expressing their deepest thoughts about painful events, the participants are somehow mastering their response to them. They are pulling all of their thoughts into a coherent narrative and they are no longer the victim of a series of events. And of course, writing about events forces you to step back and to reappraise the whole thing, to see everything in a new light. But these are not just isolated psychological changes – these are important psychological processes with a direct effect on under-lying physiology (after all, there was less physical illness in the experimental group). In the words of the authors, these changes in psychological function 'could have directly dampened neuroendocrine responding to the stress of incomplete cognitive processing, thus short-circuiting physiological stress response and concomitant changes in immune functioning that influence risk for infectious illnesses'.

If you do this experiment yourself, you will not feel euphoric afterwards. You may not even feel particularly jolly, but you are exposing yourself to the painful thoughts and lessening their power. You are also making sense of what occurred and putting things in perspective and articulating them from your point of view. In so doing, you are helping your immune system deal with the stress of the break-up, and thereby decreasing your risk of infectious illness.

It is extraordinary that this simple idea of writing about negative emotional events comes out time and time again as being a very powerful psychological technique for coming to terms with the kinds of events that can damage our psychological and physical health. The mechanisms are usually thought of as being quite general – habituation, closure, reappraisal – but it would be interesting to analyse in detail the kinds of things that people write (given the incredible freedom allowed to them by the very broad procedure used) to see how the different types of accounts that people actually write might predict psychological and physical recovery from the event. There have been some attempts to use computerized analyses of the accounts (including the *Linguistic Inquiry and Word Count* which we'll learn more about later on) but there have been far fewer attempts to analyse in detail the coherent narratives that people write, to see what it is in these accounts that actually makes the difference. If we could work this out then we could potentially provide more direction in the instructions themselves. Presumably,

people write about very different things and what they specifically choose to write about and how they express it will have a
big impact on how they subsequently feel and think. But the
good news is that regardless of the detail of what is actually
happening, the general technique is clearly doing something. It
is well worth trying.

- To mend a broken heart, you need to deal with your
  intrusive and painful thoughts

- Write about the break-up over three consecutive days

- You are doing two things here – exposing yourself to the
  powerful negative thoughts (and thus desensitizing
  yourself to them), and making sense of what happened
  through language

How to cope with criticism of your appearance

I, like many other people, hate having my appearance criticized.
I can be very sensitive when it comes to how I look and any
comments I receive. A few years ago at an awards ceremony in
Kinsale, south-west Ireland, I got dressed in my favourite dinner
jacket and trousers for the stunning black-tie dinner. I like how I
look when I am formally dressed and I was anticipating very
positive comments. I called my companion for the evening into
the hotel room. She looked me up and down, and then burst
out laughing. 'MC Hammer,' she said. That was all, but that
was more than enough. There was a long pause, filled with her

sniggering behind her hands, glancing occasionally my way to see how I was taking it. 'You can't touch this,' she added, almost unnecessarily, after a few minutes of torment. The trousers, it seems, were a little too wide at the top and narrow at the bottoms. They were also half-mast. I had never looked at them that closely in a full-length mirror. I sat for the next few minutes in my dress shirt, the trousers thrown on to the floor beside me, wondering what to wear or what to say. Eventually, because my feelings had not subsided, I started trying to insult her. I said that her clothes were hardly 'appropriate' and that she looked a little 'cheap'. She told me that my insecurity was obvious, and that my motives were absolutely transparent. During the dinner itself we sat in silence. I refused to go to the bathroom, just in case someone sang 'Hammertime'.

Research reveals that if someone criticizes your appearance, even if you feel very hurt by what they have said, you shouldn't try to retaliate. If you do, your response will be full of emotion (because you have been hurt) and your strong emotional response will just demonstrate to yourself that the criticism was justified in the first place. In addition, your retaliation will make the relationship even worse with the person who made the comment. It also turns out that retaliation (generally speaking, although there are always exceptions) doesn't make you feel better. The best way to deal with a negative comment is to just accept the comment and leave it at that. If your partner says that your hair is a mess, just say something like, 'Hey, I'll fix it when I get a chance. I've been too busy today. I've got lots on. I'm pleased you noticed it though!' It shows that you're paying attention. Don't say, 'It's not as bad as yours, love. Go and buy a mirror.' The first response will make you feel better; the second may well make you feel worse.

So what is the best way of coping with criticism of your appearance in terms of feeling good afterwards? Luo Lu and colleagues of the National Taiwan University in China considered all of the different ways in which people can respond to a negative comment like this and grouped them into three main categories. The first they called 'acceptance', which they said has both a problem-solving and an assertive element to it. According to the researchers, acceptance means responses like 'improving myself to meet the other's expectations', 'thanking the person for pointing out my deficiencies', and 'happily accepting the criticism with gratitude' (in other words behaving like a saint). The second type of response the researchers called 'retaliation', which is primarily emotion focused and verbally aggressive, for example: 'Telling the person that he/she is not perfect either', or 'mocking her/his shortcomings'. The third kind of response is what researchers called 'avoidance'. This response is primarily emotion focused and non-assertive, for example: 'Treating it as a joke and laughing it away', or 'Making excuses to get out of the scene'. But the question is, how effective are each of these coping styles in helping you deal with someone's criticism of your appearance? What impact does each of these responses have on how you feel immediately after the criticism has occurred?

The researchers' analysis revealed that the best options were either acceptance or avoidance, as both led to the person who was criticized feeling better after the event. Retaliation, which might often seem like the most attractive option ('Have you ever looked at yourself in the mirror, buddy?' or 'You think I'm fat,

Response	Behaviour
Acceptance	'Improving myself to meet the other's expectations'
	'Thanking the person for pointing out my deficiencies'
	'Happily accepting the criticism with gratitude'
Retaliation	'Telling the person that he/she is not perfect either'
	'Mocking her/his shortcomings'
Avoidance	'Treating it as a joke and laughing it away'
	'Making excuses to get out of the scene'

just check yourself out', or 'I think it's a case of the pot calling the kettle black, if you don't mind me saying') produced much more negative emotion in the participants (i.e. more depression, anxiety and shame). The conclusions of the researchers are that, 'If the criticism has some truth in it and the individual is willing to face the deficiency, this can be a rather positive and constructive reaction to criticism, which usually can effectively avert interpersonal tension in this situation. Responding with sincere gratitude may even serve to strengthen the relationship with the antagonist.' Although whether you want a relationship with a person who criticizes the way you look is a moot point. According to this research the last thing that you should do is retaliate, not necessarily to save the other person's feelings, but to preserve you own. Retaliation doesn't, in the end, make you feel better, so try to avoid it.

The problem with the study is that it only analysed Chinese subjects and in Chinese culture, the maintenance of interpersonal harmony is a core aspect of everyday social life. In a more individualistic culture like a Western culture, would the same results be found? We need some new research to find out. Another issue to do with this study is that it is based exclusively on self-reports of people imagining what their emotional response would be when they were faced with criticism and whether they would respond using one of the three strategies. It would have been interesting to get them to keep a 'you're obviously having a bad hair day' diary and use it to record their exact response along with a precise description of their innermost emotion at that point in time. This could potentially give us new insights into how people really feel when they're confronted by an attack on their appearance and when they try to respond as best they can.

- If someone criticizes your appearance, avoid retaliation (it will only make you feel worse because it will be obvious to you and to them that they have managed to hit a nerve)

- Take criticism on the chin (thank them, if necessary: that will deflate them)

How to deal with shame

Some people are consumed with shame and guilt. According to some clinical psychologists, if you want to deal with shame, you need to learn to be a lot less self-critical. You need to be able to reassure yourself more effectively; essentially you need to be able to soothe yourself. When you start to feel shame, think of a positive mental image and keep it in your mind and think of acts of caring that you have shown to other people. So when shame starts to come to mind, think of that feeling of caring for other people. This simple imagery technique should reduce the self-critical thoughts and the feelings of inferiority connected with shame. You are remembering the good things that you have done and associating them with powerful, positive, mental images to overcome the negative feelings of shame.

Shame is a major emotion for many people. According to Paul Gilbert and Sue Proctor of the Mental Health Research Unit at Kingsway Hospital in the UK, shame can make people more vulnerable to mental health problems and can affect an individual's ability to talk to a therapist about their problems. People can be, quite literally, too ashamed to talk about the nature of their psychological issues.

Shame, according to Gilbert and Proctor, has two major components. They are:

External shame	} The thoughts and feelings that other people view you with anger or contempt.

Internal shame } Involving a high degree of self-criticism.

When people experience shame, both of these things come together and an individual can feel that the world is against them, and their own evaluation of themselves becomes more critical and more hostile. The psychological impact of this can be huge. In Gilbert and Proctor's words, 'Under this type of threat the self can feel overwhelmed, easily fragmented and simply close down – there is no safe place either inside or outside the self to help soothe or calm the self.'

The other problem with shame is that people cannot get it out of their minds. They focus on it and can ruminate about it for hours or days. Gilbert and Proctor say that shame has a certain 'stickiness' about it. It is very hard to get rid of.

So what can be done about it? Cognitive behaviour therapy (CBT) has been used to try to deal with shame and as part of a CBT programme, individuals have to attempt to generate alternative thoughts to the self-critical thoughts that they normally feel. But the problem would appear to be that although people who suffer from high levels of shame are able to generate alternative thoughts when instructed, they do not necessarily feel that reassured by what they manage to come up with. So it is almost as if something is missing here. The cold logic of the alternative thoughts might not be enough to help these people, and therefore they might have to be taught a different type of response in order to soothe themselves, something more emotional and less coldly logical.

Gilbert and Proctor distinguish two different types of positive emotion systems within human beings. One system revolves around achieving certain goals and anticipating rewards associated with the goals. This system involves the neurotransmitter dopamine and according to the authors is an active arousing system. The second system is connected to affiliation and care; it involves things like stroking and holding, a warm tone of voice and positive facial expression and involves neurohormones like oxcytocin and the endogenous opiates. This second system develops in the brain in the earliest years of life where parents act as caregivers who protect and soothe their children. Without positive beneficial experience, Gilbert and Proctor argue, the system does not develop in the normal way and this may help explain why certain individuals are particularly sensitive to self-criticism and shame. Children without the necessary secure bonding experiences end up being dependent on others and focus on others as sources of threat. In the words of the authors, 'In that context they become highly social rank focused, especially on the power of others to control, hurt or reject them.' They go on to suggest that high levels of criticism are fundamentally linked to insecure attachments. Their solution to this problem is to train individuals to engage in self-soothing strategies and self-reassurance. Their basic philosophy is that, 'some people have not had opportunities to develop their abilities to understand the sources of their distress, be gentle and self-soothing in the context of setbacks and disappointments but are highly (internally and externally) threat focused and sensitive. When a setback, failure or conflict occurs they rapidly access internal schema of others as hostile rejecting (Baldwin, 2005) with (well-practised) self-focused, self-attacking.'

The researchers investigated whether people could be taught to be self-soothing and whether people could be taught to generate internally 'feelings of compassion' when they are feeling threatened and whether people can be trained to have quite a different emotionally laden inner conversation. This was examined by asking people to create a vivid mental image of warmth and either 'by thinking or recalling one's own compassionate motives and feelings flowing *outwards* to others (e.g., imagine compassion and warmth for a child or someone one cares about)'. And they also used other forms of imagery as an aid, whereby the participants in the research had to learn to conjure up a compassionate image when required (this could be something warm and soothing like a tree, the sea or a particular type of animal). Then when they had this particular image in mind, and a sense of what compassionate feelings are like, they had to learn to generate this image every time they felt shame coming on, and then examine their thoughts in a more detached way. Using this quite basic technique the researchers found that the self-critical thoughts decreased in frequency, they also started to lose their power and became less obtrusive. On the other hand, their self-serving thoughts became 'more powerful and accessible'. There were also reductions in their feelings of inferiority and the experimental participants became more assertive.

This is a novel approach to an age-old problem. It goes beyond normal treatments of cognitive therapy to introduce emotion and warmth into directed self-talk. It essentially suggests that the next time you feel shame and self-loathing, conjure up a positive image and imagine warmth coming from this image, warmth of the kind that you know and recognize, because you yourself are capable of it. It is not an arithmetic substitution of one thought for another, but an attempt to change the emotional balance of a thought by conjuring up a different emotional context for it. The idea is that while some people develop these kinds of strategies naturally and instinctively through normal processes of development, some people do not (but through no essential fault of their own). Some people learn how to deal with things that go wrong in everyday life in their own way by soothing themselves first, and by not jumping to the stage of self-criticism immediately. Gilbert and Proctor's study suggests that we can all learn a new approach.

This is an interesting clinical study which introduces some basic neurophysiology into psychological treatments and the results look very promising. But the limitation of the study is that it was very restricted in its scope; it was a very small study involving nine patients of which three dropped out. This new therapy might not work for everyone but it has some face validity. It is extraordinary the way that some people direct criticism on themselves in the most irrational of ways and perhaps it is stating the obvious to say that some of these individuals need to develop ways of comforting and reassuring themselves before allowing the self-criticism and shame to kick in. What Gilbert and Proctor are asking us to do here is to think of a number of self-comforting words, thoughts and images and produce them in our heads whenever we need to. This could be a real dividend for many people, who need to care more about themselves and to treat themselves better, even with a number of simple procedures.

- Many people punish themselves with feelings of shame
- Learn to comfort yourself by evoking a strong positive mental image of something good whenever you feel shame coming on

How to combat loneliness

If you are feeling really down and lonely and think that you have no significant support from any close friends, then deliberately bring to mind an event from your past that evokes nostalgic feelings. When you think nostalgically about the past it should bring to mind not just a whole series of positive emotions, but negative emotions as well. But critically it will remind you of the connections you had with other people and it will increase your feeling of connection with the people and the world around you. This helps reverse the effects of loneliness. It reminds you of the closeness you had in the past with people and encourages you to think about the connections that you can have again.

Loneliness is an unpleasant state of negative emotion characterized by a general level of unhappiness, pessimism and, often for many people, self-blame. The normal (and obvious) cure for loneliness is to encourage people to develop more social relationships. But can you combat loneliness without necessarily involving other people? This was the question posed by Xinyue Zhou of the Sun Yat-Sen University in China and his colleagues. This group acknowledge the research of Tim Wildschut (2006), of the University of Southampton, who proposes that nostalgia, which is a certain kind of 'sentimental longing for the past', can work to re-establish a symbolic, if not a physical connection, with other people. Wildschut and his colleagues asked research participants to think of a nostalgic event and then write about it. They asked an additional set of people to think of an ordinary event and write about that. They found that participants who had been asked to reminisce nostalgically reported feeling more bonded with others and more securely attached.

So Zhou and his colleagues pushed this idea further by suggesting that we may be able to counteract feelings of loneliness by asking people to draw on nostalgic memories. Following the earlier study, their experimental participants were asked to, 'bring to mind a nostalgic event in your life. Specifically, try to think of a past event that makes you feel most nostalgic.' They found that inducing nostalgia in this way led their experimental participants to feel more social support on the standardized measure which included responses such as 'I can count on my friends when things go wrong'. They also found that asking people to think nostalgically meant that they listed a greater number of friends (who would volunteer for a task when asked to do so). In other words, merely asking people to have nostalgic thoughts increases their sense of connection with the world around them. It reminds them of their social bonds and gives them a more optimistic view of their friends and how they might help.

Loneliness has the opposite effect to all of this. When you are feeling lonely, you feel isolated, lacking in social support and much less optimistic about the role of friends in your life. The researchers thus suggest that nostalgia, and the process of consciously and deliberately bringing to mind nostalgic thoughts, might be a useful alternative coping strategy in dealing with loneliness. In the words of the authors, 'the past, when appropriately harnessed, can strengthen psychological resistance to the vicissitudes of life.'

This is an interesting result in that we normally think that loneliness can only be cured by increased social contact. This study suggests there is something we can do in the meantime. We can allow ourselves to have nostalgic thoughts – this will not make our feeling of loneliness worse, it will have the opposite effect. The instruction given to the participants was very broad ('bring to mind a nostalgic event in your life') and in some sense the results are even more impressive given the broad instruction and presumably the diversity of the response. However, there is always the possibility that some nostalgic thoughts might be best avoided, but this study doesn't allow us to identify what these might be. This particular study was carried out on university students and factory workers in China, and the researchers argue for the universal nature of their findings. Loneliness is found in all cultures, and nostalgia, with its curious blend of positive and negative emotions, would also seem to be a more or less universal phenomenon and a possible antidote to the effects of loneliness.

My mother suffered terribly from loneliness as she got older. I was in England with a family of my own to look after while she was stuck in Belfast, quite alone. Her old girlfriends had either moved away or were married. 'I've no wee chums any more to go out with,' she would say. She liked to talk nostalgically about old times and about me and my brother Bill when we were young, to combat this terrible sense of isolation. She always said that all she ever wanted was for us all to be together again. 'I remember coming over the Hightown one night, with your father and you and Bill in the car, and I was scared because it was dark. But then I thought that we were a family all together and that if we went off the road and we died then we'd still be together. And then I realized that I wasn't scared any more.' This was the nostalgic thought that she clung to and told over and over again. This desperate, and from my point of view slightly alarming, thought seemed to help her a little, but I always wished that she would try other images and other thoughts as well.

But one good thing was that she didn't bottle up her feelings regarding her sense of isolation – quite the opposite in fact – she would tell anyone who would listen how lonely she was. In the 1990s she came with me to an awards ceremony for the Ewart-Biggs Literary Prize when my book *We are the People: Journeys through the Heart of Protestant Ulster* was shortlisted. The great and the good of Belfast milled around in a posh bank in the centre of Belfast, bathed in the bright, white lights of the television cameras. Some of the Ewart family were themselves present that night. My mother had worked in Ewart's linen mill all her life so this event meant something special to her. 'We're mixing with the nobs tonight, alright,' she said. The prize was in honour of Christopher Ewart-Biggs, the British Ambassador to Ireland, who had been murdered by the IRA in 1976. My mother had a few glasses of wine, which she gratefully accepted off the trays from smiling waitresses in starched white uniforms. 'You don't even have to go to the bar yourself, they bring it over to you,' she said, and she stood chatting to Brian Keenan, who was also shortlisted for the prize. He told my mother all about his book and his life and about how he had been taken hostage in

Beirut by Shi'ite militiamen and held in captivity for four and a half years.

Brian spoke in a whisper after all those years locked in a Beirut cellar. I could hear the conversation. 'Speak up, Brian,' my mother kept saying to him. 'I can hardly hear you. Speak up, Brian, for God's sake. You don't have to whisper now.' Brian kissed her gently on the cheek when he was called forward to receive the prize for his wonderful and desperately harrowing book *An Evil Cradling*. 'He deserved it,' she said to me, as the applause started to subside, 'for all those years sitting in the dark in that bloody cellar. He told me all about it. I couldn't believe it. What did they want with him? But I said to him, don't worry about it, Brian, I know what it's like. I never bloody well get out either. We both know what it's like to be stuck in night after night with nowhere to bloody well go.'

Brian hugged her when he came back with the cheque in his hand, a shy smile on his face. 'Do you still drive, Brian?' my mother enquired. 'That captivity hasn't put you off, has it? Remember, if you're ever up in North Belfast, and you've got a nice wee car, you could always take me out for a wee drink. After all, you and I both know what it's like to sit in night after night staring at those same four bloody walls. You just have to get out.'

I don't think that Brian ever made it up to that particular part of Belfast, but if he had, my mother would, I am sure, have overwhelmed him with her nostalgic memories of how things were, and I am confident that this would have done her a power of good, and helped, at least temporarily, with her terrible sense of loneliness and isolation.

- Combat feelings of loneliness by allowing yourself to have nostalgic thoughts
- These nostalgic thoughts will remind you of your social bonds in the past and will make you feel better about the present

How to forgive and forget

If you want to forgive someone for doing something bad to you, the best way is to get a blank sheet of paper and write about what happened, focusing on the positive aspects. Specifically, write about the ways in which this event has led to positive consequences for you:

Has your life become better as a result of it?
Have you learned anything about yourself or about the world because of it?
Have you become better at communicating your feelings because of it?
Has it allowed for new life experiences?
Have you discovered unknown strengths?
Have you become more compassionate?
Have you learned to stand up for yourself?
Have you learned what to look for in a romantic partner?

The secret in writing about it is to really let go and to be totally honest, but focus not just on the event itself but on the positive effects on your own life. Research has shown that focusing on the positive benefits of the event in this way leads to more insights about the event and it allows you to forgive. The reason that it is important to forgive is that we know that those who cannot forgive are more prone to depression and stress. Writing about the event in this particular way, focusing on the positive benefits for yourself, can have a major impact on this negative emotion and therefore can protect you, to some extent, from further harmful effects in the future.

In everyday life people can sometimes do things to others which can be very hurtful. When you are on the receiving end of these hurtful acts, it is often very difficult to get over them, no matter how hard you try. Take, for example, infidelity. Research has shown, for example, that if your partner is unfaithful to you, you are six times more likely to suffer from a major depressive disorder (Cano and O'Leary, 2000). When you are on the receiving end of hurtful acts, a whole series of negative psychological effects starts to occur. You often want to avoid the person in question (difficult, if it's your partner), and you will often be overcome by your desire for revenge. These vengeful thoughts lead to anger and arousal of the cardiovascular system and you can get very stressed as a consequence. In addition, when you feel vengeful and unforgiving you become more prone to depression. So clearly helping people to deal with the consequences of these kinds of interpersonal transgressions becomes an important psychological issue. In the words of Michael McCullough, Lindsey Root and Adam Cohen of the University of Miami, 'Helping people modify their response to transgressions may be useful for helping them improve their relationships as well as their psychological and physical health.'

The way that these researchers attempted to examine this was by focusing on the psychology of forgiveness. Forgiveness is a complex and somewhat mysterious process by which an individual becomes more positive about the person who has caused the hurt. But the key questions are: How do people forgive and why? Can some people forgive easily and not others. Is there any way of facilitating forgiveness?

According to the researchers, there is one critical component of forgiveness, and that is the process of the victim of the hurt finding some benefit in what has happened to them. In the words of the researchers, 'Transgressions come with costs to the victim (e.g. loss of trust, self-esteem, material resources, physical or psychological well-being, etc.). However, focusing on the benefits that one has gained (or might gain in the future) from a transgression could help to negate some of the transgression's psychological costs and, by doing so, encourage forgiveness.' The kinds of benefits that the researchers refer to are things like the sudden realization of your inner strengths, the realization that you have not been destroyed by what has happened to you, a new, deeper appreciation for your life and other things in your life (like children), improved relationships with other people, or the fact that you have become wiser because of the process and maybe have had to deal with things on your own for the first time, thus developing a degree of confidence. The researchers report other work in this area by Zechmeister and Romero (2002), who had asked participants to write about events that had happened to them in the past, in which they viewed themselves as either the victim or the perpetrator. They had to say whether what had happened was either forgiven or not. The researchers found that only 2 per cent of the victims who did not forgive the other person for what had happened wrote that the incident had any positive consequences at all, whereas 21 per cent of victims who forgave the other person for what had happened reported a number of positive outcomes.

From these results, therefore, it might appear that there might well be some relationship between forgiveness and a natural focus on positive consequences. But which way round is the relationship? Do you forgive someone for something because you can see the positive aspects of it for yourself? Or do you see the positive aspects of something because you have forgiven the other person for it? And, perhaps even more importantly, can you facilitate forgiveness by specifically getting people to focus on the positive consequences of what happened? That was the question that McCullough and his colleagues asked, by getting their research participants to write about 'a harmful thing that someone that you know did to you in the past'. They asked participants to focus on what happened, how they felt about it and also how they were affected by it. A second group was asked to write about the same thing but this time focusing on the positive outcomes of the event and the personal benefits in the outcome. Specifically they were prompted by questions like, 'In what ways has your life become better as a result of the harmful thing that occurred to you?' and 'In what way is your life or the person you have become, better today as a result of the harmful thing that occurred to you?' The researchers took a number of measures of forgiveness by measuring motivation to:

avoid the transgressor – '*I live as though he/she doesn't exist*'

and

revenge – '*I will make him/her pay*'

They also used *Linguistic Inquiry and Word Count* (LIWC) to analyse what was written. LIWC is a computer program for categorizing words into seventy grammatical, linguistic or psychological categories. Here, the researchers focused on positive emotion words, negative emotion words and words indicating a high level of mental processing, including words that identify possible cause-and-effect relations and words displaying insight:

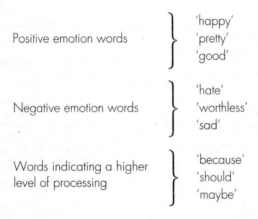

Positive emotion words	'happy' 'pretty' 'good'
Negative emotion words	'hate' 'worthless' 'sad'
Words indicating a higher level of processing	'because' 'should' 'maybe'

They also created two new categories, one based on benefit-related words and one based on cost-related words:

Benefit-related words	Cost-related words
'learned'	'devastation'
'recovered'	'violated'
'blessed'	'betrayed'
'benefited'	'unfair'
'stronger'	'broken'

The researchers found that the kinds of transgression written about in the essays were mostly committed by boyfriends or girl-friends and the most common forms of 'transgressions' were:

- Romantic infidelity (30 per cent)
- Insults by a friend or betrayals of confidence (20 per cent)
- Rejection, neglect or insult by a family member (15 per cent)

When participants simply wrote about the trauma, they tended to focus on the event itself, their thoughts about it (e.g. disbelief, confusion, attempts to rationalize or justify the event), their feelings (e.g. anger, pain, sadness, shock, humiliation) and their psychosomatic response to the transgression (e.g. dizziness, vomiting, sleep problems) as well as their subsequent behaviours (e.g. aggression). The researchers found that participants often went on to describe other types of negative consequences as well (e.g. changes in self-esteem, problems with body image, even changes in perception of themselves as a potential partner for future relationships). On the other hand, in the condition where they had to focus on possible benefits, the participants tended not to describe the actual event itself in quite so much detail; instead they listed (as they were requested to do) the perceived benefits for themselves of what had occurred. The computer program demonstrated that in the condition in which they focused on the trauma, a higher proportion of the individual words used were cost related, whereas in the condition where they were told to focus on the benefits, a higher proportion of the words were benefit related.

The big question was how did each of the instructions that were provided in terms of how to write the essays affect forgiveness? The results were clear. When people focused on possible benefits in their essays, this significantly lowered the avoidance score and also the revenge score. So in other words, when you explicitly instruct people to write about the benefits of a harmful event that another human being has done to you, they are more likely to forgive that person, less likely to want to avoid them and less motivated to seek revenge on them. The benefits which the participants came up with (quite readily, according to the researchers) were things like:

- 'grew stronger or discovered unknown strengths' (55 per cent)
- 'became wiser' (44 per cent)
- 'allowed for new life experience' (29 per cent)
- 'strengthened other relationships' (26 per cent)
- 'became better at communicating feelings' (25 per cent)

So what these researchers had done was to demonstrate that you can foster forgiveness by asking people to focus specifically on the benefits obtained from someone doing something wrong to them. The one thing that characterized these particular written accounts was that there was a greater proportion of words indicating a higher level of thinking (words identifying cause-and-effect relationships, and insight words). When people are asked to focus on the positive aspects of bad things that have happened, they do think differently about the event and spell out the implications. So if you want to forgive someone who has done something bad to you, think about how this whole sorry event may have benefited you, think about how it may have helped you and develop and change as a person. Forget revenge.

This is clearly an interesting and practical study, limited slightly by the fact that all of the measures of avoidance and revenge are self-reported measures rather than actual behavioural observations. There is also no indication in this study of how long or how permanent (or temporary) the effects might be. So does focusing on the positive benefits of a negative event like this have short-term effects or does it produce more enduring changes? This particular study doesn't tell us this but the authors seem well aware of the possible limitations and they may set out to answer some of these questions in subsequent years. Given the possible health benefits of forgiveness, this would seem like an important and urgent task. The other problem with the research is the transgressions that were written about were those that would typify the student population used as the experimental participants. Whether the results can be generalized to much more serious transgressions like sexual assault or rape or even marital infidelity (where you have spent a lifetime and not just a few months with your partner) does remain to be seen.

- Learn to forgive and forget by focusing on what positive things have come out of the experience

- All experiences change us. Ask yourself how this particular experience has changed your life for the good. Has it made you more independent, has it made you less naive, has it made you mentally stronger?

- Write about these changes. The more honest and the more thoughtful the account the better

How to stop yourself getting stressed by harbouring a grudge

If you want to avoid harbouring a grudge towards another, you need to learn to develop feelings of empathy for the perpetrator and to grant forgiveness by letting go of the extreme negative feelings.

When people are asked specifically to think about what factors may have influenced the perpetrator's behaviour and are asked to let go of the negative feelings associated with the offence, this has a major impact on the physiology of the body. Both the heart rate and blood pressure lower, there are fewer frowns and lower skin conductance is as a good indicator of sympathetic nervous-system activity.

The alternative response to transgressions in which people rehearse the hurt that has been caused to them, by endlessly reliving the memory of the painful experience, seems to have the opposite effect on the body's physiology by producing an endless series of stress responses which can have a major impact on health. So if you want to avoid harbouring a grudge think about what factors may have influenced the perpetrator. Don't just focus on the act itself; try to imagine the factors leading up to it. Try to take his or her perspective when you are trying to forgive them. Remember that this does not involve condoning or excusing the act, rather it is about letting go of those extreme negative feelings. If you can work on your empathy and the letting go of the negative emotions, this will have long-term emotional and physical benefits.

When someone has done something bad to you, there are a number of different responses that people usually have. Some rehearse the hurt and pain and relive the memory over and over again. Some hold a grudge, remembering themselves as the victim of the other person's selfish behaviour. These are both types of unforgiving response. Others do try to forgive, however; sometimes they try to develop feelings of empathy towards the perpetrator, trying sometimes desperately to understand why they might have done what they did in the first place. Still others try to forgive the person for what they have done and let go of the negative feelings towards the perpetrator (and as we have seen previously this may well involve recognizing the potential positive effects of the act itself).

According to Charlotte van Oyen Witvliet and her colleagues at Hope College in Holland, Michigan, these different types of response (holding a grudge versus forgiveness etc.) may have a big impact on the body's basic physiology and on our psychological and physical health. The way they tested this was to ask a set of participants to think of one particular person who they blamed for mistreating, offending or hurting them in some way, and then they had to imagine vividly each of the four types of unforgiving and forgiving response ('rehearsing the hurt', 'harbouring a grudge', 'developing feelings of empathy' or 'granting forgiveness'). The researchers measured the participants' heart rate and blood pressure throughout as well as taking measure of facial behaviour (as a sign of their emotional response to what they were talking about). They also measured skin conductance level as a measure of sympathetic nervous-system activity. While the participants rehearsed their hurt or imagined harbouring a grudge, they reported feeling significantly higher levels of arousal; in addition they were angrier, sadder and felt less in control. As well as their facial expressions showing more frowning, the skin conductance scores were higher as were their heart rates and blood pressure. This could have a major impact on health because unforgiving responses, in particular, seem to perpetuate anger and heighten arousal and cardiovascular response.

This was the first study to explore the psychological effects of consciously using forgiving or unforgiving strategies for dealing with real-life events. It tells us that trying to understand the perpetrator's point of view and trying to let go of all of the negative emotions ultimately protects our body and our health.

One of the more surprising features of forgiveness is how some people seem to be able to forgive more readily than others. You hear of people who have lost family members to terrorist bombs saying that they forgive the perpetrators, while other people look incredulously at this response. This study does not tell us anything about why some people are more inclined to forgive than others, but it does tell us that if you specifically request people to think in certain ways it can have a big impact on mood state and cardiovascular activity. It would seem that we all should, regardless of our natural inclinations, try to develop more forgiving responses to transgressions, because in the end unforgiving responses just ultimately harm ourselves.

- Remember that if you are able to forgive someone, you will be able to release a lot of negative feelings
- Forgiving someone will make you healthier and stronger
- Think about why they might have done what they did
- Try to take their perspective, to understand what occurred from their point of view

How to stop being tortured by regret

Many people have their lives ruined by regret: 'If only I had revised more thoroughly,' they say, 'I would have passed my exam and my life would have been a success' or 'If only I hadn't stayed out with my friends that night I wouldn't have got into trouble'. Regret seems like a difficult emotion to deal with sometimes and it can have a big influence in subsequent decision-making, such that many people will avoid trying something which could lead them to fail by a narrow margin because they think it could lead to higher levels of regret and self-punishment. They would rather not try at all than fail badly so that there is nothing to regret. But there is evidence that people are not good at predicting or anticipating how much regret they will feel when they narrowly fail to achieve something, and that the size of margin by which you fail may influence the anticipated level of regret but not the actual level, at least in some domains. So don't let the anticipation of regret rule your life and govern your decisions. When a major task is looming, just go for it and sideline thoughts of possible regret because these thoughts will not tell you how you will actually feel anyway.

The fear of regret plays a major role in decision-making. Research in psychology appears to show that the possibility of regret, and the anticipation of it, has a major effect on people's decision-making. We feel regret when we behave foolishly, when we have accepted bad advice and when we have failed by a narrow margin. According to Daniel Kahneman and Dale Miller (1986), regret is a 'counterfactual emotion' that arises when we recognize that some negative event is attributable to our own actions. Self-blame is often a major feature of regret. Regret is much worse when we have a near miss at something (and nearly got it right) than when we have done something really badly and failed altogether. Most people believe that a near miss makes the whole process of self-blame that much worse.

According to Daniel T. Gilbert of Harvard University and his colleagues, these expectations may be quite wrong and they argue that too many people allow the anticipation of regret to rule their lives. Gilbert says that people are very good at rationalizing negative outcomes once they occur and in his words people 'may be better at avoiding regret than they realize'. To test this, he set up an experiment which mimicked the game show *The Price is Right*, in which people had to set supermarket items in the order of price and then identify which set was most likely to be the correct one. The experimenters always told the participants that they had chosen the incorrect set, but in one condition they were told that the other set was also incorrect (the wide-margin condition) whereas in the other condition they were told that the opposite set was correct (the narrow-margin condition). After the experiment, participants were asked how much regret and disappointment they felt. But, in addition to this, they were asked how much regret and disappointment they thought they would feel given the other possible outcome. The results were quite striking in that the size of the margin of the error (narrow versus wide) influenced anticipated regret but did not have a significant effect on actual felt regret. In other words, it affected how they *thought* they would feel but didn't actually affect how they did feel.

In a second experiment, Gilbert and his colleagues studied people who had missed a train at a subway station in Cambridge, Massachusetts, asking them how they felt (a risky bit of research, if you ask me). The commuters were told either that they had narrowly missed their train or that they had missed the train by some margin. Others were asked how they thought they would feel if they narrowly missed their train or missed it by a much wider margin. The researchers found exactly the same pattern of results, with the size of the margin influencing the forecast of regret but not the experienced regret.

The conclusions of the researchers are that regret is not as bad as it may appear in prospect. People think that they would feel really bad if they narrowly failed to do something compared to failing it by a wider margin, but this is not necessarily the case. The size of the margin only influences anticipated regret not experienced regret. According to Gilbert's team this is not a trivial phenomenon because in everyday life many people will often 'favor gambles in which bad outcomes are likely but unregrettable over gambles in which bad outcomes are unlikely but regrettable'. This strategy only makes sense if we are accurate in predicting what level of regret we will feel. It turns out that we are not very good at this process.

This is an interesting study which suggests that people do not know themselves or what emotions they will feel in particular situations as accurately as they think. Many people's lives are overshadowed by regret: 'If only I had done this, if only I hadn't done that.' This overshadowing causes them to avoid doing things in particular ways.

When it comes to the possible limitations of the study there are two obvious issues. The first is the nature of the tasks used and whether they are capable of generating the kind of regret that can be genuinely debilitating. One might suggest that judging a list of items in a 'Price is Right' game, or narrowly missing a train, do not produce the high levels of regret found in many of our lives. The second problem is that the participants were specifically asked about what level of regret they felt three minutes after making the wrong 'Price is Right' judgement or just after missing the train. Regret is such an insidious emotion that almost seems to have its own will in tormenting us. It arrives at unpredictable intervals and can stay with us for long periods of time. Whether it can be accurately measured in a fixed interval is a major question.

- We are not good at judging the level of regret that we will feel in any situation
- Don't let the fear of regret inhibit your life

---

5. FOSTERING INTIMACY

'It is not enough to conquer; one must
know how to seduce.'

Voltaire, *Merope* (1743), 1.4

How to laugh someone into bed

You can laugh a woman into bed by telling her a funny story or a joke with a punchline that is much funnier than she expects. The secret is that you need to think about how to increase that psychological gap between what they expect at the end of the joke and what they actually get. It is the unanticipated nature of the funniness of the punchline which seems to have a big impact on the female brain and affects the neural pathways connected with reward. To laugh a woman into bed you need to build on the gap between expectation and delivery. For example, make out that you are not a very funny guy and then hit them with that killer witty line of your own making. Or alternatively, find a really, really funny joke that they won't have heard before. This should also do the trick for you (without necessarily the same level of creative input from yourself). It won't do if it's a joke that they have heard before, because they might well be able to anticipate the level of funniness of the punchline (without necessarily being able to remember what the actual punchline is). It is much harder to laugh a man into bed, however, because they seem to expect much more once a joke or story has started.

The scientific basis to this advice goes something like this. It is a common belief that women really do find men who make them laugh attractive. A man's sense of humour (and their ability to make someone laugh) is an attribute typically rated very highly by women. The reason for this is usually understood in terms of a simple psychological mechanism. It is normally argued that humour demonstrates (and signals) a man's confidence and, the argument is, women tend to go for confident men because from an evolutionary point of view confidence reflects something positive about reproductive success. The reverse, however, doesn't seem to hold, in that female humour often doesn't seem to have the same effect on men (and some people have pointed out that male comedians are often perceived as sexually attractive in a way that female comediennes are not). Research by Eiman Azim and his colleagues at Stanford University, which analysed how the brain responds to humorous material, may help us to understand why there are important sex differences in our appreciation of, and response to, humour (and perhaps also our psychological response to the teller of the joke).

The researchers point out that there are two basic types of process involved in the appreciation of humour. Firstly, there are those processes involved in the understanding and the integration of the humorous material ('Oh, I get it!'), and then after the material has been comprehended, there are those processes involved in the feeling of amusement and of positive emotion ('That is really good. Ha! Ha! Ha!).

The researchers scanned the brains of healthy volunteers as they read a series of funny and unfunny cartoons. The participants had to respond with a button press if they found the cartoon funny. The researchers found that comprehension of the cartoons was associated with activity in the area of the brain known as the temporal-occipital junction and temporal pole. The prefrontal cortex was also involved because it is responsible for managing the response to the incoming material. The feelings of amusement and positive emotion involve a different part of the brain known as the mesolimbic reward system and particularly the dopaminergic reward pathways.

What the researchers found was that when you scan the brains of men and women looking at non-verbal cartoons, you find activation in the left temporal-occipital junction and the temporal pole in both sexes, but women use specific brain regions to a greater extent than men when presented with the humorous material, particularly the left prefrontal cortex. This suggests greater use of executive functions in women. These are the functions key to understanding the cartoons, things like working memory, verbal abstraction and the screening out of irrelevant material. In other words, women's brains do more work on the incoming material than men's, and in addition they show more activation of the mesolimbic reward region (i.e. they get more of a buzz out of it). In the words of Azim *et al.*, 'This small brain region has been implicated in psychological reward, including situations of self-reported happiness, monetary reward receipt, the processing of attractive faces, and cocaine-induced euphoria.' And this occurs even with cartoons which are rated just as funny for the men as for the women. Azim goes on to assert, 'Because equivalent amusement seems to be processed differently, the patterns of activity observed here may provide compelling insight into sex-based differences in humour at the neural level.' In other words, women's brains process humorous material differently to men and they get much more of a reward from it when the punchline finally arrives.

So how do you laugh a woman into bed? You need to build on the chasm between expectation and delivery. Give them the impression that you are not a funny guy at all and then start to tell a joke (their heart will sink); they will have very low expectations about how good the punchline will be and then you hit them with a great final line. Their prefrontal cortex will have been activated throughout and then you will have stimulated their mesolimbic reward system in a way that they wouldn't have thought possible. It will be like cocaine-induced euphoria. The rest is up to you.

This is new science in which brain-imaging studies are telling us things about how the brain actually works as it processes the world around us. There was always the feeling that males and females reacted differently to humorous material, and now we know a little more about the possible nature of sex differences in terms of actual neural processes. How general are the results which were found? It's an important question because not every form of humour requires the types of integration sometimes necessary with sophisticated cartoons. What happens in the brains of men and women when they process the kinds of funny stories usually heard in bars or restaurants? We have no idea. But there are some grounds for optimism here. What we might guess is that the low expectations of women regarding punch-lines might be even more intense in this context, so the unexpectedly funny punchline could be even more effective in these kinds of situations.

- Women find funny men very sexy
- Women's mesolimbic ('reward') system is more activated than men's when they process funny material

- Men anticipate the punchline too much in humour, and are often disappointed when the punchline finally comes

- Women have lower expectations about what the punchline will deliver, and get more of a hit when the punchline is funnier than expected

- To laugh a woman into bed, tell them a joke with a punchline that is actually funnier than expected

- Alternatively, make out that you're not a funny guy to begin with and then hit them with a great punchline

- In laughing a woman into bed, it's all about the gap between what is expected and what is delivered. The bigger the gap the greater their brain activation

How to flirt more effectively with one simple (mental) step

Here is a simple tip to help you flirt more effectively – think about it differently. It's meant to be fun (men especially need to remember this). Research shows that males and females approach flirting, and view the fundamental nature of flirting, with a somewhat different mindset. For women, flirting is often about fun and enjoyment, and it is often regarded by them as an essentially playful form of activity. It is a way of getting attention from a number of men, and once a woman has got that initial attention, she can be selective and pick and choose between them on the basis of more information, such as how they respond and behave in the flirting situation. For females, flirting is also a subtle way of changing the intimacy of the relationship between two people. Males tend to view flirting as being much more serious than that, and primarily they see it as a form of activity directly linked to sex. In order to flirt more effectively, men need to change their mindset and tune in more to the playful nature of flirting. Women need to think more about the non-verbal signals which are responsible for escalating flirting from playfulness into something else. If men and women could align their thinking about flirting, the whole process would be much more enjoyable for both parties. Men, however, might need to do the most adjustment in terms of their thinking.

It is surprising that flirting is so much of a problem for so many people. It's meant to be fun, but sometimes it isn't because it is often difficult to interpret the intentions behind each of the individual behaviours. There is a perennial danger of miscommunication in this area, where the meaning attributed to the message by the receiver can be at odds with the meaning intended by the sender. Women frequently complain that behaviours that they intended as just a bit of fun are misinterpreted by men as overt displays of sexual intent. The problem is that many of the behaviours that are displayed in flirting (eye gaze, lip lick, hair toss, etc.) are exactly the same behaviours displayed if one or both parties are interested in a sexual encounter. Over forty years ago the American psychologist Albert Scheflen (1965) called these behaviours 'quasi courtship behaviours'. David Henningsen of Northern Illinois University investigated sex differences in the perception of the motivations that underlie flirting. He identified six different possible motivations, as follows:

Motivation 1	}	The desire for sex.
Motivation 2	}	The motivation to change the intensity of a relationship, in other words, people will often flirt in order to engineer a more intimate relationship.
Motivation 3	}	To explore whether other people are interested in you, before making any subsequent decision about what type of interaction you want to have with them.
Motivation 4	}	Flirting for the sake of fun, and because it is enjoyable.
Motivation 5	}	The desire to build one's own self-esteem, in that if others respond to you in a positive way because of your flirting it can make you feel better about yourself.
Motivation 6	}	'Instrumental motivation', which is flirting with someone to get some reward (for example in a bar in the hope of being bought a drink).

Henningsen asked his experimental participants to think about the kinds of behaviours that people show in a typical flirting interaction and to write down all of the words that would be used during the interaction, describing all of the non-verbal actions associated with the conversation. They then had to go back through this detailed script identifying each and every single flirting action and to code each of the behaviours in terms of the six possible motivations that could underlie the flirting (for example, 'sexual', 'relational', 'exploration', 'fun', 'maintaining self-esteem' or 'instrumental'). Participants had to identify the *main* motivation underlying each act (even though, on occasion, there might well be a variety of motivations underlying a single behaviour, e.g. 'exploration and fun').

The analyses revealed that men systematically identified more sexual motives than women, and women identified significantly more flirting behaviour as being primarily connected with changing the intimacy of a relationship. In other words, this study reveals clearly what many people already suspected: that men and women read the signals of flirting quite differently, because they assume that they have very different underlying motives. Henningsen uses an evolutionary perspective to try to understand the findings and he argues that women might flirt more for fun because this allows them to practise different flirting strategies so that they can work out which is effective and which is ineffective. Women need to be better at flirting than men because they can use it to keep men interested and it allows them to find out more about potential suitors during the sustained flirting period.

So how should you go about flirting? The single most important thing to remember is that men and women flirt with a very different mindset and that successful flirting involves not just the convergence of behaviours, but also the convergence of minds. Men need to learn that for women flirting is a fun and enjoyable form of interaction rooted in evolution and that it holds no promises. If they could accept this simple idea, then some of the common miscommunication simply wouldn't occur. Women need to ensure that the playfulness of the flirting is signalled throughout, with smiles, laughter and teasing, so that the men understand that this is a bit of fun (and just that), and needs to be treated as such. They need these playful signals accompanying the talk (so called 'meta-signals') to play more of a role in directing the whole thing.

However, the one thing that Henningsen didn't do was to show examples on video tape to men and women in order for them to identify the underlying motivations. His participants simply had to note (and then rate) their own list of behaviours in written form. An interesting extension of his research would be to determine how subtle changes in the forms of behaviour that accompany the talk (the meta-signals) can affect the attribution of underlying motivation. There is always the possibility that men and women read some of the subtle playful signals of flirting quite differently and immediately jump to automatic and wrong conclusions about why the behaviours occurred in the first place. In summary, there is much additional research to be done in this area before we fully understand why men and women are often at such cross-purposes when it comes to flirting.

- To flirt more effectively, remember that men and women approach flirting differently

- Women are more likely than men to see flirting as just a bit of fun

- Men should focus on the fun element and enjoy it differently and more. It does not have to be that serious

How to get your partner to be more intimate in a relationship

You can get your partner to be more psychologically intimate with you by deliberately sending signals that unconsciously and subtly remind them of sex. The outcome is that individuals want to disclose more to another person; they want to sacrifice themselves more for their partner; they want to be more cooperative in terms of how they deal with conflict within the relationship; and they are more ready to think about intimacy when they have been unconsciously exposed to sexual stimuli. If you want your partner to be more intimate, take them to an art gallery; works of art naturally stimulate our aesthetic values, but there may well be more than a hint of sex in a few of them. Flick through some glossy magazines together and look at the adverts; some of them contain sexual 'embeds' that unconsciously provoke your imagination. Or simply wear an item of clothing that you had on the last time you had sex. It will unconsciously remind your partner of your most recent intimacy and it may well result in the stimulation of certain parts of the brain and, as a consequence, increase in the desire to make the relationship closer.

Omri Gillath of the University of Kansas and his colleagues tested the idea that one way of getting people to form and maintain closer intimate relationships is by unconsciously stimulating their sexual interest. Their theoretical starting point is the notion that the secretion of oxytocin during sexual foreplay and during sex itself, not only produces highly rewarding sensations and emotions, but it also activates neural or brain pathways which mediate social bonding and attachment. This research, however, derives mainly from animal studies in which the levels of oxytocin can be measured. Gillath suggests that, 'these findings support the idea that sexual stimuli and sexual behaviour may be part of a system that contributes to relationship formation and maintenance. This suggests the possibility that exposing people to sexual stimuli will motivate them, implicitly or explicitly, to initiate and maintain a close relationship.' In some senses this is not that surprising. In most people's minds, sex and the intensity of a relationship would seem to be closely connected, but the next step is perhaps a little surprising. The researchers carried out five experiments in which they exposed people to either sexual or neutral stimuli and tested whether this exposure increased their tendency to initiate and maintain close relationships. The extraordinary thing about the experiments is that the researchers tested whether the stimuli had to be presented in such a way that participants had to be consciously aware of them, or whether they would also work when they were presented without the conscious awareness of the recipients, i.e. when the stimuli were presented subliminally.

Gillath's previous research using brain-imaging techniques had shown that when pictures of naked people were presented subliminally, there was increased activation in sex-related regions of the brain (e.g. the thalamus and Brodmann's area 7), which are areas of the brain normally associated with sexual stimulation, orgasm and ejaculation. Subliminal exposure to pictures of naked people, however, did not result in activation of those parts of the brain connected with the control of behaviour (the orbital frontal cortex). You would appear to need stimuli which can be consciously perceived to affect these areas. In the study itself, the participants *thought* that their task was to decide how similar the names of two pieces of furniture were. The presentation of the names was preceded by a brief flash, but the flash was actually a subliminal prime (i.e. trigger) – the prime was either sexual (an erotic picture) or neutral (an abstract picture) presented for 30 milliseconds.

In the first study the researchers looked at the willingness of their participants to disclose information to a romantic partner depending upon whether they had been exposed to the sexual prime ('an attractive, naked reclining man shown from the groin up for the female participants; an attractive, naked kneeling woman photographed from behind for the male participants') or the neutral prime (an abstract picture with no obvious or subliminal sexual content). In a second experiment, they looked at the effects of the different sorts of prime on the willingness of the participants to sacrifice themselves for their partner (basically to suspend self-interest, to promote the well-being of one's partner). In a third experiment, they looked at the effects of the prime on the accessibility of intimacy-related thoughts. In another experiment, they looked at the effect of the prime on how the participants liked to restore conflict situations with their partner and particularly on whether they used positive strategies (including compromise) or negative strategies (principally trying to dominate and control the other person).

The results were extraordinary in that, for all the experiments, the subliminal sexual prime led to a greater willingness of the participants to self-disclose and to engage in self-sacrifice for their partner. It also resulted in greater accessibility of intimacy-related thoughts (in that they recognized statements about the intimacy of their relationship more readily than other more neutral statements) and a significant preference for positive versus negative conflict-resolution strategies.

In this research, the experimenters also compared the subliminal sexual prime with the same pictures presented for a duration that participants could actually see (for 500 milliseconds rather than 30 milliseconds), thus bringing the sexual stimuli into consciousness. What they found was again extraordinary in that it was the subliminal sexual primes that were found to have the most pronounced effects (and the same or very similar effects on men and women). The researchers also demonstrated that this effect of subliminal priming was found not just when pictures were used, but even when the word 'sex' was flashed up very briefly for a duration such that it would not be consciously registered.

The conclusions of this research are quite dramatic. Their studies, in their own words, 'suggest that even very basic and unconscious sexual stimulation (subliminal exposure to an attractive opposite-sex nude of reproductive age, or a sex-related word) activates relationship-related motives, causing people to become more interested in, or inclined to, engage in behaviours that would foster initiation and maintenance of a more extended couple relationship.' They say that this evidence of how closely the sexual system and the attachment system are bound together is 'in the ultimate service of reproduction and the survival of offspring'. So, according to these researchers, how do you get your partner to be more interested in working on the intimacy of your relationship? How do you get them to disclose and open up more? How do you get them to put your interests and concerns before their own? How do you get them to choose cooperative rather than competitive strategies to resolve conflict in the relationship? And how do you get them to think more intimately? The answer would seem to be to employ unconscious sexual cueing. It is the merest hint of sex which seems to affect the neural circuitry of the brain and feeds into that great link between sex and intimacy. It seems that we can do this quite successfully without the other person even being aware of it.

This is a striking finding which uncovers the close relationship between our sexual system and our desire to be romantically linked to another person. The subliminal primes affected the brains of the individuals even without them knowing about it. These primes were images and words that were flashed up so quickly that people did not even report seeing them, but a whole host of behaviours seemed to be changed by their unconscious reception.

The main limitation of the studies, however (and to their credit, the researchers seem aware of them), is that the measures they took were all self-reported ('How would you interact with your partner? To what extent would you consider ending your relationship with your partner if it meant you could not continue with your education?'). These sorts of measures were taken rather than measures of changes in actual behaviour. So, for example, participants were asked what they thought they would disclose rather than being tested as to what they actually did disclose following the experimental procedures. But, nevertheless, there were a number of converging studies reported which do clearly point to a significant role for subliminal sexual priming as a major factor in the desire to increase the intimacy of a relationship. Research in the future will, I am sure, add actual behaviour into this inventive paradigm.

- Get your partner to be more psychologically intimate with you, by 'priming' them with sexual stimuli

- Take your partner to an art gallery – at one level it is all about high art but at another level they will 'see' more basic human concerns (lust, sex, sexual longing)

- Get your partner to be psychologically closer to you by wearing something that unconsciously reminds them of sex. Do this in a subtle way, well below the level of consciousness, for maximum effect

How to make someone like you without them even noticing

If you want someone to like you on first meeting, use a hint of perfume so subtle that they are not consciously aware of the smell. If the perfume is very subtle it will produce a positive response in the other person which bypasses all conscious processing. If people become consciously aware of the smell ('that's a very nice perfume you are wearing') the smell doesn't seem to have the same kind of effect. So before you meet someone for the first time, dab a very small amount of perfume on, ask a friend to smell it and say, 'Have I forgotten to put on my perfume?' If they say yes, then you know that you are wearing exactly the right amount to have the most impact on the person that you are just about to meet.

According to Wen Li and her colleagues of North Western University in a study published in 2007, you can make yourself more attractive with a very subtle hint of perfume. We know from other research in psychology that information impinging on the senses below the level of consciousness (so-called 'subliminal information') can have a significant effect on our response to various things. Research has demonstrated that by subliminally presenting emotionally charged pictures and words, you can affect people's preference for what follows these subliminal primes. Wen Li and her colleagues tested whether it is possible to have olfactory primes which would affect the evaluation of whatever was presented to follow it. They suggested that this is highly likely given the very close connection between the olfactory system and the limbic region in the brain which is concerned with affective and emotional processing.

The way the experimenters tested the hypothesis was to have three odours: citral ('lemon'), anisole ('ethereal') and paleric acid ('sweat'). These were considered pleasant, neutral and unpleasant smells respectively. On each trial, participants took a sniff from a bottle containing one of these smells (some bottles didn't contain anything) and the participants had to press a computer key to indicate whether the bottle contained an odour or not. Then, the computer screen displayed one of eighty pictures of a face with a neutral expression and participants had to rate how likeable the face was. The respiration and heart rate of the participants were also measured.

The results were extraordinary in that when the odour was present but below the level of conscious awareness, faces were rated as 'less likeable' following the unpleasant odour than following the pleasant odour. However, in the case of the participants who could (consciously) smell the odour, this difference did not emerge. Heart rate increased following the unpleasant odour, but this was independent of conscious awareness.

So this study provides clear evidence that subliminal odours do significantly affect likeability judgements and the heart rate of individuals. The most striking result of this study was that the odours had to be subliminal to affect the likeability judgement. As the researchers say, 'It is in the absence of conscious awareness that odours best exert their effects.'

So if you want someone to like you from the word go, simply wear the most subtle hint of beautiful perfume. Use just a drop so that they are not consciously aware that you are wearing any perfume at all. If you do this, it will subliminally prime their affective response to you and make them like you more.

This study demonstrates that smells work best when they are below the level of consciousness. Most people go out of their way to cover themselves in expensive perfume when they are out to make a lasting impression on another. However, in the case of smells, less is most definitely more.

The main limitation of this study is that it just compared one positive odour with one neutral and one unpleasant odour, so it gives us no way of determining which pleasant smells are most effective and why. It also did not try to investigate the 'match' between the pleasant smell (or perfume) and the person wearing the perfume, which might seem to be a critical issue in everyday life. One particular perfume might smell fantastic on one person but not on the next.

The authors finish their research article by saying, 'We can only hope that the subtle smells we emit make a pleasant impression on other people.' I think we can be a bit more direct here. I think that we need to make sure that when it comes to first impressions we use very subtle smells to prime other people in exactly the right way.

- Attract someone to you by wearing a perfume so light and so subtle that it isn't consciously detected
- 'Prime' strangers to like you in this way, using very subtle smells

How to make yourself more attractive to men

You can make yourself more attractive to men by wearing the colour red. It is not necessarily about putting on a red dress or a red blouse, it can be much more subtle than that. In a series of experiments it was demonstrated that men rated pictures of women as more 'attractive' when the photos were presented briefly (for five seconds) on a red as opposed to a white background. Men were also more likely to find women more 'sexually desirable' when the photos were presented on the red background. In other words, brief exposure to the colour red, again below the level of consciousness, seems to influence judgements of attractiveness.

The reason for this seems to go far beyond culture, and the fact that we use red to symbolize love in many cultures across the world i.e. red roses, red hearts, red underwear etc. Rather there may be a biological basis to redness signalling love and, therefore, a biological basis to our cultural use of red to symbolize love. After all, many non-human female primates display red on their genitals when they are in ovulation. The reddening of the skin is related to higher levels of oestrogen, which increases vascular blood flow beneath the surface of the skin which is then shown as a reddening in colour. In other words, the colour red in female primates represents a clear sexual signal to attract a mate. So if you want to make yourself more sexually desirable display the colour red, but do it briefly and subtly and below the level of consciousness: a red watch strap, red shoes, a red scarf – the subtler the better.

Will this always work? It's hard to say but what was interesting was that in the same set of experiments, brief flashes of the colour red did not affect women's perceptions of the attractiveness of other women and it also didn't affect whether men saw the women in the pictures as 'likeable', 'kind' or 'intelligent'. In other words, brief flashes of the colour red just seemed to affect sexual interest and positive sexual judgements (rather than positive judgements more generally). And, given that one of the questions that the psychologists asked was the rather basic and unambiguous 'Would you want to have sexual intercourse with that person?' (on a scale from 1 meaning 'definitely no', to 9 meaning 'definitely'), there cannot be too much ambiguity about the actual results. The participants in the study were more likely to want to have sexual intercourse with the woman in the photo when the colour red was present. Of course, looking at a photograph is not real life, so how would brief flashes of the colour red interact with the effects of the other things which can influence sexual desirability? We don't know, but in the meantime buy the watch with the red strap, if that's what you want.

- Sexual attractiveness is influenced by a range of unconscious factors

- The colour red is an unconscious signal of sex in women

- Men rate women as more 'attractive' and more 'sexually desirable' when pictures of the women are associated briefly with the colour red

- Use brief flashes of the colour red to attract men to you, e.g. buy a watch with a red strap

- Work the unconscious to make yourself attractive to the opposite sex!

6. MARRIAGE AND RELATIONSHIPS

'If married couples did not live together,
happy marriages would be more frequent.'

Nietzsche, *Human, All too Human* (1878), 393,
tr. Helen Zimmern

How to have a happy and successful marriage

In order to have a happy and successful marriage, you have to be on your guard against certain behaviours that precipitate the end of any marriage. They are:

- Criticism
- Defensiveness
- Contempt
- Stonewalling

If you really want your marriage to succeed, you need to be less critical, much less defensive, you need to engage in less stone-walling and you must avoid the display of contempt at all costs. The display of contempt in marriage seems to be especially destructive and a strong prelude to divorce. If you are the wife, and you want to criticize your husband – who doesn't at some time in any marriage? – then you need to introduce the criticism relatively gently and to reassure him during the criticism. If you are the husband, when your wife criticizes you, you need to listen and understand what she is saying rather than refusing to listen or blocking it. Both partners need to avoid displaying contempt at all costs. Research has shown that in a marriage the display of contempt by the husband actually results in an increase in infectious illness in the wife. Contempt doesn't just finish off the marriage, it goes some way to finishing off the wife as well.

According to research by John Gottman and his colleagues

of the University of Washington, a happy marriage and a stable relationship are predicted by certain core sequences of interaction and behaviour that can be readily identified. For the past thirty years Gottman has investigated the behavioural sequences that characterize successful marriages, compared with marriages that end in divorce, and he has written a number of important and influential books on the subject with ominous titles such as, *What Predicts Divorce: The measures*, and (perhaps even more frightening) *The Mathematics of Divorce*. What is different about Gottman's work is its detailed analysis and identification of the actual elements that are associated with happy marriages, and using this close observational approach he is able to evaluate other approaches to understanding marriage which did not have the benefits of his level of detailed scrutiny. Thus there are many myths and assumptions associated with what makes a happy marriage, including the view that marital anger is the kiss of death. According to Harville Hendrix (1998), 'Anger is destructive to a relationship, no matter what its form. When anger is expressed, the person on the receiving end of the attack feels brutalized, whether or not there has been any physical violence; the old brain does not distinguish between choice of weapons.' Another strongly held belief about marriage is that the 'act of listening' (as an expression of empathy in a relationship) is one of the single most important factors in underpinning a successful marriage and this, of course, forms the basis for many different types of marital therapies. Couples, and particularly husbands, are taught to listen more. They are taught to 'hear' things like complaints and to paraphrase the complaint in the conversation 'in a non-defensive way' in order 'to validate the complainant's feelings'.

Gottman, however, started his research with no such assumptions about what the key features of a happy marriage might be. He did not assume that anger was necessarily bad, nor that more active listening was necessarily the panacea for all marriages. He started with more or less a clean slate to describe what behaviourally and routinely went on in happy marriages and what went on in unhappy marriages. What he found was surprising and shocking in many ways because he discovered early on that the experience and expression of anger was not necessarily that predictive of marriage failure. He also found that active listening was rarely found even in the happiest of relationships. He did, however, find certain sequences of behaviour which correlated very highly with the success or failure of relationships.

The way that Gottman conducted his research was to recruit a sample of newly married couples who answered written questions on various measures of marital satisfaction. In the second phase of the research, 130 of the couples were invited to the lab and filmed. The mean age of the husbands was, at that time, twenty-seven and the mean age of the wives was twenty-five. Once a year their marital status and marital satisfaction were both measured. At the end of the six-year research period, there had been seventeen divorces in his sample. The couples were filmed discussing a chosen problem that was the cause of on-going disagreement within the marriage and there were also what Gottman called 'recall sessions' in which the couples reviewed the discussion of their marriage disagreement. The couples discussed the topic for fifteen minutes and then watched video recordings. The husband and wife then had to rate their emotions during the discussion both for themselves and for their partner. The emotional expressions for the individuals were analysed, focusing on facial expression, tone of voice and speech content. The five positive emotions focused on were:

'interest'
'validation'
'affection'
'humour'
'joy'

The ten negative emotions focused on were:

'disgust'
'contempt'
'belligerence'
'domineering'
'anger'
'fear/tension'
'defensiveness'
'whining'
'sadness'
'stonewalling' (or listener withdrawal)

The key research questions were what types of emotional displays were associated with happy and unhappy marriages? And what types of emotional displays predicted divorce? The analyses revealed that 'criticism', 'defensiveness', 'contempt', 'stonewalling' and 'belligerence' both by the husband and wife, when of a sufficiently high intensity, predicted divorce but did not necessarily differentiate happy and unhappy marriages. In terms of low-intensity emotional displays, 'whining, anger, sadness, domineering, disgust, fear and stonewalling' by the wife also predicted divorce but did not reliably differentiate happy and unhappy marriages. Anger in the relationship, contrary to the previous received wisdom, did not predict divorce and did not discriminate between happy and unhappy marriages.

In other words, if you want a marriage to succeed, you should not be too concerned about expressions of anger, but there are other types of emotional displays that should concern you greatly. Four of them – criticism, defensiveness, contempt and stonewalling – Gottman called 'The Four Horsemen of the Apocalypse'. When you see the four horsemen riding into view, you need to start fearing for the survival of the relationship. In Gottman's view, these behaviours characterize some of the most 'destructive patterns' that can occur in a marriage and were all highly predictive of whether the marriage would last or not. On the other hand, 'active listening', which is such an integral component of much marital therapy, was found by Gottman to be relatively infrequent even in the happiest and most successful of marriages.

Gottman moved on from the identification of individual units of behaviour to a description of interactional sequences that characterize happy and unhappy marriages and that predict divorce. The main sequence that Gottman identified was described by him in the following way: 'The pattern predictive of divorce was negative start-up by the wife, refusal of the husband to accept influence from his wife, wife's reciprocation of low-intensity negativity in kind, and the absence of de-escalation of low-intensity negativity by the husband.' And you can see that this is a pattern that merely ramps up and up – the wife brings up some irritation, the husband blocks the discussion using negative emotional signals, the wife responds in kind to these signals and the whole thing escalates from there. When couples get locked in this kind of pattern, divorce seems often to be a highly probable option.

On the other hand, those marriages that turned out to be happy and stable were those that had a 'softened start-up by the wife, that the husband accepted influence from her, that he de-escalated low-intensity negative affect, that she was likely to use humour to effectively soothe him, and that he was likely to use positive affect and de-escalation to effectively soothe himself'. In other words, in happy and stable relationships, the wife introduces the touchy topic in a less intense way and she uses some humour to soften the criticism and stop the whole thing getting out of hand, while the husband uses the expression of positive emotion to keep his own psychological state in control.

One critical finding from Gottman's research is that it is only couples in which the husbands accept influence from their wives that end up both stable and happy because the husbands' responses to the initial conversational move from the wives appear crucial. But Gottman's analysis of behavioural sequences in marriage does not just predict divorce rate, it also predicts illness within the marriage. He found, for example, that the display of contempt by your partner actually predicted an increase in infectious illness (for women at least, but interestingly not for men). In the case of men, the relationship between conflict and illness was affected by the psychological dimension of loneliness. Gottman's analysis here suggests that men are more likely than women to start to withdraw from a relationship when stressed and it is this withdrawal which mediates the relationship between conflict and illness.

So the big question is, how do you have a happy marriage? The answer would appear to be don't be overly concerned about temper tantrums, but do be concerned about criticism, defensiveness, contempt and stonewalling. Contempt appears to be particularly serious because it doesn't just finish your relationship off, it can finish your partner off as well and make them more prone to infectious illness. The secret of a happy, stable relationship is that when your wife introduces some criticism, don't block it with negativity. For the wife, the secret would appear to be to introduce criticism gently and to use humour to soften the criticism (without appearing to be too sarcastic); don't let the Four Horsemen of the Apocalypse (and their fellow rider, belligerence) carry you to a place beyond hope.

Gottman's research has been the focus of much popular discussion. In his initial experiments he used an observational sample of fifteen minutes to predict the patterns of divorce. Subsequent researchers argue that this can be done on the basis of a sample of three minutes. Three minutes, the argument goes, can tell you all that you need to know about whether a marriage will survive or fail. But there are shortcomings in the research. It is interesting that the number of divorces in the original sample is not that large and all the interviewees were drawn from the same small part of the United States, so we have to be very careful about drawing general conclusions from such a small sample. That being said, what is exciting and innovative about Gottman's work is that it does focus on behaviours that characterize happy and unhappy marriages as well as failed marriages and it does, therefore, draw attention to the small behavioural sequences of which a marriage is made. It also reminds us that we should avoid being locked into a particular sequence of behaviour all the time. We can all learn ways of de-escalating emotional intensity. The one danger with Gottman's work is that there is always the possibility that the behavioural descriptions may merely be the symptoms of some deep, underlying cause. Some basic incompatibility between the partners is being realized on a daily basis in these behavioural sequences. Only time and much larger samples will tell us if this is correct. But in the meantime, the next time you feel some contempt for your partner welling up inside you, just pause and rewind unless you know, for definite, that you want the relationship to end.

- Routine behaviours in a marriage can indicate whether the marriage will succeed or fail

- Criticism, defensiveness, contempt and stonewalling in a marriage are, unfortunately, often a prelude to divorce

- The display of contempt can affect physical as well as psychological well-being

- Women need to introduce criticism gently

- Men need to respond to criticism

- Outbursts of anger in a marriage do not necessarily signal the end of a relationship

- Active listening in a marriage is good but not critical

How to spot if your relationship is in trouble

If you want to tell whether your marriage or relationship is on track, listen out for how your partner uses pronouns to describe the two of you. There are a number of different pronouns that can be used:

First-person singular – 'I', 'me', 'my'
First-person plural – 'us', 'we', 'our'
Second-person – 'you', 'your'

If the second-person pronoun ('you', 'your') is used, this is a bad sign. It indicates that the relationship is pretty negative (with lots of criticism, disagreement, justification and negative attitudes). Use of the first-person plural is a very good sign because it tends to indicate a relationship characterized by compromise and positive solutions. First-person singular pronoun usage is also particularly good because it is related to marital satisfaction.

Rachel Simmons of the University of Pennsylvania and her colleagues examined the relationship between the words people use in interaction and their marital satisfaction. She focused on the use of first-person and second-person pronouns.

On the basis of previous research, she says that 'highly committed partners' tend to use 'we' pronouns more frequently than 'less committed partners' when describing their relationship, whereas the second-person pronouns 'you' and 'your' are more often used when the focus is on creating psychological distance from the other person. The researchers recorded fifty-nine couples discussing the top issues facing their relationships and the researchers took measures of marital satisfaction and the relative number of you-focus pronouns ('you', 'your'), we-focus pronouns ('we', 'us', 'our') and I-focus pronouns ('I', 'me'). They also scored how positive and negative the interaction was. They found that the use of second-person pronouns was more common in negative interactions and that the use of the pronoun 'I' was more common in positive interactions. The use of 'we' pronouns was connected with more positive problem solving (which included both the number of constructive solutions offered as well as compromises in the conversation). In summary, the pronouns we use in conversation do seem to be related to the quality of the relationship.

Of course, the problem with this study is that it may be the kinds of things that people are talking about that is direct-ing their pronoun use and it may not be a good independent measure of a sound relationship. But the researchers clearly think there is a possibility that 'individuals perceive and respond to their partner's pronoun use independently of speech content'. In other words, they may feel threatened by the use of the pro-noun 'you' in conversation because it sounds vaguely accusatory. I'm not so sure.

- The pronouns that couples use when they are talking about their relationship can reflect how healthy and happy the marriage is

- Overuse of the pronoun 'you' may be a bad sign; it can appear accusatory

- The use of the pronoun 'we' is a good sign because it reflects compromise and the search for constructive solutions to problems

- The use of the pronoun 'I' is another positive sign. It reflects the taking of responsibility

How to make someone judge you less harshly

You can make someone judge you less harshly by choosing the moment that you reveal your guilty secret very carefully. The secret is to tell them after they have washed their hands (say before dinner). Research has shown that moral judgements do not depend solely upon reasoning and conscious decision-making, but are affected by intuitive factors and physical conditions. It is no accident that we can describe some immoral acts as disgusting; there seems to be a connection between the underlying judgement of how bad an immoral act is and physical aspects of behaviour. Psychologists have demonstrated this by exposing people to a bad smell, or getting them to work in an unpleasant environment and then asking them to judge the severity of a moral judgement. The physical aspects of the environment seem to impact on this judgement. Simone Schnall and her colleagues from Plymouth University looked at people's response to six (particularly disgusting) moral dilemmas, including:

- Eating a dead dog
- Switching the tracks of a trolley to kill one workman instead of five
- Using a kitten for sexual arousal

Schnall and co primed the participants in the study by asking them to form sentences from words related to cleanliness, e.g.:

pure
washed
clean
immaculate
pristine

or neutral words

The researchers found that when the participants were primed with the cleanliness words, they gave lower ratings to how wrong the various dilemmas were. So, for example, 'eating a dead dog' was rated as 6.55 on a scale from 0 (perfectly OK) to 9 (extremely wrong) when the participants were primed with neutral words, whereas it was judged as 5.70 on the same scale when the participants were primed with the cleanliness words. 'Using a kitten for sexual arousal' was judged at 8.25 when neutral words were used compared to 6.70 when cleanliness words were used. These were significantly lower (meaning more acceptable) in both cases. In other words, the participants in this experiment found these moral dilemmas to be not quite so awful after concepts of cleanliness were activated in their brain without their conscious awareness. In a follow-up study, the researchers looked at the effects of allowing people to wash their hands before making a moral judgement and found exactly the same effects in that allowing people to wash their hands led to less severe judgements. The conclusion of the psychologists was that 'dramatic purity can serve as a basic intuition when judging the moral quality of an action'. So if you want to have a clean conscience and get things off your chest, make your confession when you have just done the housework, confess just after your partner has washed their hands and never confess in a dirty room (unless you really want to suffer, that is).

- Moral judgements are affected by unconscious factors, including aspects of the physical setting

- Moral judgements are less harsh when the brain has been 'primed' to think of cleanliness

- Always confess in a clean room

- Tell your dirty secrets when your partner has just washed their hands

---

How to tell if your marriage is heading for disaster

You can tell if your marriage is heading for disaster by getting yourself and your partner to talk about the early days together. Reminisce about how you met and how you courted, talk about the wedding day, the bridesmaids' dresses, and the father of the bride standing tipsy in the aisle. Then step back and think about what was actually said. What about the wedding itself, how was that discussed? Was the focus on:

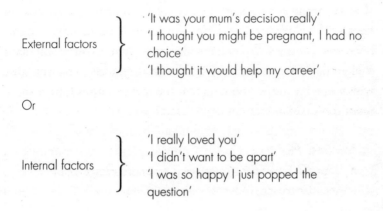

External factors
} 'It was your mum's decision really'
'I thought you might be pregnant, I had no choice'
'I thought it would help my career'

Or

Internal factors
} 'I really loved you'
'I didn't want to be apart'
'I was so happy I just popped the question'

What about the early days? Was it a story of overcoming adversity together? Or was it a story of disappointment? Was it all about the challenges that you faced and was the focus on two people acting together, or was it about a series of disappointments and separation? Was it a story about 'we'? Or was it a story about 'you and I'? And what fondness was expressed in the account? Did feelings of pride just slip in naturally and effortlessly? Or were all the positive feelings most noticeable by their absence?

The way couples frame and tell the story of how they get together and their early years together seems to be a reliable indicator of the future course of the marriage. If the signs are negative rather than positive, it might be time to take stock. But remember, repair is always possible.

According to John Gottman, one of the most reliable ways of telling if your marriage is in trouble is to listen to you and your partner talking about your shared past. In Gottman's words, 'when a marriage is unravelling, we found that husband and wife come to recast their earlier times together in a negative light.' Your recall of previous disappointments and slights becomes dramatically enhanced. Where once you might have looked back fondly on your first dance together or buying your wedding rings, now you focus on the jarring notes that seem to foreshadow your current dissatisfactions – your fiancé showing up tipsy or the late-night argument over the wording of the invitations. The key point is that putting a negative spin on your past is an early warning sign that your marriage is in trouble. Rewriting history may begin well before you become aware that your marriage is in serious danger.

Gottman studied fifty-six couples and asked them a whole series of questions about the history of their marriage including its early days, how they met, how they got together and how they overcame all of the obstacles together. When they were first interviewed, none of the couples had plans to break up, but three years later 15 per cent had divorced and Gottman noticed something very interesting in terms of how they had talked about their past together. He says that there are a number of distinctive features you can look out for. Some couples look back on their early days 'as a time of great confusion, uncertainty, and anxiety', and they often viewed their coming together as an essentially stressful, 'almost haphazard occurrence'. According to Gottman, this is a very negative sign. If they say that external factors led to the marriage, such as pressures of money or something like pregnancy, this is also a negative sign. In psychological terms these things are called 'external attributions', where you explain an event as a result of external factors rather than internal factors (such as 'I just wanted to get married') where the stress is very much on a person making an active decision.

Couples who ended up divorcing also looked back on the early days as being a source of disappointment rather than with the kind of pride associated with overcoming obstacles. The more a husband and wife talk about the early years as a 'joint undertaking' with them working together (as in 'when we moved in we kept the house tidy together'), the more positive the sign that the marriage will work in the future. Perhaps not surprisingly, Gottman found that husbands in stable marriages spoke about their wives with greater fondness. Gottman claims that these indicators are highly predictive. He writes, '. . . 100 per cent of the time we were able to predict which couples [divorced] based solely on how they had answered our questions about their marriage's history three years earlier!' It is interesting to see features of conversation which can forewarn of a negative event several years in advance and it is crucial for us all to look out for signs that a relationship might not be as robust as we would like to think it is. In his research, Gottman identifies a number of features but does not give us any way to rate the importance of each of them. So, for example, how important is the 'sense of control' versus the romanticization of the difficult, early years? Say that someone was pushed into marriage by their partner's parents (thus essentially making an external attribution) but nevertheless have a romantic view of getting by without any money in the first few years: is that better or worse than taking an essentially internal attribution for getting married ('I really felt like it at the time') but not having such a romantic view of the early years ('we had no money and it was horrible')? Gottman doesn't really allow us to weight each of these factors but he details things that we might well look out for. The other issue with this study is that the size of the sample was quite small. Only seven couples actually got divorced. This, of course, is a very small sample so may not be truly representative of a wider trend.

- You can tell if your marriage is in trouble by what you say when you are reminiscing jointly about the early days of your relationship

- Is the story about the earlier days of the marriage positive or negative? This is highly predictive

- Are the early days of the marriage seen as stressful and unpredictable? If they are, this is not good

- Do you both say that 'external' factors led to you getting married in the first place? This is also a negative sign

- Remember, it's never too late to repair a marriage but you need to understand the warning signs

How to apologize

The secret of a good apology is that it has to be perceived as heartfelt and it must also contain several key ingredients. In order to be regarded as heartfelt, the person doing the apologizing has to be perceived as really meaning it. Key to this is the delivery of the spoken part of the message. In terms of timing and pause patterns and the accompanying facial expressions, the apology must not be too rushed. Filling devices like repeating a word can be used to slow it down, thus 'I am really, really sorry' is nearly always better than the simpler 'I am sorry'. If this section of the apology is produced too quickly, it may be seen as over-planned and therefore not spontaneous and real. In terms of facial expressions, eye contact must be made during the apology because the function of the apology is partly to make the recipient feel better and therefore it is important to have a connection with the recipient.

In terms of content, the apology must have a number of different components including:

- An expression of *remorse* or sadness about one's actions, e.g. 'I am really, really sorry.'
- An acknowledgement of *responsibility*, e.g. 'I know what I did was wrong.'
- A promise of *forbearance*, e.g. 'I promise that it won't happen again.'
- An *offer of repair*, e.g. 'I will try to make this up to you.'

If any of these components are missing then there is a significant effect on how the apology is perceived; the higher the number of these components that are absent, the more the recipient will blame the speaker for what they did and the more they will want to sanction them. So in order to make an effective apology ensure you have all four components in place and watch your delivery, take it nice and slowly and be sure to make eye contact.

The classic research on the essential components of

an apology was carried out by Steven Scher of Eastern Illinois University and John Darley of Princeton University (1997). They looked in detail at four of the principal components of an apology:

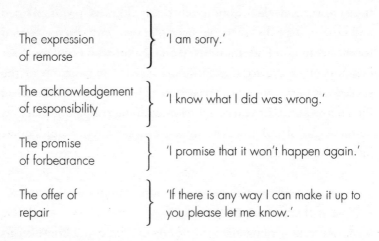

The expression of remorse	'I am sorry.'
The acknowledgement of responsibility	'I know what I did was wrong.'
The promise of forbearance	'I promise that it won't happen again.'
The offer of repair	'If there is any way I can make it up to you please let me know.'

The researchers presented participants with a story about a character who failed to carry out an important promise for a friend. In the story the main character had promised to call his friend with some information crucial to a job interview. However, he forgot to call and instead called several days later. The participants received an account in which remorse, responsibility, the promise of forbearance and the offer of repair was either present or absent. After the participants read the story they had to judge to what extent the main character felt bad about what he had done, how much they would blame him for what he had done and how much they would condemn him for his actions.

In terms of the results, this study showed that the components that people include in an apology 'have clear and independent effects on the judgements people make about the transgressor. The addition of each strategy seems to have had an additive effect on judgements of how appropriate the utterance of the transgressor was and how much the transgressor was blamed and sanctioned for the transgression, and on judgements related to the identity of the transgressor'. In other words, all four components seem to work and to be very important to the success of the apology. If you want to make an apology effective, then make sure that you do express remorse, make sure that you admit responsibility, make sure that you promise it will never happen again and then offer to make it up to the person in any way possible. The more of these components you include, the more effective the apology will be.

The main limitation of this study is that it only used one scenario so it is not necessarily obvious that all transgressions require each of these components. Are there some things that we do wrong that we cannot make amends for (even if we were to try our very hardest)? Is the apology less effective because of that? But what this research does tell us is that spoken apologies have multiple components and it is important to ensure that we remember to include as many components as possible.

- Apologies need to be seen as heartfelt, so make the apology slow and 'thoughtful', with good eye contact to show that you mean it

> - Good apologies have four essential components (remorse/responsibility/promise of forbearance/repair)
> - Make sure that all four components are present when you apologize. The more components are present, the more effective the apology will be

How to get your partner to clean the house

If you want someone to clean more around the house, make sure that there is a vague smell of citrus cleaner in the critical areas. Make sure that the smell is not too strong and not too obvious; this slight smell will unconsciously influence their thoughts, their plans and their actions. It will make them think more readily of cleaning products. If asked what they are going to do for the day, they are more likely to think of cleaning as one of their activities and if left alone they will be more likely to clean up after themselves. This is an example of unconscious priming of behaviour.

This is the conclusion of Rob Holland of Radboud University in Nijmegen and his colleagues. They argue that smells can *prime* both thoughts and behaviour. What the smells do is to bring certain associations to mind and guide behaviour. Holland *et al.* referred to some classic research by Bargh, Chen and Burrows (1996) who gave people a list of five words out of which they had to make a four-word sentence, in a task called the 'scrambled sentence test'. The five-word sequences included:

Shoes gave replace old the.
Sky the seamless grey is.
Should now withdraw forgetful we.
Us bingo sing play let.
Sunlight makes temperature wrinkle raisins.

You can try this test yourself, it is pretty easy. So you might get:

Replace the old shoes.
The sky is seamless grey.
We should now withdraw.
Let us play bingo.
Sunlight makes raisins wrinkle.

In their study, Bargh *et al* effectively primed their participants with words associated with being elderly, embedded in each of the original lists, i.e.

'old'
'grey'
'forgetful'
'bingo'
'wrinkle'

The participants thought they were just doing a language task but what Bargh and his colleagues were actually doing was unconsciously priming them to think about being old. The researchers then asked participants to walk down a hallway by the laboratory and incredibly they found that those people who had been primed in this way walked more slowly than those who had not been primed. In other words, people can be unconsciously cued to behave in certain ways. Holland and his colleagues asked whether we can cue people unconsciously to clean using a similar priming technique. They tested their idea with three experiments. In the first experiment, they used something called a lexical decision task. A lexical decision task is where people have to decide whether a string of letters on a computer screen is a real word or not. Participants have to press a 'yes' or a 'no' key and the researchers measure the time in milliseconds that it takes the participants to press the key. The researchers looked at the effect of a slight hint of citrus (the smell of an all-purpose cleaning product) in the experimental cubicle on this task, in which the participants had to decide whether the string of letters was a real word, which was either cleaning related (e.g. 'cleaning', 'hygiene', etc.) or not cleaning related (e.g. 'table', 'computer' etc). The participants were also asked what they thought the study was about and whether they noticed any particular smell in the cubicle (and if so, what the scent was).

Incredibly, participants in the 'scent' condition (all-purpose cleaning product) responded faster to the cleaning-related words than the participants in the control condition (i.e. no 'scent') with a mean latency of about 590 milliseconds in the scent condition compared to 618 milliseconds in the control condition for the cleaning-related words. The latency to identify the non-cleaning-related words was more or less the same in the two conditions. This significant difference occurred without them consciously being aware of the smell of the scent.

In a second study, again participants either entered a cubicle smelling slightly of citrus or the control cubicle which did not.

This time they were merely asked to write about what they were planning to do for the rest of the day. Again, extraordinarily, when they did this in the cubicle which smelt slightly of citrus, they were more likely to list a cleaning-related task as one of their activities for the rest of the day. In fact they were three times more likely to mention a cleaning activity as part of that day's plans than when they were in the control cubicle.

So it looks as if the merest hint of all-purpose cleaner affects our thinking and our plans but does it have any influence on our actual behaviour? The researchers tested this in a third study. Once again participants were put into the cubicle as before, and this time they were then taken into a separate room where they sat at a table and were given a crumbly biscuit to eat. A hidden video camera recorded their every movement. Again the results were quite remarkable. When the participants had been exposed to the smell of the cleaning fluid, they were more likely to remove the crumbs that fell on to the table than when they had not been exposed to the smell. In other words, by exposing someone to the smell of a cleaning product, it affected the accessibility of their thoughts, their action plans and also their actual behaviour in that they kept a table cleaner after smelling it. And all of this happened without any conscious awareness of the scent (only a very few participants noticed the smell at all).

This is an extraordinary set of results which again demonstrates the influence of unconscious primes on behaviour. It shows that we can unconsciously influence people to recognize cleaning-related words more quickly, to think more about cleaning-related activities in their plans for the day ahead and actually to engage in more cleaning and tidying up when we expose them to certain smells which are reminiscent of cleaning.

For every cohabiting couple who want their partner to do more cleaning around the home, the lesson here would seem to be very clear-cut.

The one limitation of this study is that it doesn't tell us whether, or how quickly, people habituate to such a smell. Can you just use this tactic on a few occasions spread out over time because otherwise we might get too used to the smell, or does it have its unconscious effect regardless of how often we do it? This is a very practical question that has not yet been answered.

- People can be unconsciously 'primed' in many different ways

- If you prime people with unconscious cues to get them to think about being old, they walk more slowly as a consequence

- You can prime people using certain smells, which they are not consciously aware of, to think about cleaning or tidying

- Leave a slight smell of cleaning products in certain rooms to make sure that your partner suddenly thinks 'spontaneously' of tidying and cleaning that room, and thereby stop arguments about domestic chores.

How to save a failing relationship

You can save a failing relationship by putting a bit more effort into it, surprising your partner, breaking out of the mould, thinking of something that they would really like to do and avoiding nasty pitfalls. One such pitfall is Valentine's Day. Valentine's Day is the most romantic day of the year for many people and expectations can be very high, so you need to beware. Katherine Morse and Steven Neuberg of Arizona State University say, 'Partners who fail to meet expectations will be easily compared to a multitude of others who apparently meet the expectations handily.' These researchers found that Valentine's Day was a great 'catalyst' for the breaking up of relationships. Couples were more likely to split up in the period around Valentine's Day than they were in any other comparison time periods. The problem is that on Valentine's Day, people think critically about their ongoing relationship and if their expectations on that day are not met they will often finish the relationship in the days immediately afterwards.

To keep a relationship going, you need to surprise your partner in good ways, and if your relationship is already weakened, make sure that you take the trouble to do it on Valentine's Day itself. Otherwise the consequences may be severe.

- Valentine's Day is a minefield for relationships that are already in trouble, because it is a chance to compare one's relationship unfavourably with those of other people

• Do something surprising and fun on Valentine's Day to
please your partner, or you may be in real bother

How to make yourself feel better in a relationship

There is one very simple thing that you can do to make yourself
feel better in a conversation with your partner, and that is to
ensure that you make time to ask them how their day went.
Angela Hicks and Lisa Diamond of the University of Utah found
that couples who had the opportunity to talk about the most
positive experience that they had had that day felt much better
(as measured by a screening instrument called the Positive and
Negative Affect Schedule). The way that Hicks and Diamond
conducted the research was to get couples to fill in a daily diary
for twenty-one days, recording the most positive experience that
they had had that day, and whether they had told their partner
about it. They measured mood state as well as taking measures
of bodily changes including cardiovascular and neuroendocrine
reactivity. It turns out that men and women have very similar
patterns of talking about the good things that happened to them
during any given day. Women in the sample said that they
disclosed the most positive events that happened to them that
day 44 per cent of the time and men 42 per cent of the time. And
the researchers critically found that disclosing the most positive
events of the day were associated with significantly higher end-
of-day positive emotions for both partners. In short, relating
positive news makes both the teller and the recipient feel good.

196

The advice on the basis of this research is very simple – make sure that you find time each day to hear the good things that happened to your partner. This will help you both.

- Make time to ask your partner how their day has been
- Ask your partner about what good things have occurred that day
- This simple sharing will make you both feel better, psychologically and physically

---

How to tell if your partner is lying

In order to discover if your partner is lying, do not look at their face to begin with. People give out too many contradictory signals with their face when they are lying. This occurs because the face is a great sender of information – there are, some psychologists say, two thousand different facial expressions – but we have excellent feedback about what our face is doing at any point in time and therefore we fight to control our facial expressions when we are lying. Instead, watch the hands. When people talk, they characteristically make spontaneous and un-conscious hand movements to illustrate what they are saying. When people lie, the rate of these illustrative hand movements decreases. Indeed, liars will often lock their hands together to stop the hands from revealing too much. Once the hands fall silent during conversation you have the first clue that everything is not right. Then, and only then, glance at the face for further information to settle the matter one way or another, but still avoid looking at the eyes. The eyes are not the gateway to the soul, as some believe; they are the gateway for good liars to get away with yet more fabrication.

- There is no single 100 per cent reliable sign that someone is lying, but there a number of cues that are significant

- When people lie there are sometimes signs that they are having trouble making up the lie (longer pauses), and signs of their emotional discomfort (negative micro-expressions) while telling it

- The cues depend upon the seriousness of the lie and the damage that will be caused if the lie is discovered. The more serious the lie the more likely the presence of very brief micro-expressions of negative emotion

- People often lock their hands when they are lying in order to unconsciously inhibit their revealing hand movement

- Don't look closely at the eyes to tell if someone is lying or not. Most people (except very inexperienced liars) are very good at controlling their eyes when they lie because they know that the person that they are talking to will be monitoring their eyes carefully

7. WORK

'It is only by labour that thought can be made healthy, and only by thought that labour can be made happy, and the two cannot be separated with impunity.'

John Ruskin, 'The Nature of Gothic',
The Stones of Venice (1851–53), v. 2.6

How to see the bigger picture

If you are working on a project and you need to see 'the bigger picture' instead of being overly focused on the detail, go and pick up a feel-good DVD and watch a short, happy section of it. The positive emotion induced does affect your cognitive processing of the world around you and it will give you a more global perspective on the information that you are processing. You will be able to see the bigger picture in the task more easily and quickly.

This is what Barbara Fredrickson and Christine Branigan of the University of Michigan demonstrated in 2005. They started their research with an absolutely fundamental question in psychology, namely why do we have positive emotions at all? Happiness, joy, contentment and serenity may feel good but what are they actually for? The researchers argued that the function of *negative* emotions (like anger, fear and anxiety) is pretty clear, in evolutionary terms. Negative emotions get you ready for specific action sequences like fight or flight. These are the kinds of actions that meant (in evolutionary terms) that you survived in everyday struggles of life or death. But what corresponding purpose do positive emotions serve? Fredrickson and Branigan point out that we don't really know because, unlike the fight-or-flight response, the actions associated with positive emotion often seem a little vague and non-specific (for example 'free movement' and 'joy', 'inactivity' and 'content-ment'), and they say that positive emotions are often associated with a lack of autonomic (or bodily) reaction. But they do have a theoretical hunch, which is that 'many positive emotions *broaden* individuals' momentary thought-action repertoires, prompting them to pursue a wider range of thoughts and actions than is typical (e.g. play, explore, savour, and integrate)'. In evolutionary terms, they say that this works because the thought-action patterns associated with negative emotions work well in specific threatening situations, whereas 'The broadened thought-action repertoires of positive emotions were likely adaptive over the long run.' Part of this adaptability is that it builds personal resources, and they use the word 'resources' here carefully in that these are resources that can be drawn upon to improve coping during the course of a lifetime. They cite the research by Danner *et al.* (2001) which found that elderly nuns who expressed the most positive emotion in the early part of their life (whilst they were taking their vows, in fact), lived on average ten years longer than those who expressed much less positive emotion. In other words, the experience and the expression of positive emotion can affect an individual's longevity.

But what evidence is there that positive emotion does significantly affect patterns of thinking? This is what Fredrickson and Branigan tested. They used a stimulus which contained three figures, with one figure on top and two figures to be used for comparison printed beneath it. Participants had to simply judge which of the two figures was more similar to the standard figure. Judgements could be made either on global configuration (for example, the fact that the standard figure is a triangle) or could be based on more local concerns (for example, the fact that the figure was made up of square elements). The more they focused on global configuration, the more the researchers took this to reflect a global bias in thinking, which they say is linked to a broader scope of attention.

The second measure they took was an open-ended twenty-statement test, where participants had to rate their emotion and then write up to twenty statements reflecting what they would like to do at that point in time, e.g. I would like to . . .

'go to bed'
'do homework'
'go for a swim'
'take a walk'
'look at old pictures'
'have fun'
'visit friends'
'hit someone'
'yell for help'
'fly'

The way that the researchers changed emotional state was to get participants to watch short films (just two minutes in duration on average) of:

Penguins waddling (*amusing*)
Fields and streams (*serenity*)
People being taunted and insulted (*anger and disgust*)
A climbing accident (*anxiety and fear*)

Their analyses revealed that the positive-emotion films (the film about penguins and the film about fields and streams) produced a global bias in the processing, in that after watching these films participants used the broader features of the stimulus pattern for comparison (the overall shape). In addition, having watched either of the two happy films, participants wrote more responses in the open-ended twenty-statement test than they did when they watched the negative films. In other words, having watched these happy films, participants were in the right frame of mind to do lots of different things whereas, when the participants watched the negative films (in particular the film which involved the taunting and insulting), they felt like doing much less.

This was the first direct experimental test of the hypothesis that positive emotions do have an evolutionary function, particularly with regard to thought-action repertoires. When you manage to get yourself into a positive state of mind, you can see the broader picture (you don't get bogged down in the specifics), and you can think of more things to do. The extra-ordinary thing is that it is not difficult to get into this psycho-logical state. These were short two-minute films, but they did the trick. So the next time you can't see the wood for the trees, reach for the DVD player and watch something funny.

What is exciting about this research is that it tackles a fundamental question in psychology: what is the evolutionary significance of positive emotions? The assumption, of course, is that if these emotions did not have some evolutionary signifi-cance, then they would not have evolved. What the researchers did in their study was to demonstrate that positive emotion seems to broaden attention and broaden what they call 'thought-action repertoires'. My only problem with this research is that I am a little concerned about the actual tasks they used. The advantage of the comparison task used is that you can easily distinguish the two types of bias that people might show when they are making comparisons and you can do this clearly and unambiguously. But how will this generalize to other tasks when seeing the bigger picture is that much more difficult? And what happens if you get stuck on a task, unable to take a broader perspective – does positive emotion still work then? And as for the second measure, the twenty-statement test, how do we know that seeing pictures of penguins in the Antarctic, or a film of mountains, fields and streams didn't just get people thinking about nature and all the things they could do out there in the wild? In other words, how do we know that this wasn't more to do with the priming of certain types of memories than anything else? But as usual, with psychology, you have to start somewhere and their results are clearly very interesting and potentially very important in terms of their applicability. So the next time you are stuck on a task, take a two-minute break and watch a happy film, it's worth trying.

- The evolutionary reason that we have positive emotions (like 'joy', 'happiness' and 'contentment') is to allow us to build resources for when we need to draw upon them

- Positive emotions help us live longer

- In a work context, positive emotions help us see the bigger picture

- To avoid being bogged down in the detail of something, watch a happy film

How to work out if you will succeed in business

You are most likely to succeed in business if you have the right sort of personality; it is as simple and as complex as that. You are most likely to succeed if you are an optimist and have an optimistic disposition. The good news is that optimism can be trained. Optimists are people who look on the bright side of life, but from a psychological point of view the most important thing about optimists is that they take credit for the good things that happen to them in their lives but don't blame themselves for the bad things that happen. They seem to intuitively think that the negative things in life tend to be the result of many factors (other people, the situation, the time of day, the economy) and they make their attribution accordingly. They are not so analytic (or thoughtful) when it comes to the positive events that surround them ('Of course, the project was successful, I was in charge!'). So if you want to train yourself to be more optimistic, the next time that you feel that you are about to put some failure down to yourself, just think more carefully about it – tell the little voice in your head that it could be someone else's fault. A little more analysis here will mean that you will not internalize failure quite so readily. But be quite prepared to internalize success immediately and readily! Feel good about success. The reason that optimists do so well in business is that they believe that good things are just around the corner and that is why they are so successful, they keep going when others would have packed up and gone home.

So if you want to work out whether you will succeed in business or not, ask yourself how optimistic you are:

- Are you a glass half full (*optimist*) or half empty (*pessimist*) sort of person?
- The last time you passed an exam was it because you know that you are very bright or good at exams (*optimist*)?
- Or was it because the exam was easy and everyone did well at it (*pessimist*)?
- The last time you failed an exam was it because the exam was very difficult (*optimist*)?
- Or was it because you're not that clever or good at exams (*pessimist*)?

If you haven't got a naturally optimistic outlook you will need to rethink how you spontaneously explain why all of the small things of everyday life turn out the way they do. You need to start making the immediate assumption that all of the things that turn out well in your life are down to you, and the things that turn out not so well might not be anything to do with you. Herein lie the roots of optimism and business success.

According to Fredrick Crane of Northeastern University and, his colleague, Erinn Crane of Suffolk University Law School, there is one key psychological factor that any entrepreneur needs to have in order to achieve success, and that is what these researchers called 'dispositional optimism'. Optimism is a particular way of thinking about the world and why things happen the way they do; optimists believe that they will experience positive outcomes in the vast majority of situations that they find themselves in (pessimists believe the opposite). Dispositional optimism means that some people have this kind of optimism as a personality trait. Optimism, in other words, is essentially a belief that they carry around with them. The psychological benefit of being an optimist is that you will try harder and not give up in any situation because you believe that good things are just around the corner. Pessimists, of course, think the opposite and they give up much more readily. Given that entrepreneurial success is not just inspiration but perspiration, and that it is very much about sustained effort over a protracted period of time, optimists have a huge advantage when it comes to success in business.

Crane and Crane reviewed the literature on personality factors and entrepreneurial success and they cite the work of Kim Owens (2004) who reported that a range of factors predicted financial success: 'Goal setting, emotional resilience, ability to sell self, social networking, and work-related locus of control were positively related to both financial performance and work satisfaction.' Crane and Crane's review found that 'optimism', 'work ethic', 'energy', 'goal orientation', 'capital' and 'business skills' were the six characteristics which most typified successful entrepreneurs. However, the most important characteristics were 'work ethic' and 'optimism', with dispositional optimism being the most important of them all. To put it simply, it doesn't matter how good your work ethic is, how hard you work, how good your energy level is, how goal-oriented you are, what capital you have at your disposal to put into your business or what your business skills are, if you aren't fundamentally optimistic then there is a major chink in your armour and you may have to think of an alternative career.

So how can you tell if you are a born optimist or not? One simple method was devised by Martin Seligman, who looked at people's spontaneous attributions for success and failure.

Whenever something goes right, optimists tend to put it all down to themselves (they make what are called 'internal', 'stable' and 'global' attributions for what has occurred), assuming that cause is specific to themselves ('internal'), will always be present ('stable') and will influence many aspects of their lives ('global'). For example, 'I made the right decision in that business deal because I'm a pretty smart guy.' This attribution is essentially internal ('it's all down to me'), stable (you don't, after all, suddenly become stupid) and global (it influences every aspect of your life, or at least most). However, when things go wrong, optimists do not tend to internalize the cause of the failure; they assume it can be down to other people or the situation. They also assume that the cause will not be stable over a long period of time and therefore will not influence other events in the future. And they tend to make a specific attribution for the negative event and therefore it will not influence every aspect of their life. For example, 'I didn't make the deal but they weren't ready to negotiate' is essentially external, unstable and specific. You are not blaming yourself for why it did not work out.

The extraordinary thing about the work of Martin Seligman is that he shows that what is called 'attributional style', i.e. our tendency to make one type of attribution rather than another, can be changed. So if you are not naturally a dispositional optimist, then don't despair, you just need to start monitoring your processes of attributions of success and failure and you need to learn to put success down to you (the way that others naturally do). Instead of assuming that all failure leads directly back to you, think more carefully about other possible causes. Could it be due to another person? Could it be due to the situation? Could it be due to the task? Could it be due to some complex interaction between the other person and the task?

If you want to succeed in business you need to think about your underlying personality. Do you have the sunny personality of the optimist who believes that everything will be all right in the end? If you haven't, then you either need to change your career plans, or you need to think about your everyday pattern of attributions because this is the cognitive foundation of both optimism and pessimism. If you start thinking and believing like an optimist then anything may well be possible.

Crane and Crane reviewed the literature on entrepreneurial success of the last twenty-five years or so in an attempt to identify what distinguishes successful entrepreneurs from unsuccessful ones. They argue that psychology can play a major role in the development of entrepreneurs. My only issue with this study is that it can be dangerous to look at one psychological characteristic in isolation. A long time ago, I wrote a book about entrepreneurs in Thatcher's Britain (Beattie, 1987) and it was clear to me even then that although many of the most successful entrepreneurs I interviewed were great optimists, so too were some of the entrepreneurs with some of the most ridiculous business ideas I have ever encountered. I was desperate to suggest to some of them that perhaps they should give up, and that their ideas were never going to work. But they were just too optimistic and they believed that success was just around the corner. Some of them persisted with their dream for years; they needed a sense of realism to temper their optimism. It is this appraisal skill – in addition to optimism – that helps us identify the really successful entrepreneurs. It seems clear that optimism may be a necessary cause of entrepreneurial success (because the ability to persevere in difficult times is crucial) but it's not enough on its own. We may be able to train optimism, but what about realism and the ability to step back and appraise entrepreneurial progress? Can we train these skills effectively as well?

- You will succeed in business if you are an optimist because you will persevere when things are not going well (pessimists will often just give up)

- Optimism derives from an identifiable pattern of thinking, hence optimism can be trained

- If you're not naturally an optimist you need to learn to dispute that internal voice in your head that puts all failure down to you (one of the main characteristics of the pessimist)

How to work more effectively on a project

If you are working on a project over several days or weeks, think more carefully about how you talk about what you have done so far. If you are talking to a colleague about what you have achieved, use the imperfect past tense rather than the perfect past tense:

Imperfect past tense } 'I was mapping out all of the options'
'I was deciding on the best way forward'
'I was thinking about the alternatives'

Perfect past tense } 'I mapped out all of the options'
'I decided on the best way forward'
'I thought about the alternatives'

The reason for this is that although we sometimes think of these two verb tenses as being interchangeable and essentially synonymous, the brain recognizes that the perfect past tense:

'mapped'
'decided'
'thought'

signals completion, whereas the imperfect past tense:

'was mapping'
'was deciding'
'was thinking'

signals that things might not yet be complete. The imperfect tense keeps our brains in a state of readiness to complete the project. It enhances memory for what we have been working on, it makes us more ready to resume our action and it keeps core thoughts more firmly in mind.

Research in this area was carried out by William Hart of the University of Florida and Dolores Albarracín of the University of Illinois at Urbana-Champaign. Their underlying philosophy is that thoughts and behaviour are intimately linked and the way we describe actions and events may have a profound influence on our behaviour. They tested this by asking people to talk about events using one of two verb tenses:

Imperfect past tense	Perfect past tense
'I was walking'	'I walked'
'I was doing'	I did'
I was working'	'I worked'

The critical difference between the imperfect and the perfect past tenses are that the imperfect ('I was working') represents a past action as ongoing and not yet complete, whereas the perfect tense of the verb ('I worked') represents the past action as complete. However, we often use them more or less as interchangeable without much conscious reflection, as in 'Yesterday I was working on a project, it was going pretty well. I was just finishing it when the bell went' or 'Yesterday I worked on a project, it went pretty well. I had just finished it when the bell went'. Hart and Albarracín say that, 'Although at first sight the distinction might seem relatively inconsequential, we propose that the choice of aspect can influence memories of a described behaviour, as well as the likelihood of re-enacting that behaviour at a later time.' The specific idea that the researchers tested was that the imperfect past tense (because it is signalling the action is not yet complete) facilitates memory for action-relevant knowledge. The way that they tested this hypothesis was to ask people to write an essay arguing against black stereotypes in either the perfect or imperfect past tense. They then looked at the effects of the tense of the verb used in the essay on subsequent stereotypical judgements about black people. They found that the tense of the verb had a significant effect on these judgements, with the descriptions in the imperfect tense leading to less harsh judgements. In the second experiment, the researchers had participants do an anagram task, but they were interrupted several minutes into the task 'because of time constraints'. Then participants were asked to describe what they had been doing in either the imperfect or perfect past tense and finally their memory for the particular anagrams was tested. Their willingness to resume the task was also measured. Again, quite extraordinarily, participants who wrote about their task in the imperfect tense were more willing to resume the task and had better memories for the anagrams than those in the perfect tense condition. In other words, by simply changing the verb used to describe your behaviour, you can affect your subsequent behaviour, your memory for what you were doing and even (in the case of the black stereotype experiment) the accessibility of your underlying beliefs. This is clear evidence for a strand of thought that has been around in psychology for a long time called 'the linguistic relativity hypothesis'. The basic idea behind this hypothesis is that the language we use can affect the nature and pattern of our thinking. What these researchers have demonstrated is that something apparently as inconsequential as verb tense can influence thought and behaviour in significant ways. In the words of the researchers, 'An aspect marker that described experiences as ongoing rather than completed enhanced memory for action-relevant knowledge and increased tendencies to reproduce an action at a later time.'

The linguistic relativity hypothesis has been around for a very long time and it is normally illustrated by showing that the presence of linguistic labels can affect the kinds of discriminations that you can make in your everyday life. One of the most frequently cited observations is that the Inuit of Alaska have many different words for types of snow and, the claim is, they can differentiate many types of snow because they can attach these linguistic labels to them. But the problem with this argument is that it works equally well the other way round. The type of snow is very important in the world of the Inuit and thus the necessity to make perceptual distinctions may well have driven the diversity of linguistic labels. The research by Hart and Albarracín takes us beyond the circularity of this reasoning and demonstrates that one aspect of linguistic form, the tense of the verb, has a significant effect on thinking, on action and on memory. Of course, the extraordinary thing about verb tense is that we normally take it for granted, but the argument here is that the imperfect tense signals that the action is not yet finished and primes our brain to get ready for future actions. Use of the perfect tense signifies that the action has finished and this would seem to allow our brain to move on that much more readily.

- The language and the words we use can affect our thinking and the activity of our brain

- Words that may look interchangeable and synonymous may have very different effects on our brain

- Use the imperfect past tense of the verb when you are working on an on-going project, and talking about your work so far ('I was mapping out all the options'), rather than the perfect past tense ('I mapped out all the options')

- The imperfect past tense keeps our brain in a state of readiness to act again

How to help someone remember
what you have just said

If you want people to remember better what you have just said, make sure that your hands are free to make spontaneous gestural movements while you talk. These gestures will display all kinds of meaningful patterns, and will illustrate the content of what you are saying. Supporting gestures also mean that listeners will receive information that is closely related in terms of meaning, in two forms, at the same time. This means that the information will be stored in their memory in two different ways and will be more effectively recalled.

After all, one well-known technique for remembering basic information in everyday life is to form a mental image of the things that you are trying to remember. So if you are trying to remember a list of objects, say:

'chair'
'banana'
'picture'
'boy'
'hat'

then it often helps if you visualize a boy wearing a hat, holding a banana, sitting on a chair with a picture in the background. This visual image which ties the various objects together into one picture helps you to recall the individual items, so there is the strong possibility that in everyday life, by making these gestural movements (both spontaneously and unconsciously) it helps others remember the content of what you are actually saying.

If you are making a very important speech and you have time to plan what you are going to say, then it is possible to plan and (to some extent) even choreograph these gestural movements to produce positive effects on both the comprehension of what is said and to improve the memory of your speech. The gestures must be selected very carefully and the form of the gestural movement must link closely with the content of the speech. Say you are just about to make a speech about the current economic crisis and say that you hold the belief that we really do not understand fully all of the factors that were responsible for it. The sentence that you might have planned to include could be: 'There is a wide gap in our current understanding of the critical factors that led to the economic downturn.' Then if you want people really to get the point and remember that there really is a large gap in our understanding, make sure that the hands open widely as 'a wide gap' is mentioned. That way the audience will remember that the gap is wide because they have both *heard it* ('wide gap') and *seen it* (as depicted in the accompanying gestural movement, which is unconsciously processed along-side the speech). The fact that these types of movements are also usually generated unconsciously alongside speech (we are usually totally unaware of the specific movements that our hands make) gives them a special premium in communication. When people gesture we know that they mean it, and some of the most important things they say are reflected in the gestures. The timing of these gestural movements, however, is crucial because the apex of the movements and the speech must coincide. This means that the starting point of the movement must slightly precede the speech so that the hand can be in a critical position to make the movement as the relevant bit of speech occurs.

Thus if you are going to say: 'The { re is a [wide gap] in our current understanding of the critical factors that led to the economic downturn', the gestural movement needs to start at {, with the hands starting to move towards the chest, and at [the hands need to start moving apart (with the stopping point of the movement at]).

If this all seems a little tricky, watch how people gesture in everyday life to see how the gesture starts relatively early in the sentence. If you are going to send the information through the gestural code effectively you need to become a good observer of human action. (Some politicians who try to use gestural movements effectively in political speeches must not be good observers of human behaviour because their timings are often badly out!) But the possible dividends are enormous. By putting the same message into the speech and into the hands, you will be delivering a message that is both clear and very hard to forget.

I did some of the basic research on this topic with Heather Shovelton, also of the University of Manchester. We noted that when people talk, they spontaneously move their hands and these gestural movements map out images which are connected to the content of what is being said. These movements are typically generated below the level of consciousness. They often display some of the same basic content as that described in the speech, sometimes exactly the same but at other times adding important new information. So, to take a very simple example like the description of a basic action, if someone was describing watching their friend sliding on ice, they might say, 'He slid along the pavement.' The accompanying gestural movement exactly timed with the speech will display the basic action of sliding but in addition it will show the speed and the direction of the actual movement (which is not mentioned in the sentence itself). There is a good deal of research to show that people who see these spontaneously generated movements in addition to hearing the speech, pick up a good deal more information about the original event being described.

So these gestures can add to meaning, but they also do something else as well. They can help you remember the content of what has been said, because the information is essentially put into a verbal code (the speech) and an image code (the gesture) at the same time. That is what Heather Shovelton and I tested as we devised a number of scripted messages (in the form of advertisements) for a range of products (holidays, cars, mobile phones) and choreographed appropriate gestures to accompany the speech. One set of participants saw the advertisement with the speech on its own, another set watched the advert with appropriate gestures and a third set just read the text of the advert. Those who watched the advert containing the speech and gestures got a lot more information about the products, and it was retained for a significantly longer amount of time (with a very small reduction in the amount of information retained after a three-month period in the case of some of the core messages).

In another study (for a fresh fruit drink 'F') we made a broadcast standard TV advertisement, comparing the effects of certain gestures with more traditional images that advertisers might normally use. We focused on three core messages that we wanted to send (and be remembered) by an audience:

The fruit in the drink was *fresh*

The drink was for *everyone*

The bottle was very *small*

We devised the gestures for inclusion by studying the kinds of spontaneous and unconscious gestures that people use in their everyday life to illustrate these kinds of things (we had to do this because, of course, there is no dictionary that you can look in for these kinds of spontaneous movements). The movement for *fresh* that most people produced was curled hands opening rapidly, for *everyone* it was a large, sweeping movement, and *small* was very easy to represent – the hands simply coming together and falling stationary six or so inches apart showing the actual size of the bottle. The alternative images were devised by an actual advertising agency (*fresh* – juice on a piece of fruit; *everyone* – a *Sun* headline saying 'Phwoar! Everyone's drinking it'; and the *small* bottle size – a hand holding the actual bottle) and we found that the imagistic gestures had the edge again in terms of communication and memory, because they are very good at isolating the core feature that you are trying to communicate. Thus, one critical bit of the message was that in this new drink you have 'five fruit portions crammed into every tiny little bottle', the accompanying gestural movement showing the size of the bottle just draws attention to that one feature. The alternative image, the actual bottle held in the human hand showing the size has lots of other information (the colour, texture, shape, etc.) which can potentially distract from the core message.

So, if you want someone to understand and remember better what you are saying, make sure that your hands are free to make these spontaneous unconscious movements. If you have time to think and plan a particularly important message, you may even want to include deliberate gestural movements in your description. The accompanying gestures mean that the content will be stored in both a speech and an image format and this will facilitate recall.

- Allow your hands to move while you are talking to help people remember what you have just said

- Gesture represents the content of the speech in a visual code which reinforces what is said in the linguistic speech code

- We always remember material better when it is stored in two codes simultaneously

- If you have to give an important speech, plan a gesture to coincide with the most important speech content. The same basic message will then be received in a visual and verbal code, which will make it that much more memorable

---

How to start the day well

If you want to start the day well, make sure that you have cereal and coffee (or tea) because breakfast helps you work more efficiently. The cereal improves memory (and particularly spatial memory), while the caffeine makes you process information more rapidly and more efficiently. Breakfast is also beneficial because it puts you in a good mood and we know that people in a good mood set higher goals at work. Those who eat breakfast regularly tend to be less depressed, they also appear to be not as emotionally distressed and they also have lower levels of perceived stress than those who do not have breakfast regularly.

These assertions are supported by research conducted by Andrew Smith and his colleagues of the University of Bristol. According to their research, both cereal and coffee have a big impact on psychological functioning. Previous research has shown that breakfast significantly improves memory by increasing glucose into the brain. Coffee, on the other hand, doesn't seem to have much of an effect on memory, but has a big impact on attention span, and previous research also suggests that caffeine speeds up the processing of new incoming information. As well as affecting levels of glucose in the brain, existing research also suggests that breakfast cereal increases positive mood by affecting the level of serotonin in the brain. So when Smith started his research, there was already considerable evidence that breakfast consisting of cereal and coffee does affect aspects of psychological functioning. He wanted to try and pinpoint exactly what specific psychological functions were affected. What was different about his study was that it worked with a model which set out the basic components of human memory to see exactly where the effects lay. He used a wide variety of tests of things like 'serial recall' (eight numbers were presented one at a time on a computer screen and participants had to write them down in the order in which they appeared) and 'spatial memory' (participants observed a sequence of lights coming on and they had to memorize the sequence on a spatial array), as well as assessing mood and blood pressure. His analysis revealed that breakfast cereal has a big effect on memory, but particularly on spatial memory. Caffeine didn't affect memory performance, but in a task involving attention, caffeine had a big effect on reaction times and breakfast was also associated with improved mood state including feelings of 'calm'. Other researchers found that regular consumption of cereal for breakfast is linked to lower levels of cortisol production (a good indicator of stress). Indeed, more generally, Smith concluded that, 'Those who consumed a cereal breakfast each day were less depressed, less emotionally distressed and had lower levels of perceived stress than less regular consumers.' The extraordinary thing about all of this is that recent surveys of people's early-morning habits in the UK have suggested that many people skip breakfast. The research suggested that 33 per cent of people don't eat breakfast at home and 42 per cent of young people between the ages of 18 and 25 don't eat breakfast at home. For this group of young people, in terms of early-morning priorities, breakfast is behind fixing their hair and having a shower or a bath; nearly as many young people from this sample watch TV in the morning rather than eating breakfast. The main reasons given for this are that some people say they don't feel hungry in the morning (33 per cent), some people reported having too little time (27 per cent) and some people said they just couldn't be bothered (13 per cent). When asked what they would do if they had an extra quarter of an hour in the morning, 40 per cent said that they would stay in bed and 53 per cent of the young people said that they would stay in bed. Of the sample, 47 per cent also said that they breakfasted alone. So the early-morning routine of many people in the UK seems to be primarily focused on appearance; with many of the sample reporting that they spent between forty-five minutes and one hour getting ready.

However, these priorities seem completely wrong from a

psychological point of view. The message should be clear that something that makes you feel good is actually very good for you. If you have breakfast you will feel better, work more efficiently be less stressed, less depressed and be in a better mood generally.

- Always eat breakfast
- Breakfast cereal improves spatial memory
- Caffeine improves attention
- Breakfast improves mood state
- A better mood means that you set higher goals at work
- Give up early-morning TV, or give up the extra fifteen minutes in bed, in order to make the time for breakfast

---

How to train yourself to persist in a task

If you want to persist in a task, there is one very simple thing that you can do; fold your arms before the task starts. Research has shown that folding arms is linked, not just to defensiveness, but also to a certain kind of persistent attitude. However, bodily movement does not just reflect the underlying psychological state; it has an effect on that psychological state. This has been demonstrated in a number of areas where instructing people to adopt a certain type of behaviour seems to affect their underlying attitude and emotion. If you ask people to fold their arms it has an impact on how long they persevere with a task and it also seems to affect how efficient they are at the task. Arm-crossing and persevering at a task are linked unconsciously in memory and the occurrence of one of them seems to automatically trigger the other. So if you want to persevere at a task, train yourself to fold your arms and let your unconscious associations take over.

Ron Friedman and Andrew Elliot of the University of Rochester, USA looked into the subject of persistence. They conducted two experiments in which people carried out anagram tasks. First of all, participants were given a number of anagrams that were easily solvable (you can try this for yourself):

'WODN' and 'TOBOR'

Then they were given a final anagram which was unsolvable (you can try all you like with this one!):

'OCHERSTE'

The participants were told that they had as much time as they needed for the task. In one condition the participants were told to cross their arms before the study started and in the second condition they were told to place their arms on their thighs. The researchers wanted to know how long the participants would persevere for. They found that when the participants were told to fold their arms before the anagram task, they persisted for an average of fifty-four seconds, whereas in the other condition, they persisted for less than thirty seconds. In a second study the psychologists looked at the effects of arm-crossing on the success of a task, this time using only anagrams which were solvable. Again they found that people who crossed their arms before the task persisted longer than those who didn't and they also solved more anagrams.

The psychology behind this is that arm-folding is a 'proprioceptive cue', which 'acts as embodied manifestations of an underlying subjective experience'. Everyone knows that how we feel inside affects our behaviour but we have also known for some time that our behaviour itself can affect our subjective experience. Charles Darwin, for example, speculated that an individual's emotionally expressive movement has an impact on his or her underlying emotional state. This was demonstrated experimentally by Stepper and Strack (1993), who asked people either to furrow their brow or adopt a slight smile while they engaged in a task. They found that those people with furrowed brows actually reported putting more effort into the task (furrowed brows, are of course, associated with greater effort). Even more incredibly, Wells and Petty (1980) asked people either to move their head vertically or horizontally while listening to a recorded message and they found that those people who were asked to nod their head while listening reported that they were more likely to agree with the recorded message. In other words, we get feedback from our body which affects our subjective experience. This gave Friedman and Elliot the theoretical underpinning for their work. Their assumption was that, although sometimes arm-crossing can be associated with defensiveness, in other situations it is associated with signifying 'an unyielding attitude'. In the words of the researchers, 'Arm crossing tends to occur in situations where people are working hard to solve a problem or accomplish a task, and are determined to continue until successful completion. With repeated experience, arm crossing in achievement settings is presumed to become deeply linked with a behavioural tendency to persevere. As such, over time, the act of arm crossing in achievement contexts should activate a perseverant behavioural tendency, and this should occur without intention or awareness.' This is exactly what they found and they produced clear evidence that merely crossing your arms before you start a task means that you will persist longer at the task and perform better.

This in many ways is an extraordinary result given that arm-crossing seems to be affected by different psychological and emotional states and does appear to be linked to things like defensiveness as well as persistence. How universal will these results be? For example, if you are asked to take part in a test and you feel very negatively towards the person making the request, and consequently fold your arms, will this also result in persistence? Or will the same behavioural configuration – arm-folding – lead to a different subjectively experienced state like hostility?

- Folding your arms can increase your determination
- To persevere in a task, fold your arms before you start

How to get the most out of a new job

If you want to get the most out of a new job you need to recognize that any change in life circumstances will be associated with a range of emotions and sometimes conflicting thoughts. There may be all kinds of anxieties and worries just below the surface which, despite the excitement of change and progress, might come to the fore. The best way of dealing with this is to sit down and write for twenty minutes about 'your deepest thoughts and feelings' associated with the change. Do this for twenty minutes at a time on three consecutive days; this not only improves how you feel generally but it seems to have a direct effect on a core component of mental processing, namely working memory capacity. This means that you will be able to process and store information more efficiently and therefore work more effectively in your new job. What you are doing is tying all of your thoughts and feelings together and making these thoughts and feelings easier to inhibit. This provides you with more cognitive resources to deal with the job at hand.

When taking on new challenges it is important to work as efficiently as possible, but sometimes because of the confusing emotions created by conflicting thoughts, this can be difficult. Kitty Klein and Adriel Boals of North Carolina State University studied working memory as a means of dealing with difficult transitions. Working memory is the ability to store and process information; this processing requires activation of a particular part of the brain called the prefrontal cortex. Working memory, which is a central component of all mental tasks, however, has to compete for the limited resource of all the other thoughts that may be flying about in our heads. So Klein and Boals suggest that one way of improving working memory is to deal with all of the thoughts that will be particularly prevalent during a major life transition. Their suggestion is that we need to write about the transition in order to make a coherent narrative about it: 'The result of moving from many representations to a single mental model of the event will be that fewer resources are required for its inhibition, with the consequence that more resources will be available for other working memory requirements.'

The researchers got first-semester college students to write about their 'deepest thoughts and feelings about coming to college'. They used three twenty-minute writing sessions over a two-week period. The students had to write about their thoughts and feelings in such a way as to 'tie it all together'. In the control condition students had to 'write about everything they had done that day and to write about how they might have done a better job'. The measure of working memory that the researchers used consisted of some arithmetic followed by a word memory span task. What the researchers found was that asking the students to write about their transition to college significantly improved their working memory capacity and those students who showed the greatest improvement in working memory scores achieved the highest test scores in their college exams. They also found that those students who used the highest proportion of insight words in their essays showed the greatest improvement in working memory scores. In a second study, the researchers found that participants who wrote about negative experiences also showed a reduction in the amount of intrusive thinking that they were experiencing.

In other words, writing about major events can have a major impact on the efficiency of our memory and our thinking. We know from other research that writing about negative events has a major impact on psychological and physical health; this particular study suggests what the mechanism might be. Unwanted, intrusive thoughts can impact on working memory and thereby interfere with problem solving to the extent that coping responses will become less likely. Writing about the transition to college (and the homesickness, loneliness and study difficulties associated with this) may mean that the whole thing is tied together into a coherent narrative and is made sense of and can be suppressed more easily. Writing three short essays over two weeks seems to have an impact on working memory. It means that you can work more efficiently and enjoy college life more. But this is not limited just to college students. Any job or work transition is characterized by a range of emotions and often conflicting thoughts and can be dealt with in the same kind of way.

- Get the most out of a new job by recognizing that there will be some negative emotions associated with taking the job. This is not a sign of weakness

- Work more efficiently in a new job by writing about your thoughts and feelings (including the negative feelings) associated with the move

- This writing process will tie all the issues together and make you feel better, and, in addition, it will improve working memory. So you will now work more efficiently

How to enhance someone's self-esteem in twenty seconds

High self-esteem is a very important attribute in everyday life. If you think positively about yourself then it stops you from getting too deflated by criticism and if you have high self-esteem and you are not doing very well at something, you will persist for longer at the task, because you know that you will be able to do it in the end. But is the level of self-esteem fixed over a period of time or can it be changed? And if so, how can it be changed? It seems that you can change how people feel about themselves inside by pairing positive words or non-verbal expressions every time they use the word 'I'. Every time the person talks about themselves make sure that there is a positive response associated with it. The positive response could either be verbal (such as saying 'good' or 'well done'), or non-verbal (a smile or head nod). We now know that implicit self-esteem can be boosted through this simple conditioning technique, which occurs without any conscious awareness. The more subtly this is done the better.

It is extremely important in everyday life to have high self-esteem because we know that if you have a positive view of yourself it promotes happiness and is good for your mental health. People with high self-esteem are less sensitive to the debilitating criticisms of everyday life and they can persist for longer at work-related tasks. For many years psychologists have studied conscious or explicit self-esteem, which is how we consciously reflect on ourselves, but in the last few years psychologists have started examining implicit (or unconscious) self-esteem, which is not subject to reflection, but nevertheless is thought to underpin our everyday social life. The advantage of measuring implicit self-esteem is that it is not subject to the same kinds of biases that plague explicit measures. People may after all tell you that they feel good about themselves, but how do we know if they really do deep down inside? How do we know that they are not just putting on a brave face?

Psychologists have begun to use the Implicit Association Test (IAT), which we came across earlier, and this measures people's ability to pair self-related words or words not related to the self with positive and negative evaluative words. The basic idea here is that the closer you associate self-related words with the category 'good' (and the higher your self-esteem) the faster you will be able to do this in a computerised test and the fewer errors you will make in doing it. Another measure of implicit self-esteem that has been used is the initial-preference task (IPT), which was developed and produced by Nuttin (1987). The IPT is based on the assumption that letters are evaluated more favourably by people with names which contain those letters compared to people with names that do not. It turns out that this effect is even stronger for the evaluation of people's own initials, and people with high self-esteem rate the letters from their own names and their own initials as particularly positive (without any conscious awareness of what they are doing). So we can now measure implicit self-esteem, the big question then is, can we change it?

This is what Ap Dijksterhuis from the University of Amsterdam studied. The method he introduced to promote change was classical conditioning, presenting the word 'I' (the Dutch word 'ik') on a computer screen immediately followed by a positive-trait word like:

'nice'
'smart'
'warm'

This was a technique designed to enhance implicit self-esteem. Participants were told that this was a psychological task where they had to decide whether a string of letters was a word or a non-word, but in one condition the pairings of the word 'I' with the positive-trait words was also presented. The IPT was given to the participants before and after and it was found that when the word 'I' was paired with the positive words, the IPT scores improved significantly. In other words, this simple procedure seemed to elevate their level of self-esteem. In another experiment, the researcher showed that you got exactly the same result when you used the IAT measure instead, and amazingly, this result was obtained even when the word 'I' and the positive-trait words ('nice', 'smart' and 'warm') were presented subliminally for seventeen milliseconds, which was below the level that participants had any conscious awareness of what was going on. At this level of presentation, one participant said that 'she had seen flashes on the screen during the lexical decision task, but she did not report having seen any words'.

This basic conditioning procedure also worked independently of whether the participants had low or high self-esteem to begin with. The experimenter then rather unkindly lowered people's self-esteem by giving them false feedback on how they had performed in an intelligence test, and what they found was that the conditioning procedure worked even when the participants had had their self-esteem lowered by giving them negative feedback.

In the final set of experiments the researcher tested the effects of higher levels of self-esteem on other aspects of behaviour. The researcher speculated that the beauty of high self-esteem is that it gives you some protection against criticism and it means that you persist longer at various tasks. So this time the researcher elevated people's self-esteem through the conditioning procedure and then they were given negative feedback, and were given the chance to do other tasks which could potentially restore their level of self-esteem. They found that those participants whose implicit self-esteem had been enhanced by the conditioning procedure showed no effects of negative feedback on mood. In other words, these people were feeling so good about themselves that telling them that they had done poorly on a task did not seem to affect their emotional state. When they received the negative feedback, those who had their self-esteem boosted persisted longer at the new task presented to them.

The results of this set of experiments are very encouraging, they tell us that we can do something about the implicit self-esteem of ourselves and those around us. Boosting self-esteem helps enormously; it acts as a buffer against criticism and helps you focus on the task at hand. One other significant detail in this experiment needs to be pointed out, namely that the conditioning procedure only took twenty-five seconds. So you can do something (at least temporary) about someone's self-esteem in less than half a minute.

This remarkable set of studies suggests that we can do something about someone's self-esteem in a very short amount of time. The researcher used two different measures of implicit self-esteem, both of which had been tested in other studies and appeared to be reliable indicators of self-esteem. The only caveat to this study is that we do not know how long the effects will last; the researcher only tested the new levels of self-esteem immediately after the manipulation had taken place. The question is, will this elevated level of self-esteem last for minutes, days, weeks or months? At the moment we don't know.

- People's implicit self-esteem is not fixed; it can be changed in a relatively short space of time

- You can boost the implicit self-esteem of others by using a conditioning procedure, without their conscious awareness

- To enhance self-esteem, associate nods and smiles when others talk about themselves

8. INTERVIEWS

'A man willing to work, and unable to find work,
is perhaps the saddest sight that fortune's
inequality exhibits under this sun.'

Thomas Carlyle, *Chartism* (1839), 4

How to appear more intelligent without even opening your mouth

If you want to appear more intelligent when you first meet someone (say in a job interview) remember to smile naturally and if you want an unfair advantage, invest in some blue contact lenses. We judge people with blue eyes as more attractive and surprisingly, more intelligent than people with any other eye colour. We also rate people who display natural Duchenne smiles (discussed in Chapter 2) as more attractive, sociable and intelligent than those who do not. When blue eyes and Duchenne smiles are combined, you have a winning combination. Why should people with blue eyes be perceived as more intelligent? It doesn't make much rational sense, but because we find this eye colour attractive, we attribute other positive characteristics to the person. When we see someone smiling in a natural way it is hard not to reciprocate the smile. This emotional display affects how we feel inside and it makes us feel good. So again, we attribute more positive characteristics to the person in question. Paul Newman, with those eyes and that smile of his, had it easy.

In 2002 Heather Shovelton and I investigated how eye colour and facial expression can affect interpersonal perception. We knew from previous research that eye colour is a very important aspect of social interaction. For example, Lynn and Shurgot (1984) analysed 395 advertisements in a singles magazine in

Ohio, and found that 173 of these advertisements contained information about the person's hair and eye colour. Jacobi and Cash (1984) analysed the ideal physical attributes that people look for in a partner and found that there was some tendency for people to look for an eye colour similar to their own, but both sexes thought that the opposite sex preferred blue eyes over any other colour. So there is research to suggest that eye colour is important, but how does it affect judgements on issues such as sociability and intelligence? In psychology we sometimes get what is called a 'halo effect' – when something is seen as positive it can influence other judgements, which in principle shouldn't really be connected at all. So if people think that blue eyes are the most attractive eye colour, does this influence judgements not just of attractiveness, but judgements about other attributes like intelligence and sociability?

And does this same process work with things like facial expressions? Michael Cunningham (1986) and Cunningham, Anita Barbee and Carolyn Pike (1990) found that smiling faces, generally speaking, are rated as more attractive than faces that are not smiling.

The way we tested this was to have four confederates who wore different-coloured contact lenses – blue, brown and green or none. The photographs were taken either with a neutral expression or smiling. We got them to smile by using a whole series of prompts (jokes told by the author). The smiles that we were looking for were genuine smiles, or Duchenne smiles, which we eventually managed to elicit. We used a total of thirty-two stimuli, three different-coloured contact lenses plus their own natural eye colour, with either smiling or neutral expressions. We showed the thirty-two pictures as slides to a set

237

of judges who were asked to rate each of the photographs on the following three criteria:

'attractiveness'
'sociability'
'intelligence'

The results were in many ways very striking. Eye colour did significantly affect judgements of attractiveness. Both the male and female judges rated the blue-eyed pictures as the most attractive. We also found that the smiling faces were judged as more attractive than the neutral faces by both our male and female judges. Eye colour did not have a significant effect on judgements of sociability but facial expression did. The faces shown smiling were judged as more sociable than the neutral faces. But the extraordinary thing was the effects of eye colour on judgements of intelligence. There was a general tendency for both men and women to rate the pictures with blue eyes as the most intelligent. The female judges rated both female and male faces as most intelligent when they had blue eyes, the male judges rated the male faces with blue eyes as the most intelligent (the male judges only rated the female face with blue eyes as most intelligent when they were smiling as well!).

So we do seem to have something of a halo effect operating here. Blue eyes are perceived as most attractive and more intelligent. We also found that both male and female judges rated a smiling face as significantly more intelligent than a neutral face, again, more evidence of the halo effect.

The take-home message from this study is that if you want to give the impression of being intelligent on first impressions, invest in some coloured contact lenses, think of something funny and show a natural smile. You will not only be perceived as more attractive, but more intelligent as well.

This study was tightly controlled and the same faces were shown over and over again to a set of judges with the eye colour and the facial expression systematically varied. The participants in the experiment had to make a series of very simple judgements and, in most cases, the purpose of the experiment would have been pretty obvious to them, but of course you could argue that these would be grounds for getting no effects for rating eye colour and facial expression. Why not give the same ratings as the same faces pop up time and time again? We do, therefore, seem to be influenced by eye colour and facial expression. Blue eyes and Duchenne smiles seem to be particularly effective. We prefer them in combination and the halo effect seems to work outwards to encompass judgements of intelligence as well as attractiveness. Of course, this study is based on the very first impressions of people who never had the opportunity to open their mouths. I am sure that as the words come tumbling out, many other factors will also influence these judgements, but for the first few seconds of silence, before the conversation starts, blue eyes and natural smiles seem to have a big effect.

- You will be judged, on first impressions, as more 'attractive', 'sociable' and 'intelligent', if you smile naturally in an interview

- Wear blue contact lenses if you want an unfair advantage. We find blue eyes attractive, and blue eyes produce a positive halo effect. This means that we judge blue-eyed people as more intelligent, as a consequence (even when they do not open their mouths)

How to make an impact in a job interview

If you want to make an impact in a job interview then some degree of ingratiation will help enormously. When you ingratiate yourself with another person, you are essentially agreeing with what they say and reflecting some of their opinions and attitudes back. This technique works because we like people who have got things in common with ourselves and if you ingratiate yourself subtly, people will like you without necessarily realizing why. The other typical verbal strategy that people often use in employment interviews is self-promotion. Self-promotion seems to have much less of an effect and appears to be the weaker of the two strategies.

Chad Higgins of the University of Washington and Timothy Judge of the University of Florida examined this topic by comparing the effectiveness of two different verbal strategies that people use in employment interviews, namely 'self-promotion' and 'ingratiation'. There are good psychological reasons why both of these strategies might work. There is a well-known theory in psychology that we are attracted to those that we have something in common with, and this is why ingratiation should work. Similarly, self-promotion should work because employment interviews are all about finding competent people with the right knowledge, skills and ability to fill the post. Therefore it would seem that by promoting your own skills and ability, this should have a positive effect. Researchers analysed the relationship between what applicants said they did in the interview and the outcome. They found that, although both strategies are commonly used, one is much more influential than the other. Ingratiation was the one that worked, whereas self-promotion had a weaker effect. Those who used ingratiation were thought to fit in well with the organization and meet the requirements of the job better than those who did not.

This study is limited by the professional background of the people being interviewed; they were graduates in business and liberal arts and they were being interviewed for positions in sales and management. The ability to get on with people is an essential part of such jobs and the ingratiation tactic might generally be a powerful indicator of one's ability to draw people to you. In other words, self-promotion might be very effective in certain other domains and it should not be ruled out entirely.

- In interviews for certain types of jobs, ingratiation seems to work better than self-promotion

- When you agree with what the interviewer is saying and reflect back some of their opinions and attitudes, you will be seen to 'fit in' better

How to be more relaxed in an interview

If you want to be more relaxed in an interview, spray yourself lightly with perfume or aftershave beforehand. The parts of the brain connected with the processing of smell are closely connected to those neural substrates that are responsible for emotion. Wearing perfume or aftershave not only affects other people, it affects how you feel about yourself. People wearing fragrance feel more relaxed and show fewer 'self-adaptors', or self-comforting movements, during the course of an interview. They also tend to be rated as more confident by female observers (but not male observers). So, the next time you have an interview, reach for your favourite perfume or aftershave and spray yourself very lightly. It only needs the merest hint to relax your brain and make you perform to your very best.

These were the findings of a study conducted by Takahiro Higuchi of Tokyo Metropolitan University and his colleagues. The psychological reasoning behind this is that those parts of the brain responsible for smell have direct neural connections with those responsible with emotional processing. This means that perfume may not only affect the person you are interacting with, it may affect the wearer as well because of these very close neural connections. Higuchi and his colleagues tested this in a very simple way. They studied young females involved in an interview. Half of the interviewees sprayed some perfume at the midpoint of the interview while the other half did not. Higuchi and his colleagues then had observers rate the non-verbal behaviour of the interviewees all the way through the interview, focusing on three main types of behaviour: smiling, eye contact and 'self-adaptors'. (Self-adaptors are those self-touching movements that are designed to comfort and soothe and they tend to be a reliable indicator of negative emotion.) In addition to analysing the non-verbal behaviour, the experimenters also asked participants to rate their mood on a number of scales.

What the researchers found was that perfume had no effect on the frequency of smiling or the amount of eye contact, but it had a major effect on the frequency of self-adaptors used, in that those who were wearing the perfume showed far fewer self-comforting movements as the interview progressed. Perfume also had a significant effect on the degree of relaxation that the participants felt.

In summary, what this simple experiment demonstrated was that something as basic as spraying oneself with a pleasant-smelling perfume can have a major impact on how you feel and how you behave. In an interview it is very important to be able to relax and to show a low frequency of the kind of movements that could be interpreted as indicating anxiety and negative emotion. Those participants who sprayed themselves with a hint of perfume showed the highest degree of relaxation and were rated by female observers as being more confident. It seems that perfume is not just something we can wear for other people; it is something we can wear for ourselves.

The main issue with this study is that it only used simulated interviews, so in real interviews when the stakes are much higher, would the effects be so pronounced?

- Spray yourself with perfume very lightly before a job interview. This will help you relax and make you appear more confident

- When you are relaxed in an interview, you will display fewer self-comforting movements, and you will be perceived as more confident

How to get the best job in the world

Some people perpetually strive for the very best in all areas of their life. When making a decision, they use a procedure that involves 'an exhaustive search of all the possibilities'; they need to know what is out there in order to properly evaluate each option. These people differ from those who are looking for options that are 'just good enough' to satisfy what they need.

So how can you find the very best job in the world? The answer is that you can't, and that this psychological drive to try to find the best job may make you very unhappy. Those people who explore all the options and push themselves to get the best possible outcome tend to find jobs with a salary on average 20 per cent higher than those who do not, but potentially at a huge cost to themselves. They tend to be 'more pessimistic, stressed, tired, anxious, worried, overwhelmed and depressed throughout the process than others'. You will never find the best job in the world, but you may find one that fits you well. If you are the kind of person who needs to search out every possible alternative, then you need to do something about this natural tendency – pause, reflect and relax because it may be driving you on to a slightly higher salary but it might make you much more miserable in the process.

When it comes to any kind of decision-making, people fall into one of two groups – maximizers and satisficers. Maximizers are only content with the very best and in order to find the best they need to do an exhaustive search of all the possibilities. Satisficers, on the other hand, just need to find something that is 'good enough'. Their search procedure is quite different; they will search only until an option that crosses some threshold of acceptability and then they stop. This was a distinction that was first introduced over fifty years ago by Herbert Simon (1955) and formed the basis of an important study at Columbia University by Sheena Iyengar and her colleagues. Iyengar illustrated the difference in the two types of individual in the following way. Say you were looking for something to watch on the TV, a maximizer would surf across a range of channels and may well spend so much time channel-surfing, and deciding about which programme to watch, that they have little time left for viewing the actual programme. The satisficer, in contrast, would channel-surf only until they encountered a show which was good enough to watch; then they would put down the remote and actually watch it. There is psychological research to suggest that although maximizers spend much more time and effort trying to make a decision, and explore far more options than the satisficers to achieve greater satisfaction, they tend to feel worse about the outcome. In the words of Iyengar and her colleagues, 'Results showed that maximizing tendencies were positively correlated with regret, depression, and decision difficulty, and negatively correlated with happiness, life satisfaction, optimism, and satisfaction with decision outcomes.' The question that these researchers asked was this: even though maximizers might feel worse about the decisions they have made, does their search procedure and their desire to find the very best option allow them to reach outcomes that are in some sense objectively better than those reached by satisficers? In short, does the whole maximizer strategy give you some objective benefit when it comes to making a decision?

The way the researchers measured this was to contact students graduating from eleven different universities. They analysed their 'maximizing tendencies' with a questionnaire which presented statements such as:

> *'When I am in the car listening to the radio, I often check other stations to see if something better is playing, even if I am relatively satisfied with what I am listening to.'*

If you are always checking what is on alternative stations, then you clearly have 'a maximizing tendency'. Another statement was:

> *'When shopping, I have a hard time finding clothes that I really love.'*

Again, if you have a hard time finding clothes that you really love you will also tend to have maximizing tendencies. The psychologist had the participants rate each of these items on a 9-point scale ranging from 1 (strongly disagree) to 9 (strongly agree). The researchers measured how many jobs the participants aimed to apply for as a measure of their search procedure, and they also tested the emotional state of the students before, during and after they had made their applications. Finally, they also measured the participants' satisfaction with the job offers they accepted by asking two very simple questions:

'How satisfied are you with the job you have accepted?'

And

'How confident are you that you've made the right choice about where to work next year?'

As predicted, those participants who had the highest maximizing tendencies were intending to apply for more jobs than those with lower maximizing tendencies (the satisficers). Further, they found that 'students with greater maximizing tendencies reported that they wished that they had pursued still more options . . . and they were also more reliant on external influences during the job-search process'. But the researchers did find that maximizers, rather than the satisficers, achieved outcomes that were objectively better in that the mean salary of the maximizing job seekers was over $44,000, whereas the mean salary for the satisficers was over $37,000.

So to summarize, if you are the kind of person who needs to find the best job available, you will tend to engage in a different type of search process that will bring in the financial rewards. But – and it is a very big but – in the study, maximizers tended to experience more negative emotion and reported less satisfaction with their accepted job offers. According to the researchers, 'Compared with satisficers, maximizers do better financially in their job search, but feel worse. In their quest for placement after graduation, students with greater maximizing tendencies not only pursue and fixate on realized and unrealized options to a greater degree, but also rely on more external sources of information than do more satisficing job seekers. These efforts result in higher payoffs: Maximizers earn starting salaries that are 20 per cent higher than those of satisficers. Yet, despite their relative success, maximizers are less satisfied with the outcomes of their job search, and more pessimistic, stressed, tired, anxious, worried, overwhelmed, and depressed throughout the process.'

So in other words, always searching for the very best job may have severe psychological costs. If you are by nature a maximizer, always wanting to find the best radio station, the best programme on TV or the best job available, you might need to think about this aspect of your personality because although it may drive you to better outcomes, it will not necessarily make you happier; indeed it may leave you unhappy and dissatisfied for a long period of time. In the damning words of the authors, 'Even when they get what they want, maximizers may not always want what they get … If the subjective well-being of the decision maker and the objective value of the decision outcome are at odds, which should be prioritized? What should people do when "doing better" makes them feel worse?'

One obvious issue with this study is that it could be the case that maximizers might simply be high achievers who have very high expectations and that no matter how well that they do, maximizers are less happy because their accomplishments do not match their expectations. But this is an issue that the researchers have thought about; although they found that there were more maximizers in top-rank universities than in other universities, they did not find any relationship between maximizing tendencies and the average grades that the participants obtained. It's also not the case that maximizers are just unhappy people by nature because even when you control for happiness level you still find that maximizers are less happy after the ob search is over. The main issue with this study is that the researchers took only one measure of objective success (namely, salary) and ignored the other aspects of the jobs that the students found which might have been making them unhappy. In other words, could the higher salaries be associated with higher responsibility and a more competitive environment that could affect their psychological state? It would be good to know because it is important to discover (as the researchers say) why when some people get what they really, really want, they do not always want what they get.

- Some people have a tendency to strive for the very best in everything, including the very best job in the world; this tendency may well stop them from ever being happy

- In reality, you will never get the best job in the world, no matter how much you try, or how much you push yourself

- If you push yourself in this regard you may get a better-paid job but you will ultimately be less happy

How to make yourself smarter in ten minutes

If you want to elevate your IQ, it is possible to do this in a very simple way. Just listen to some Mozart for ten minutes. The Sonata for Two Pianos in D Major will do nicely. It has been found that listening to Mozart significantly elevates IQ performance. The way this works is to improve mood and arousal level.

The so-called 'Mozart effect' has recently been studied by William Forde Thompson at York University, Canada and his colleagues. This effect was first demonstrated by Francis Rauscher, Gordon Shaw and Katherine Ky (1993), who found that their experimental participants did better on standard tests of spatial abilities after listening to ten minutes of Mozart than after being told to relax and just being left to sit in silence. Thompson and his colleagues followed up this research by comparing the effects of a Mozart sonata with an adagio by Albinoni. The Mozart sonata was expected to elicit a positive mood in the participants and a heightened sense of arousal whereas the adagio was expected to generate a sad mood in participants and a low level of arousal. The researchers played ten minutes of either the Mozart (Sonata for Two Pianos in D Major) or ten minutes from Albinoni's Adagio in G Minor for Organ and Strings and afterwards the participants had to perform 'a paper folding and cutting subtest from the Stanford-Binet Intelligence test'. What the participants had to do was watch a rectangular piece of paper being folded and cut; their task was then to choose the correct option from five unfolded pieces of paper. The researchers also measured the mood state and the arousal level of the participants. What they found was that the participants performed better on the test of spatial abilities after listening to Mozart than after just sitting in silence. However, when they listened to the music by Albinoni instead, this had no effect on their spatial abilities. After listening to Mozart the participants also scored higher on positive mood and arousal and lower on negative mood. The authors conclude that the 'Mozart effect is not that mysterious after all' in that listening to Mozart seems to make us perform better at parts of the standard intelligence test because it increases our arousal level and puts us in a better mood and it is these variables which produce the change. Nevertheless the message is the same: if you want to perform better on the spatial subtest of a standard intelligence test, put some Mozart on.

But what if (like me) you don't like classical music? Or what if classical music simply reminds you of your lack of knowledge of classical music and culture? Could these feelings of inferiority interfere with the positive effects? And if the so-called 'Mozart effect' is not that mysterious after all but is just down to mood and arousal level, would some mood-inducing rock music do instead? The answer is probably yes. So if you really don't like Mozart then listen to some rock music, hip hop, or R 'n' B, or indeed anything else that puts you in a good mood and makes you feel energized.

- You can raise your IQ performance by listening to Mozart. Listening to Mozart particularly affects spatial abilities in the standard IQ test

- The so-called 'Mozart effect' is not limited to the work of Wolfgang Amadeus; this effect occurs because the music improves mood state and increases arousal level

- If you don't like Mozart, try Dizzee Rascal

How to read a handshake

Many people believe that the handshake is a crucial feature of the first impressions they have of another person. We see the confident stranger walking into the room for the job interview, he maintains good eye contact and has a confident stride, we shake his hand and he has the limpest, clammiest handshake we have ever experienced; we suddenly think that the eye contact, the purposeful stride and the confident manner are all just an act. But does the way that someone shakes your hand really tell you anything about their underlying personality? The answer would appear to be yes, according to William Chaplin and his colleagues of the University of Alabama. In their study, they trained researchers to shake hands 'in a neutral way', and evaluated the response. The way they did this was as follows: 'The hand was extended straight out from the waist with the palm facing to the left and the thumb raised at a 45 degree angle. On contact with an individual's hand, the hand shaker closed their hand around the other's hand, but waited for the other to initiate the strength of the grip and the upward and downward shaking. In addition, the raters were instructed to release their grip only when the participant began to relax his or her grip or otherwise showed signs of wishing to terminate the handshake. Raters practiced their handshaking technique on each other and on other individuals until we were satisfied that each had mastered the technique.'

It took them exactly one month to perfect this technique! They then had to rate each participant on eight dimensions:

1. Completeness of grip (1 = very incomplete, 5 = full)
2. Temperature (1 = cold, 5 = warm)
3. Dryness (1 = damp, 5 = dry)
4. Strength (1 = weak, 5 = strong)
5. Duration (1 = brief, 5 = long)
6. Vigour (1 = low, 5 = high)
7. Texture (1 = soft, 5 = rough)
8. Eye contact (1 = none, 5 = direct)

The personality of the participants was also measured using standard tests. What the researchers found was that people whose handshakes were firmer (characterized by 'a more complete grip, stronger, more vigorous, longer in duration and associated with more eye contact') tended to be more extrovert and outgoing, more open to new experiences and less neurotic and shy. In other words, this briefest of human contacts can reveal aspects of fundamental personality. They also found that a firm handshake can lead to a very favourable evaluation, particularly for women. Women with a firm handshake were perceived as more 'confident' and 'assertive' than those with a more feminine handshake.

So how can you read a handshake? The secret is to focus simply on firmness (rather than dryness, coldness or clamminess) and if you are looking for someone for a particular position who is 'extroverted' and 'open to new experiences', then go for the strong grip. On the other hand, if you are meeting someone for the first time and you are keen to show how extrovert and open to new experiences you are, make sure that your own handshake is firm.

- Handshakes can reliably reveal aspects of personality
- Firm handshakes are associated with people who are more extroverted and outgoing, more open to new experiences, and less neurotic and shy
- Women with a firm handshake are perceived as more 'confident' and 'assertive' than those with a more feminine handshake

9. CHILDREN

'Your children are not your children. They are the
sons and daughters of Life's longing for itself.'

Kahlil Gibran, 'On Children', *The Prophet*

How to help your child achieve academic success

If you want to help your child achieve academic success, then encourage them to do as much group work as possible at school because group work helps them to develop academically in a number of distinct ways. Group work obviously encourages them to develop peer relationships with other children, and this in turn provides them with emotional support and encouragement during the course of the work. Research has demonstrated that these social and emotional features of group work have a big impact on the level of academic achievement of children.

Group relationships can either be school based around academic work, or home based. Some types of relationships seem to encourage and help academic achievement, and some seem to have the opposite effect. But what are the crucial factors in this regard? One feature that has been looked at with regard to school-based relations is how social groups are constructed around certain types of goals. Cary Roseth, David Johnson and Rodger Johnson of the University of Minnesota did a major analysis of all the studies (totalling nearly 14,000) that had looked at the impact of different types of goal structure on academic achievement and social relations among adolescents (between 12 and 15 years old).

The researchers looked at cooperative goal structures ('where the goals of the separate individuals are so linked together that there is a positive correlation between their goal attainments'), competitive goal structures (where adolescents are essentially in competition with each other) and individualistic goal structures ('when individuals perceive that they can reach their goal regardless of whether other individuals attain or do not attain their goals'). The researchers examined the relationship between the level of academic achievement and how positive the peer relationships actually were. The analysis revealed that 'for early adolescents, cooperative goal structures were associated with higher levels of achievement than were competitive or individualistic goal structures'. In other words, when young adolescents are encouraged to work cooperatively, this tends to promote interaction between them, and this interaction helps them with the 'assistance, information and resources needed to achieve their mutual goals'. In addition to this, the study also found that higher levels of positive peer relationship tended to be associated with cooperative rather than with individualistic goal structures. Getting young adolescents to cooperate in a task facilitated patterns of interaction between them, allowed them to build up their trust and their relationships, helped them to make better friends and gave them the help and resources that they needed to work better. The conclusion from this important study is very clear: if you want your child to do well at school do not encourage them to pursue an individualistic, competitive agenda (no matter how tempting individually gifted students may find this). Persuade them to work in groups on a common class project, persuade them to build trust and confidence in other people. This does two things simultaneously – it helps them to build their relationships with their peers, which psychologically is enormously beneficial, and it helps to promote academic excellence.

In some ways, the results of this study might seem obvious

but they are far from being so. There is no reason why academic excellence and the strength of peer relationships should be related at all. They could even potentially be negatively correlated. This study gives the definitive answer on the connection between the peer relationships in early adolescents and achievement, and it gives us a clear indication that any task that is essentially cooperative will improve both the nature of the relationship and academic accomplishment. But of course, like any study that performs an analysis of so many other studies, it gives us the broadest picture possible and, within this, there may be differences in individual routes to academic success. Some adolescents may perform better with a more competitive route. However, it is clear from this important study that the majority do not and group work should be encouraged and prioritized wherever possible.

* To help your child perform better academically encourage them to do group work

* Group work encourages children to develop their peer relationships, and this provides them with emotional support during the course of the work

How to help your child learn

If you want your child to learn a concept more quickly, for example a mathematical concept, encourage them to use their hands while they are trying to grasp it. You should model the appropriate movements for them. For example, if you want your child to learn how to identify the missing elements in an equation, instead of just explaining how to do it, show them how to do it, by saying 'I want to make one side equal to the other side', while moving your left hand to the left side of the equation and your right hand to the right of the equation. By asking your child to repeat both your words and your hand movements they become much better at the task. The reason this works is that these gestures are easy to produce and they free up mental resources to work on the new information. They also help the child maintain the information and connect their mental processes to the task in hand. The hands show where they are up to, where they should direct their attention and keep them focused. So if you want your child to learn effectively, don't think of the hand movements they might spontaneously produce as distractions, or signs of nervousness or uncertainty, think of them as an essential part of what it is to acquire and learn new concepts. Encourage them to use such movements and help them to learn more effectively.

These were the findings of Susan Wagner Cook of the University of Rochester and her colleagues Zachary Mitchell and Susan Goldin-Meadow of the University of Chicago (2008). There is considerable evidence that the hand movements we spontaneously make when we think and talk are an essential component of the complex mental activities that underpin speech. Previous research by Goldin-Meadow had demonstrated that in the case of children, if they gesture when they are learning a task, it is a good predictor that they will soon master the task. She also found that those children who gesture spontaneously when they are learning a task are more likely to remember what they have learned. The problem with the earlier research was that it did not allow psychologists to discriminate between two different interpretations of the results, namely whether the production of gestures 'merely reflects a readiness to learn new knowledge', a sort of signal that they have just grasped the concept and it is about to be shown in their actual behaviour, or whether the production of gestures is somehow actively involved in constructing this new knowledge. So in a new experiment, Cook and her colleagues instructed children to use gestures while learning about various mathematical concepts. The concepts were of the kind:

$$4 + 3 + 6 = \_ + 6$$

The children had to fill in the missing number and then explain how they solved this problem. The group of seven- and eight-year-olds were tested in one of three conditions:

(1) a 'speech condition' in which the experimenter told them 'I want to make one side equal to the other side'.

(2) a 'gesture condition' in which the experimenter 'moved her left hand under the equation's left side, paused, then moved her right hand under the equation's right side, and asked the child to repeat her hand movements'.

(3) a 'gesture plus speech condition' in which the experimenter said 'I want to make one side equal to the other side' while moving her left hand under the left side of the equation and moving her right hand under the right side of the equation. In each case the child had to repeat what the experimenter did. After the experimenter demonstrated this a few times the children were given problems of their own to solve and what the experimenters

found was that by instructing children to gesture when solving these problems had a significant effect on their performance. (There was not, however, a reliable difference between the 'gesture' and the 'gesture and speech' conditions.) But all those children who were instructed to gesture (either on their own or in combination with speech) showed improved performance across time in the task, compared with children instructed just to speak (an 85 per cent success rate compared with 33 per cent of children told to speak but not to gesture).

This is in many ways an extraordinary result. The conclusion of this research is that, 'when children are asked to instantiate a new concept in their hands, learning is more lasting than when they are asked to instantiate it in words alone. Indeed, in our data, it was primarily when children were encouraged to produce gestures (with speech or without it) that they retained what they had learned from the instruction. Many children who expressed the equalizer strategy only in words during learning evidenced a fleeting memory for the new concept. These findings suggest that using the body to represent ideas may be especially helpful in constructing and retaining new knowledge.'

The question of why gesture facilitates learning in this way is hugely important, but the researchers say that a number of different theoretical interpretations are still possible. One possibility is that because gestures are so effortlessly produced, they free up mental resources that could be used to process other information. In other words, it is more efficient to represent some information relevant to solving the problem in bodily movement than in speech or instead of just trying to keep it all in the head. Alternatively, gestures may help the storing of the information in the long-term memory and 'may produce stronger and more robust memory traces than expressing information in speech'. The fact that you have made a gestural movement representing a part of the solution may help you remember that bit of the process more effectively. A third possibility is that gestures may assist learning through their interaction with the external world – the gestures are essentially building connections between the mental representations and the world out there. They keep you focused on exactly where you have got to in solving the problem.

Despite the relative uncertainty about the correct theoretical interpretation (indeed there may be some truth in all three theoretical accounts), this research tells us that if you want a child to learn new concepts, encourage them to make appropriate gestural movements while they are trying to learn the new concepts. These gestural movements can assist even in complex mental operations such as mathematics.

The biggest question mark over this study is how general the effects are with respect to the role of gesturing in learning. The gestural movements used by the adults and the children here were quite simple ones and essentially directed the child's attention from one side of the equation to the other. But would other kinds of gestures be as beneficial? After all, when people, including children, talk they will often make quite complex gestures representing more complicated ideas. There is always the possibility that some gestures might not facilitate performance at all and could hinder reasoning if they were not appropriate. But generally speaking, when people make gestures, they are entirely appropriate for the mental operations that they are engaged in and that by recognizing and encouraging these gestural movements we are facilitating the acquisition of core mental skills. I really do like the last sentence of this paper: 'One way to promote lasting change in children's minds may be to change what they do, rather than what they say.' This is an important idea with obvious practical implications, only some of which are now becoming apparent.

- Help your child to learn by encouraging them to gesture while they learn new concepts

- These gestures free up mental resources

- Hand movements help the storing of the information in long-term memory and produce stronger and more robust memory traces

- Gestures build connections between mental operations and the external world

How to enhance your child's IQ

If you want to improve your child's intelligence, get them music lessons. Music lessons involve significant periods in which the child has to focus his or her attention, and require the discipline of daily practice, the memorizing of musical passages and conventions for expressing emotions in music. Learning to play a musical instrument involves a whole series of mental and physical processes that could impact on the brain during its development. Six-year-olds who were given thirty-six weeks of training in music improved their IQ by an average of seven points, which was significantly higher than the control groups (who either took drama lessons or had no lessons at all). The group of six-year-olds who had the drama lessons did, however, significantly improve in terms of their social behaviour as a result of their training. The group who had music lessons performed particularly well in terms of lower distractibility and faster processing speed. So if you want your child to be smarter, make sure that they have music lessons early on; if you want them to be smarter and more sociable, make sure that they have music and drama lessons.

Glenn Schellenberg of the University of Toronto says that there are a number of reasons as to why music lessons might improve a child's IQ. Music stimulates exactly the kind of mental processes that could positively affect the development of the brain. Previous research had demonstrated that aptitude for music is associated with a range of mental activities including general intelligence, achievement level in maths as well as memory performance. But of course the problem with this is that causality may be the other way round, such that more gifted children may be more likely than other children to take music because they might do well at it. Schellenberg designed an experiment to unravel the processes, and assigned a large group of six-year-olds to one of four conditions: two involved music lessons (one with the focus on the keyboard and one on the voice) and two were control conditions (one involving drama and one involving no additional lessons). What the researcher found was that compared with the control groups, those who had music lessons significantly improved their IQ, their level of distractibility was lowered and their processing speed increased. What the researcher also found was that drama significantly improved social behaviour based on the parents' ratings of a whole series of categories of behaviour.

Music lessons obviously involve a range of experiences that could affect IQ because they involve processes of attention and memory as well as avoiding distraction. This research does not allow us to isolate which of these factors has the biggest impact and of course there is always the possibility that it could be a more general factor. If children are doing well in music lessons, this could have an impact on self-confidence and the ability to excel in other tasks including IQ.

- Music lessons will enhance your child's IQ
- Music lessons involve a whole series of mental and physical processes that affect the brain during its development
- Drama lessons assist in social development but don't lead to any changes in IQ

How to choose a pencil for a test

If you want to do well in a test (or you want your child to do well in a test), avoid using a red pencil. Red is a danger sign which evokes activity in the part of the brain (the right frontal cortex) associated with avoidance behaviour. The colour red seems to have an impact on people's performance; they do less well on a variety of tests, including IQ tests, when they have just seen the colour and, when given the option, will choose easier rather than more difficult tasks to do. It looks as if red unconsciously primes failure and thereby affects performance. So if you have a test coming up avoid a red pencil, avoid red books, red chairs, red walls, red anything. Buy a green pencil instead.

Andrew Elliot of the University of Rochester, USA and his colleagues carried out a series of experiments to look at the effects of the colour red on performance and his conclusion is that, almost regardless of the task, red impairs performance even with brief exposures. In one experiment he had participants solve anagrams, e.g.

Sample anagram: **NIDRK**   Solution: **DRINK**

What the experimenters varied in this study was the colour of the participant number on the test. What they found was that when the participants were left to solve anagrams for five minutes when the participant number was written in red, they solved (on average) less than 4½, whereas when the participant number was written in green or black, they solved, on average, more than 5½. The researchers then looked at the effects of colour on the subsection of an IQ test (analogy subtest) and they looked at the effects of colour of the cover of the test on performance. Again they found that participants in the red condition did not do as well as participants in the green or white condition. This was also demonstrated with maths performance. Subsequent EEG measures of brain activity revealed that those participants in the red condition showed relatively more right frontal activation than those in the green or grey condition. Previous research had demonstrated that right frontal activation is associated with avoidance behaviour and the researchers linked this to another task they used in which participants had to choose either easy or difficult analogy tests. Those who had been exposed to the colour red were more likely to choose the easy task rather than the difficult task.

The conclusion of these researchers was that the perception of the colour red prior to an achievement task has a negative impact on performance. Furthermore, the perception of the colour red elicits the motivation to avoid difficult tasks and it is also associated with a higher level of right-sided than left-sided cortical activity. In their words: 'The findings suggest that care must be taken in how red is used in achievement contexts and illustrate how colour can act as a subtle environmental cue that has important influences on behaviour.' This all happens well below the level of conscious awareness, but they say that the colour red needs to be avoided in achievement contexts because they are contexts in which positive outcomes (success) and negative outcomes (failure) are always possible. The problem is that red unconsciously reminds people of the danger of failure and affects performance.

The obvious lesson from this study is to avoid painting offices or schools red (or indeed any other environment where achievement is a major issue). But the researchers themselves go beyond this. They are mindful of the fact that they used IQ tests in their study: 'the administration of such tests is strictly uniform regarding item difficulty and time allotment, but factors such as the colour of the clothing worn by test proctors and the colour of the pencil used to indicate answers are allowed to vary. Our finding that a seemingly inconsequential factor such as the colour of an IQ test cover has an important impact on performance raises the question of whether these other factors are indeed inconsequential and suggests that more strictly controlled procedures in these important assessment contexts may be needed.'

The most extraordinary aspect of this research is the robustness of the effects. They demonstrated the effects of colour on a whole series of tasks and with minimal exposure to the colour itself. This is one of those effects which seem to occur completely unconsciously because red is associated with danger and avoidance and it does seem to affect the way we think. Whether the effect of the colour remains depending upon things like clothing and hue of a pencil is unclear because there might be some contexts in which the negative impact of the colour is removed. On the other hand, the biological impact of the colour red as a danger sign may be so deep-seated that it is always there regardless of context.

- Red is a danger sign in many contexts, which evokes activity in the part of the brain (the right frontal cortex) associated with avoidance behaviour

- In achievement contexts, red unconsciously primes failure and thereby affects performance

- Never buy a red pencil for a test

How to help your children acquire higher levels of emotional intelligence

Emotional intelligence is a core aspect of everyday life. It involves the ability to read someone else's emotional state from their non-verbal behaviour, or from the prosodic aspects of their speech. The prosody of the speech involves the intonation and rhythm and can signal emotions like happiness, sadness, anger and fear. Happiness, according to William Forde Thompson and his colleagues from the University of Toronto at Mississauga, tends to be signalled by 'a rapid tempo, a high pitch, a large pitch range and "a bright voice quality"'. Sadness tends to be marked by 'a slow tempo, a low pitch, a narrow pitch range and a soft voice quality; anger is associated with fast tempo, high pitch, wide pitch range and rising pitch contours; and fear is associated with a fast tempo, high pitch, wide pitch range, large pitch variability and varied loudness'.

Emotion	Tempo	Pitch	Range	Quality
Happiness	Fast tempo	High pitch	Large pitch range	Bright voice quality
Sadness	Slow tempo	Low pitch	Narrow pitch range	Soft pitch quality
Anger	Fast tempo	High pitch	Wide pitch range	Rising pitch contours
Fear	Fast tempo	High pitch	Wide pitch range	Large pitch variability and varied loudness

We learn to identify which aspects of speech are associated with emotion through our everyday conversations. This is clearly a very important skill to have because the more sensitive you are to these kinds of features, the more emotionally

intelligent you are and the more successful you will be at interacting with other people. But some psychologists have suggested
that you can enhance these skills through an activity not related
to social interaction, and this activity (again) is music. The
argument is very simple, namely that emotions are expressed
in music and speech through the same basic features, things
like rate, amplitude, pitch and stress. So Thompson and his
colleagues took a group of six-year-olds and gave them one year
of training in either the piano or singing, or they had drama
lessons, or they were given no lessons at all. They found that
those children who received the keyboard training became more
skilled at identifying the emotions contained both in speech and
in the music. They said that this was no accident as there are
very similar processes involved in extracting the emotional
meaning in both music and speech.

So, if you want your child to be emotionally intelligent and
able to read people's emotions, make sure that they have
keyboard lessons when they are young (if you can afford it).
Otherwise just make sure that you interact with them regularly,
freely and happily.

- Lots of conversation will help your child develop high
  emotional intelligence

- Emotions are expressed in music and speech through
  the same basic features, things like rate, amplitude, pitch
  and stress

- Music lessons will thus help improve your child's emotional
  intelligence

10. FRIENDS FOR EVER

'Real friendship is shown in times of trouble;
prosperity is full of friends.'

Euripides, *Hecuba* (c.425 BC), tr. William Arrowsmith

How to gossip more effectively

The way to gossip more effectively is to understand a little about why we do it in the first place. Basically we gossip in order to cement our relationships within a social group. We do this by choosing someone to gossip to and choosing someone to gossip about. Both of these choices are crucial to the success of the gossiping. We are signalling to our gossip partner (choice 1) that we have selected them (from all other possible partners) to share information about a third person, the 'target' of the gossip (choice 2). The choice of a 'target' is crucial to the success of gossip and the most effective target, it turns out, is someone of the same gender and roughly the same age as the person you are gossiping with. This is the type of gossip that they will find most interesting because the main function of gossip is to enhance our own status relative to potential rivals (and, of course, someone of the same gender and age fits the bill beautifully). By gossiping, we are also reminding our conversational partner of the rules and norms for our social group. So essentially we are reinforcing the bonds that bind us together by gossiping and punishing deviance from the group norm by selecting someone to gossip about and focusing on aspects of their behaviour. We all love celebrity gossip, but this again works best when the celebrities are of the same gender as ourselves and roughly the same age. Celebrity gossip also has the same basic function. We are reducing perceived status of a celebrity relative to ourselves, thereby building our own status relative to them.

Gossip fulfils a number of important roles within social groups. It acts as a powerful reminder of the importance of the values held in common by the group and it can be an effective deterrent to stop people deviating from the group norms. It is also an effective way of binding the group together because every time a person chooses someone to gossip to, they are essentially taking a risk that the recipient of the gossip will accept what they are saying and ideally reciprocate with gossip of their own. Gossip is a powerful force because it allows people to damage the reputation of others by spreading negative information about competitors or enemies. Given the importance of gossip within social groups, it is not surprising that evolutionary psychologists have studied it extensively. A study conducted by Francis McAndrew and his colleagues of Knox College supports the idea that gossip is designed essentially to promote our individual interests and that the most interesting gossip is about potential competitors. The study argues that 'a human propensity for gossip is an evolved psychological adaptation that enabled individuals to be socially successful in our ancestral environments'.

McAndrew and his colleagues gave participants a number of hypothetical gossip scenarios. The participants had to read the scenarios and then report how interested they were in the story, how likely they would be to pass the information on and to whom.

The results revealed quite clearly that people were most interested in gossiping about other people of the same gender, and they were much more likely to spread negative information about potential rivals than about friends. They were particularly interested in spreading gossip about the dishonest or irresponsible behaviour of potential rivals and had little interest in gossiping about any of the good things they might have done. Women were particularly prone to this. The researchers found that they were three times as likely as the men in their sample to want to gossip about their same-sex rivals as they were to gossip about their own partners.

Gossip would seem to be a ubiquitous phenomenon with many important social functions. McAndrew's study develops a hypothesis about one of the key factors that seem to drive it – the desire to enhance one's own status by attacking potential rivals. The major limitation of this study was that it used a paper and pencil test to measure gossiping rather than studying gossip in the field, so to speak, with all of those important dynamic features. It would be interesting to see how the basic details of the original story are modified and transformed in the pursuit of the status enhancement of the teller and the status-diminution of the target. One important point about gossip is surely that it gets better with repeated telling.

- Gossip is essentially about reinforcing the social bonds between people

- Gossip is a powerful force because it allows people to damage the reputation of others, by spreading negative information about competitors or enemies

- The most interesting subject for gossip is someone of the same gender and roughly the same age as the person you are talking to

- Every time you gossip you are taking a risk, by choosing a target and someone to share the gossip with. Gossiping would not have the same power without this risk factor

How to tell a secret and get the most benefit

Keeping important secrets bottled up inside is neither physically nor psychologically healthy. It's much better to tell your secrets to a trusted confidant. In order to make yourself feel better, however, the way that you get these secrets off your chest is crucial. If when divulging your secrets your focus is very much on articulating your emotions; this way may actually make you feel much worse. When you are telling secrets to a confidant the focus should be on understanding and developing new insights into what occurred. This can allow a degree of closure on the event, whereas merely airing your emotions doesn't work. This also has significant consequences for the person to whom you might choose to tell the secret. Most people naturally go to someone who is trustworthy and can keep a secret but the kind of confidant that makes you actually feel better is someone who will show a degree of understanding themselves. In other words, when you have a big secret to tell make sure that you find someone who can really understand what you are saying and focus on trying to see the situation in a new light; this will make you feel much better both immediately and in the long run.

Anita Kelly and her colleagues of the University of Notre Dame were interested in the key characteristics of sharing a secret. We already know that keeping secrets can be psychologically harmful. For example, those who keep negative information from their friends tend to be more depressed, and have lower self-esteem than those of their counterparts. There is even evidence that gay men who have not come out are more likely to develop cancer and infectious diseases over a five-year period than those who have gone public with their sexuality. But what is it about actually telling secrets that can help us to feel better? Kelly and her colleagues say that there are two broad mechanisms that could be responsible. One is connected with insight and understanding. When you get a chance to get things off your chest and tell your secrets to another person, you often get insights into what the situation meant and why it occurred. When you talk about an event, you have to weave it together into a coherent narrative and this process of sense-making means that you can understand it and assimilate it. This is the 'insight theory' of why it is good to give up your secrets.

A different mechanism is that of catharsis and this is more an emotion-based theory. Catharsis is often associated with Freud and Breuer (1895/1955), who argued that catharsis is one of the central components of therapy: 'the patient only gets free from the hysterical symptoms by reproducing the pathogenic impressions that caused it and by giving utterances to them with an expression of affect' (Freud and Breuer 1895/1955, p. 283). In Freud's mind, catharsis was the linking of the rational and the irrational, insight and emotion, although subsequently many psychologists and others have thought of catharsis as simply the venting of one's emotions. Classic research by Pennebaker and his colleagues (1990) had considered the importance of both insight and catharsis in disclosure and his research seemed to suggest that insight may be the more important of the two pro-cesses. He found that college freshmen who had written about the experience of going to college tended to report that the most valuable part of the exercise was allowing them to understand their own thoughts and behaviour, and it was only a minority (10 per cent) who thought that the experience was most useful because it allowed them to give vent to their own emotions.

These studies formed the theoretical basis of Kelly's research, who asked participants to 'select the most private, personal secret that they have ever shared with another person' and then to describe to what extent it had been a cathartic experience and to what extent they had gained new insights into the secret (and what surrounded it), after they had revealed it. The researchers took measures of how they felt after they had disclosed the secret and measured both positive and negative mood state as well as asking the participants to rate the characteristics of the person they made the disclosure to (in terms of how 'expert', 'trust-worthy' and 'attractive' they were). The results were startlingly clear. What influenced how well people felt after they had disclosed a secret was not the amount of catharsis involved, but the level of insight they had gained from sharing it. In fact, Kelly and her colleagues found that those participants who reported that they were really able to get their feelings off their chest had more negative feelings about the secrets concerned afterwards.

In deciding to whom to reveal your secrets, 'trustworthiness' and 'the ability to keep a secret' were rated as the most important attributes of the confidant. However, in terms of actually making people feel better it is the 'expertness' of the confidant that is most important. In the words of the researchers, 'the findings indicate that there may be a discrepancy between what people say they want in a confidant and what is most helpful to them.'

It is clear then, that when you are trying to make yourself feel better by telling a secret, it's much better to find someone who will understand the kinds of things you are talking about rather than being able merely to keep a secret. In a second study, participants were explicitly instructed either to 'focus on making sense out of the secret or gaining new insight into the secret. Develop this new perspective on your secret by changing your thoughts about it. Your sole purpose in writing is to make meaning out of your secret – to gain a new perspective or new understanding of the secret' or 'focus on what you are feeling about the secret and getting those feelings out in the open. Write about your feelings without rationalizing or explaining them. Your sole purpose in writing is to get your feelings about the secret off your chest – to really pour out your emotions and release them'. Again the results were clear: those participants who focused on gaining new insight by telling their secret showed the greatest improvement in mood. Those who focused on just venting their emotions did not feel significantly better after they had done it.

So if you want to get things off your chest, the important thing is to focus on developing a new perspective on it. It is not about venting your emotions; it is about understanding what you have gone through. It is important to emphasize that the kinds of secrets that were investigated in this study were not trivial; these were things like having been raped, having been neglected as a child, having had several suicide attempts, having suffered from addiction or having had an abortion or pregnancy. The authors argue that the reason why the insight route works is that it allows you to gain closure on the issue. Closure had been first systematically studied by a Russian psychologist called Bluma Zeigarnik (1927). Zeigarnik demonstrated that if you have failed to reach a meaningful end point in understanding something then it reverberates in your mind and you remember it much better. A classic example of this is that if you have ever watched a film three-quarters of the way through, you will know that you have a much better memory of it than when you have seen a complete film. Kelly and her colleagues argue that this applies to difficult events of everyday life as well, the kinds that we keep bottled up when we have failed to achieve closure by trying to comprehend them.

There is, however, one slightly puzzling result in Kelly's study which hints at the fact that there may well be aspects of the disclosure process that we don't fully understand. In the first study the researchers found that when people put most emphasis on catharsis when they tell a secret it actually led to an increase in negative emotion associated with the telling. In the second study, this increase in negative emotion (with catharsis) did not occur. In the first study there was a confidant, but in the second study the participants merely wrote about their secrets. This is an important difference between the two studies, which is not explained. It may be linked to the fact that when you tell a secret to a friend, unless the telling does display some genuine insight, then people can be very unsympathetic to the mere expression of emotion. Clearly we need more research to work out the relationship between the types of confidants that people use in everyday life and how they react to the subject matter. This is a critical issue.

- Don't just focus on letting your emotions out when you are getting a secret off your chest

- To get the most psychological benefit from sharing a secret, make sure that you develop some deeper understanding through the recounting of the secret

- Choose a friend who will understand what you are going to say, not just someone who will keep the secret

How to stop yourself (or your child) being influenced by a bad apple

Is bad behaviour always necessarily contagious? In other words, if you (or your child) watch someone doing something bad, immoral or unethical, are you, or they, naturally inclined to follow them? Does bad behaviour always somehow have an influence on us, so that there is nothing we can do about it? And for example, if a person has done something bad, like cheating in an exam, and has got away with it (and you've seen this with your own eyes), how can you stop yourself from thinking, even unconsciously, that cheating is OK? After all, the lesson that you might be learning here, possibly against your will, is that everyone does it, so why shouldn't you?

You can stop yourself from being influenced in this way by focusing on the differences between you and the person doing the cheating in terms of the social groupings to which you belong. Even if the person is very similar in age and position to you, think of the differences that exist ('he's not an A-grade student', or 'he wasn't part of the group that went to the library every afternoon'). Even if you are colleagues and belong to the same work organization, you will both belong to a host of other social groups at the same time. Emphasize those differences in your mind and in that way you will stop yourself from being influenced and being dragged down the same route as them. The same principle applies if you are trying to stop a child being influenced by a bad role model. Focus on the differences between the negative influence and the child, and bring these differences to the fore. This reduces the effects their behaviour will have on your child.

Francesca Gino of the University of North Carolina, and Shahar Ayal and Dan Ariely of Duke University (2009) looked at the effects of exposure to dishonest behaviour on individual's own level of dishonest conduct. They argued that, in principle, there are a number of different ways that such exposure to dishonest behaviour could result in dishonesty in the person who has witnessed it. The first way is that if someone cheats in front of you and gets away with it, this can change your view of how easy it is to get away with cheating. This is a concrete demonstration that, after all, cheating can work. The second way it could influence dishonesty in an individual, is that it increases the salience of the act – so you notice the act – and this brings these sorts of moral issues to the fore. So this could potentially result in a decrease in dishonesty on the part of the individual as they reflect on the morality of actions like this. The third way it could affect an individual is that by witnessing a dishonest act, it can change your understanding of what is normal, and what is not, in any situation. And this, according to the researchers, is where social group categorization comes into play because, 'The social-norms account implies another important factor that might influence the degree to which people are affected by the unethical behaviour of others around them: the degree to which they identify with those others. The idea is that when the identification is strong, the behaviours of others will have a larger influence on observers' social norms.' So the researchers argue that whether or not the person doing the cheating is seen as an in-group member could be crucial to whether the individual becomes dishonest in the presence of cheating.

The researchers tested this by having their participants exposed to someone who cheats in an experimental task. The 'cheater' was doing the task ridiculously quickly and apparently getting away with it. The participants were all university students and the way that the cheater's in-group membership was manipulated was by asking them to wear a university T-shirt that either signified the host university or a different university. What the experimenters found was that cheating was slightly higher on the part of the participants when they saw the others cheating, but it was much higher when the person cheating was from the same university. Therefore, mere exposure to dishonest behaviour does not have a dramatic effect on a person's own moral behaviour. Much more significant is how you categorize the other person in terms of social grouping. Someone from a different social group doesn't necessarily change your view about what is appropriate or inappropriate. In a subsequent experiment, the researchers even claimed that watching an out-group member be dishonest can actually increase the honesty of your own behaviour. Their dishonesty may reflect the social norm for the group to which they belong, but you become more honest to emphasize the difference between yourself and the other individual.

So if you don't want to be influenced by someone's bad or unethical behaviour (or you don't want your children to be influenced), what should you do? Don't lose heart because it is not necessarily the case that witnessing unethical behaviour will lead you or your child to become unethical. Recognize that every individual belongs to a number of social groups simultaneously and emphasize the difference between the person doing the unethical behaviour and yourself (or your child). You may work in the same organization but if he or she worked for 'the marketing department' for a number of years you can redefine the in-group and out-group in that way, which stops you being influenced to quite the same degree.

This study only considered one aspect of the in-group/out-group affiliation, which was university affiliation, but all of us belong to many social groups at any one time – even relatively inexperienced university students belong to many social groups (male, white, early 20s, 2.1-level student, currently in a relation-ship, student with gap-year experience, occasional drug user, etc.) and membership of each of these social groups becomes more or less relevant depending upon circumstances ('I don't have to cheat in an exam, I'm heading for a 2.1 anyway'). You could argue that categorization is a more active process in every-day life, as we bring to mind the categories to which we belong, rather than categorization being something that is imposed on us (like the cheater wearing a sweatshirt from the same university as us), as it was in this study. This process of *active* categorization could well ameliorate the effects of watching unethical behaviour but this is not what was investigated.

- All is not lost if you or your child is exposed to a negative influence

- If you or your child is exposed to a negative influence, point out all the differences from the person concerned

11. BECOMING WHOLE AGAIN

'The mind is a strange machine which can combine the materials offered to it in the most astonishing ways.'

Bertrand Russell, *The Conquest of Happiness* (1930)

How to trick your brain to become whole again

This is a more personal attempt to get (or maybe regain) the edge. It is also an account of loss of different sorts and the way that psychology may or may not help. But I think that there are lessons embedded here, which ultimately transcend the personal.

I was married to Carol when we were both students at Cambridge. She was my first girlfriend from the same narrow streets of North Belfast as me. She followed me across the water to university and then later she moved north with me to Sheffield and our first jobs. It should have been a time of great promise. My brother Bill had just got married in Scotland that year and bought his first house, and my mother was happier than she had been in years. 'It's all coming together for this family, at last. You've got a wee job, your brother is settling down,' she liked to say. Then a few months later my brother went climbing in the Himalayas. He was adamant it was to be his last expedition. 'I don't even know why I'm going, to be honest,' he said when I saw him last. 'I'm not into it in the way I was.' He didn't come back from that adventure; he died on a peak called Nanda Devi, and there he lay, beneath a pile of loose stones with his name scratched on one of them with hard flint. One of my last memories of my brother is his friends and I carrying him aloft to his car at his wedding. In retrospect, it was like shouldering a coffin to the grave. It didn't feel like that at the time, but it looks a little like that, in my imagination, with the benefit of hindsight.

The months after his death were an odd, unsettled time for me. For five months my main emotion was a diffuse and unfocused sort of anger. I had, of course, lost my father when I was young and it had taken me five years to cry openly about that loss. My uncle used to say of me that after my father died, 'I just pulled down the shutters.' (You can see why I could have done with some of the advice in this book.) Then one night in Hyde Park in London of all places, I drank a bottle of cheap red wine and cried over the death of my father in front of Carol. We had hitchhiked there to go to a free concert. I didn't mean to do this, to disclose emotionally in this way; it wasn't planned, it just happened. The floodgates opened. I never realized that crying could make you feel better, but it did. I always assumed that it just made you more vulnerable. When Bill died I wasn't sure what to do; was I supposed to cry again, to cry twice, once for each of the family members that I had lost, or to wail endlessly? So I just felt angry. Carol's family was very much intact, mine wasn't. Carol tried to comfort me but I told her that she would never understand what I was going through; she would never understand what it was like to cope with loss like this.

Now it was February in Sheffield, and the snow lay thick on the ground, muffling all the sounds of everyday life. Carol and I lived together in an old rat-infested coach house with no heat. We went to bed early to warm up. This is Carol's account of the next day.

I woke up feeling a bit anxious. I was working as a trainee Prison Psychologist in a borstal in Leicester and commuting every day from my home in Sheffield. I used to leave at half past six and get the bus to the station then the train, then cycle from Leicester station to the borstal, and the same again at the end of the day, two and a half hours each way. That day I had to go to Leicester Prison to interview a prisoner on remand for murder – it was going to be my first big test. I left the house with plenty of time to catch the bus to the station – leaving a note saying 'wish me luck' to Geoffrey who I knew wouldn't be getting up for another couple of hours. There was lots of snow on the ground, it had been there for weeks, and the bus was very late coming down the road so by the time I got to the station it was getting very close to five to eight. The bus stop was right outside the station entrance and in those days there was nothing between the main foyer and Platform 1. I could see the train standing at the platform and I thought that I could just make it. I had my season ticket in my hand, although there wasn't anyone checking tickets, and I was also carrying a briefcase and my hand-bag. I ran towards the train and grabbed hold of the handle of one of the doors, just as the train began to move slowly along the platform. I was running alongside it now, not quite able to get the door open enough to jump in, hampered by the things I was carrying and the leather boots I had on. The train was moving faster now and I don't know whether I jumped towards the step of the train and lost my footing or whether I was just pulled down by the gathering speed of the train, but somehow I found myself standing upright between the platform and the moving train – there was a big enough gap between the two. Then my coat must have caught on the undercarriage of the train and I got pulled under the wheels. I remember calling out for my mum, although I don't think I've ever told her this. I can't remember exactly what happened next but the train began to stop, and I must have managed to scramble to my feet again, because when people came running along the platform and shouted to me, I was standing up. One of the people told me she was a nurse, and had been on the train when it was suddenly stopped. She kept saying, 'Don't worry; I expect it's only broken' when I told her that the train had run over my arm. An ambulance came and took me through the rush-hour traffic with a police escort to the Hallamshire Hospital. When we got there people asked me over and over again who my next of kin was. We couldn't afford a phone in those days and I knew they'd have trouble waking my husband up by knocking on the door. My coat and all my other clothes had to be cut to get them off – I'm not sure what happened to my boots. I didn't see my arm but I couldn't feel anything at all and when the orthopaedic registrar said that it couldn't be saved, I wasn't surprised.

I remember waking up some time later and realizing my mum and dad were sitting by the bed, and being very puzzled as to how they'd got there. The next morning when I woke up in a ward, the radio was on and I heard a report about myself – although I guess I could have imagined this whole thing, as I was on a morphine drip. Although it didn't occur to me at the time, one thing which I have come to regret is that I didn't see my arm or know what happened to it. I do miss it and think about it still. It was part of me.

All the time I was in hospital I was fairly positive – the

doctors I saw were all very enthusiastic about developments in prosthetics and because I was young and healthy and I had no other injuries, they thought the prognosis was good. The days in hospital took on a comfortable routine, I didn't have to worry about anything much and there was nothing too taxing or difficult to do. The weather outside was still freezing and snowy, but high up in the Hallamshire I was safe from it. I found a way to wash my hair and open the individual packs of butter and jam on the breakfast tray, and I thought that I'd pretty much cracked it. Geoffrey and I even managed to sneak off for some intimacy in the hospital, quite exciting in a strange sort of way. I think that it was important for him to show me that the accident hadn't changed anything. It was his way, I suppose.

After a month I was allowed to go home. I was looking forward to it, but wasn't prepared for the desolation I felt going back into the place I'd left without thinking a month before. Things that had been familiar had become objects to be wrestled with and I realized how hard things were going to be. When Geoffrey went to work and left me alone in the cold untidy flat I cried in a way that scared me – howling and sobbing – it was the first time that it dawned on me what had changed. I think Geoffrey and I went to the Rehabilitation Centre in a fairly positive frame of mind – almost looking forward to seeing all the marvellous things the doctors had told us about. When we got there the waiting room was full of old men – no young people or women in sight. There was also a group of artificial legs lined up in a corner and other ghastly pink prosthetic body parts sitting around waiting for fittings.

To me, at my age, who'd hardly had a day's illness in my life, it was like a vision of a hell that I was about to be dragged into. The consultation didn't do much to help as it focused heavily on the different attachments (including a hook) that could be screwed into an artificial arm, which could restore the functions of holding things, sewing and knitting – none of which I cared much about. I was more interested in form than function – I wanted something to fill my empty sleeve and restore some sort of symmetry. So we moved on to 'cosmetic' artificial limbs. I would be measured up and two artificial arms would be made for me – so I had a spare in case anything happened to one of them. The arm was heavy and awkward to wear – it was secured by leather straps that went over the shoulder and across the back – and not very convincing close up. The colour was unnatural and unlike my skin colour. There was a mechanism inside the arm which allowed it to be moved into a bent position and locked there – but it was very difficult sometimes to unbend it – I certainly never mastered it in the short time I wore the thing before throwing it in the cupboard to gather dust.

It was now a few weeks after I'd got out of hospital – I still had dressings on my arm. We'd been invited out somewhere – it was the first time I'd gone out in the evening since the accident – and we were driving there in the car. We took a wrong turn or something and in no time we were having a full-blown argument. Nasty things were said, as they usually are in pointless arguments, but I was shocked – I had felt until then that I was now surely immune from that kind of thing. I had been in some kind of cocoon of being looked after, feeling that no one would ever be unkind or mean to me again. But I was wrong. The world and other people weren't going to make allowances for me. They hadn't changed – I had. From now on I was going to be at a significant disadvantage.

This all happened over twenty years ago. For me as well as for Carol, it is also a vivid, flashbulb memory. I saw Carol the morning of her accident in the hospital before they amputated her arm. I can see the position of her now, the angle of the bed, and the shine of her long, dark hair on the white pillow. I had overslept. Someone at the hospital must have tried to reach me at work, and my professor's secretary had come to my house and knocked on the door three or four times to wake me up. She told me that Carol had had an accident, but she thought that it wasn't too serious. 'I think that she's fallen off the platform, that's all,' she said. 'Platforms aren't too high,' she said. 'It's not such a big fall. She'll be all right.'

And I can remember to this day that I misinterpreted what she was saying; I thought that she meant that Carol had fallen over in her platform shoes. My mental image at that precise moment all those years ago was of Carol tottering over on big platforms with four-inch black soles with red stars on them, shoes from our student years imported into this almost dream sequence. I can recall this misinterpretation of a word after all those years and the fleeting mental image that briefly lit up my mind. My professor was at the hospital and waited with me in the waiting room and as the doctor came in to talk to me I recall jumping up and hitting my head on something and wanting my injury to be serious, but it wasn't. The doctor described what had happened at the station and explained how they would have to amputate the arm. 'Is there any alternative?' I asked, as if he had not considered any. He shook his head without looking at me, and led me in to see her. Carol was conscious when I got there. She didn't smile at me. I mention this because it's as if I might have expected a smile from her. Then she immediately apologized because she said that she knew what I had been going through with my brother's death. 'I'm sorry,' she said, and she did smile a weak, half-hearted sort of smile. I can hear her saying those words now, and I must say that at that moment, and even now, I feel deep shame that makes me feel a little sick.

I held her limp, lifeless hand in what I suppose was my attempt to show that this hand, which was to be removed, was still part of her and of us. I was wearing a white puffa jacket that my mother had bought for me that Christmas and it got smeared up and down the sleeve with her blood. And when they wheeled Carol off to theatre I had to ring my mother and tell her what had happened, and her neighbours went to the chemist's to get her some tablets and she arrived later that day, on Valium and alcohol, after the arm had been amputated and she stared at my sleeve, as if I might not have noticed the blood that was streaked right down it.

Carol never complained about what had happened to her, but she sometimes got depressed. 'It's only natural,' my mother said. But she never complained, and she never attempted to justify any failure to do whatever a busy and active life would require. She went on to raise three children and drive and cook and sew all with one arm – she would open bottles gripped between her knees, and hold dresses with her teeth as she pushed the sewing needle through, and cut meat for the family held on chopping boards with nails sticking out of them (made by her father), and play badminton with me, serving and hitting the shuttle with her one good hand, until one day when some opponent protested that this was surely against all the rules of this most English of games. Somewhere it must be written in the rules, he said, that you couldn't just drop the shuttlecock and hit it with the very same hand. 'It must give you an unfair advantage.' I thought that he was joking and I am sure that I must have laughed, but he was quite serious about it. He had this sanctimonious expression on his face as if he had caught us cheating. Carol only ever complained that she could not greet her children with her arms outstretched in the way that you should, and could not clap her hands when she saw them in concerts or getting prizes or running races, except by slapping her right palm down on her right thigh in a muffled sort of ritual that drew attention to itself with its oddness.

But the pain in her arm never left her. 'I'm surprised,' she says.

In fact, I think it's getting worse rather than fading. There's a low level of discomfort, rather than pain, which feels like tingling nerve endings, which is pretty constant, but then this can develop into other, more definitely painful things. For example, quite often at night, if I wake up or can't get to sleep, I just can't find a comfortable way to lie and my arm becomes really hot and the pain is quite intense; or if I'm very tired or maybe coming down with a cold or something, my arm starts to get these spasms of pain darting through it; also generally it doesn't react well to extreme cold or heat. I've been trying to think about the pain, because I've never really thought the sensation was like a 'phantom limb' – I don't feel like I have a whole arm there. Sometimes I have a feeling like my fist is closed very tight and I can feel my fingernails digging into the palm of my hand, and my thumb squeezed underneath my fingers, and I feel that it would be good to be able to open my hand out and spread my fingers. When it is really painful, the only way I can describe it is as being like the thing has just happened – the train has just crushed it – it is burning hot and feels like there are bits of mangled bone and nerves and sinews all jammed together – it is a feeling of compression and pressure. I don't remember whether this is actually what it felt like at the time. When I have the spasm pain it is difficult not to flinch every time it happens. These types of pain are distracting and can be a bit draining at times. I especially hate it when it happens at night as there is nothing to take your mind off it and I sometimes think it will drive me mad. I don't take pain killers, as I don't like taking medication.

I have always felt that this pain was something of a barrier between us. It's private to her; it takes her away from those around her, engulfing her and leaving others feeling helpless, and with no sensible suggestions to make. But a while ago I spent some time reading the work of the distinguished neuro-scientist V. S. Ramachandran whose book *The Emerging Mind* explores a new method for treating phantom limb pain. Ramachandran argues that there is a huge amount of plasticity in the human brain and that this plasticity has implications for how phantom limb pain can be treated. His description of phantom limb pain seemed to fit Carol perfectly. 'Often the phantom hand goes into painful involuntary clenching spasms or is fixed in an awkward painful position which the patient is unable to change. We have discovered that some of these patients had pre-existing nerve damage before the amputation, for example the arm had been paralysed and lying in a sling. After amputation the patient is stuck with a paralysed phantom . . . as if the paralysis is "carried over" into the phantom. Perhaps when the arm was intact but paralysed, every time the front of the brain sent a command to the arm saying "move", it was getting feedback saying "no, it won't move". Somehow this feedback becomes imprinted on the circuitry in the . . . brain.'

Ramachandran tested this theory by tricking the brain into thinking that the phantom arm was obeying the brain's commands. He did this by using a mirror box. A mirror is propped up on a table at right angles to the chest of a patient with the left amputated arm to the left of the mirror and the right intact arm to the right of the mirror. The patient looks into the right-hand side of the mirror so that he or she sees the mirror reflection of the intact right arm superimposed on to the location of the phantom arm. Ramachandran then asks the patient to try to make symmetrical movements with both hands, such as clapping, while looking in the mirror. Patients not only apparently see the phantom limb move but incredibly they feel it moving as well. This visual trickery, in Ramachandran's words, 'animates' the phantom limb and this sudden sense of voluntary control and movement in the phantom limb apparently can produce relief from the spasm or the awkward posture that causes so much of the pain.

I discussed this with Carol and she said that it would be very strange, perhaps even too strange for her, to see and feel her arm moving again. In dreams she has always said that she still experiences her left arm, but even dreams in which she has both arms back can be disquieting enough. A recurrent dream that she has is of her cycling, holding on with two hands to her old Raleigh, singing on the way back from choir practice along the Backs in Cambridge. It's a very happy dream and reflects the carefree years in the Norfolk fens before life changed for her and for me.

We probably would have left it at that had I not discovered that a more sophisticated version of the mirror-box treatment for treating phantom limb pain was being pioneered at the University of Manchester (see Murray, 2006, Murray *et al*, 2007). This used a virtual-reality head-mounted display to present the computer-generated environment to participants to facilitate total immersion, with sensors attached to the intact arm. It makes a virtual representation of the phantom limb by transposing the movement of the participant's opposite anatomical limb into the phenomenological space of their phantom limb. The tasks are a bit basic but demanding enough – participants have to place the virtual representation of the phantom limb on to coloured tiles which light up in sequence or they have to bat a virtual ball around a yard using this virtual representation. A few early case studies from this project looked quite promising. One participant in the study reported vivid sensations of movement in his phantom arm. 'During it, I actually felt as if it was my left arm that was doing the work and chasing the ball. My actual phantom arm rather than my right . . . and that was more like reality than phantom reality.' He also said, 'If I could harness this movement in my phantom limb maybe I could open my fingers and ease the cramping pain a little.' His pain diary showed a diminution in the intensity of pain in the days after the trial and a positive change in his sleeping pattern with five to six hours of uninter-

rupted sleep a night as opposed to two or three. Another participant in the study reported a dramatic change in her experience of
her phantom limb after just one session. Her normal experience
was a clenched fist with the nails digging into her palm, but after
just one session she reported that, 'It's funny . . . one of my fingers
is coming out, sort of pointing out now.'

But it was very early days. These were just three case studies;
the research after all has only just begun. Nevertheless, it seemed
like too good an opportunity to miss. This really was psychology
coming right to the core of one's own life. Perhaps it was me
trying to do something about my powerlessness after all those
years. Carol, from her home in Sheffield, agreed to try it but I
could see from the start that she was apprehensive, but far too
polite to say anything. Perhaps her apprehension made perfect
sense. She has coped amazingly well with the loss of her arm; the
prostheses, lumpy and dysfunctional and garish, had been
dumped years ago, after the first few months of partial use. Her
body image is very high, and rightly so. She is very fit and an
excellent runner (she got into running originally because of me,
of course), she always wins prizes in her age group in races (and
usually first prize at both home and abroad) and she enjoys seeing
her picture in *Runner's World*. I think that she's become slightly
iconic in the running world. She wears a short black sock over
her left arm and runs in a singlet, regardless of the weather. She
has nothing to hide, that's the way she thinks about it. She is well
recognized on the running circuit, much better recognized than I
ever will be, and very much admired for her basic athleticism, as
well as for her grit and determination. Her main anxiety about
taking part in the trial was whether she would have to remove
the black sock from the end of her arm.

So here we sit in a university room, with peeling paint on the wall. The head-mounted display and computer is in one corner and for some reason an old, lumpy, pink prosthesis is in another. I can see her looking at the artificial arm and I can tell what she's thinking. This is not the high-tech world that I had promised her, this is not modernity. The researcher is amiable enough and quizzes her about her experiences of pain. He gives her some background material to read, which unfortunately talks about 'patients' and the 'stump' of the arm. Carol and I look at each other again slightly quizzically. We have never called her left arm a 'stump', it's her left arm. For a second, it's as if she's being dragged back into that bad dream from years before. She has worked hard to get away from those times. I can see that she wants to leave the room but she stays there to please me, to make me feel like I'm doing something to help. The researcher puts the head-mounted display on. It's all skew-whiff at first; it looks vaguely comical, but nobody is laughing. Carol points this out politely to the researcher, and he corrects the positioning. I can see her neck reddening in silent embarrassment. Suddenly, she's in the new virtual environment, in a yard trying to bat a ball. It's a strange sort of task for her. She looks around, she glances down at her virtual legs, she looks across at her virtual stationary right arm and then up at her virtual left arm moving through space. She finds the task difficult and keeps apologizing. 'Perhaps that's why I've never been good at tennis,' she says. 'Or badminton,' I add, trying to be ironic.

The researcher asks her to clench and unclench her fingers. I can see that she doesn't like even trying this. She makes tentative, halting movements; it's like watching a child learning to walk or gesture. It's her right hand that is opening and closing but her

299

brain is being tricked into thinking that it's her left arm. She isn't very good at batting the ball but she's better at the coloured-square task, moving her virtual left arm to find the squares. She does some more clenching and opening. She touches her thumb and fingertip and for a fleeting second she says that she *feels* that this touching was happening in her real left hand. This was, however, just for a fleeting second, but an exquisite second of something comfortingly familiar from the distant, half-forgotten past, and a fleeting second that she wanted to hold on to, after all those years without experiencing it. After a few more minutes of strange, stilted bodily action, the experiment is all over and she returns to the more mundane world of an untidy experimental room and a lumpy, pink prosthesis. We thank the researcher and leave the room in silence, trying to take in what has just happened and what it might mean for her future.

But later that afternoon things return to normal, and I see her gripping her left arm in pain, with that familiar expression on her face, as she tries to cope with this, without painkillers and without complaint. She sees me looking her way. 'Perhaps, it's because it really tired me, I don't know,' she says, in an apologetic sort of way that makes me feel worse. And that night, she tells me, it was very painful again and she woke up and couldn't get back to sleep. But the next day it is bright and sunny, and she says that she feels more optimistic about the whole thing. 'I'm sure that there's something in this,' she says, and she tells me that she really would genuinely like to try the experience again. I say that she shouldn't do it just to please me, the helpless one in all of this. But she says that she would like to do it anyway, and that this was far too important not to try. 'But perhaps they should do something about that room, you know, to make it a bit more modern,' she says after a bit of reflection. 'And make the virtual hand a bit more lifelike and feminine; the fingers were far too big for me. My brain needs to think that it's my hand actually moving and I don't think that it's fooled properly at the moment.' Then I see this smile creep across her face. 'And perhaps give the virtual figure some athletic gear to wear, and a slightly more athletic build, and maybe get the character, who is supposed to be me, moving a bit, perhaps even running. Then I might feel more immersed in the whole thing.' And we both laugh together very loudly indeed in the way that you sometimes have to.

But that, for the moment, is the end of the story. She never went back for more to that messy lab. 'But maybe one day,' she said. 'At least I now know that there are things that I can do if I need to. I'm more content with myself.' And I caught myself smiling, not because of the experience itself, nor even because of the funny bits of what we'd just been through (even Carol said that you had to laugh at how the whole thing had been managed by the researcher), but because of the thought, maybe even the genuine heartfelt realization, that psychology could potentially help with almost any aspect of people's lives, no matter how personal or profound. Psychology was not just about tips for flirting, or getting your partner to clean up after you by nudging his or her unconscious impulses, or about getting them to be nice to you by unconsciously reminding them of sex (as important as these things undoubtedly are); rather it can be introduced to almost any problem in your life, no matter how big or small, including your own most personal and private concerns. It could give hope, where previously there was none.

This was a genuinely empowering sort of thought, empowering

for the discipline and, I have to say, empowering for me personally because it is within this domain of psychology that I have chosen to spend my life. And Carol, without any reluctance or persuasion, agreed with this fundamental idea, when I later discussed it with her, even though her initial experience in this new virtual world was perhaps not all that she had hoped for. She said that she liked this new thought that her feelings of bodily symmetry and completeness may not be lost for ever and that her brain could be tricked in ways that could potentially help her to feel different and to feel less pain and that she could return to this whenever she chose. We can now, it seems, because of what we know from psychological research, direct the human brain in many ways that can allow you not just to get the edge but to regain the edge in life, the edge that you once had when you were capable of anything, the edge that we all should have as we live our daily lives, the edge that we all deserve.

- Nothing is fixed forever, not even deep emotional or physical loss

- Even the loss of an arm does not have to be permanent from the brain's point of view. You can get the brain to 'see' an arm that isn't there

- Psychology can help us in ways that we thought unimaginable even a generation ago

- We are all capable of becoming more 'complete', regardless of our individual circumstances

REFERENCES

Avni-Babad, Dina and Ritov, Ilana (2003) Routine and the perception of time. *Journal of Environmental Psychology* 132: 543–550.

Azim, Eiman, Mobbs, Dean, Jo, Booil, Menon, Vinod and Reiss, Allan L. (2005) Sex differences in brain activation elicited by humor. *PNAS* 102: 16496–16501.

Bachorowski, Jo-Anne and Owren, Michael J. (2001) Not all laughs are alike: Voiced but not unvoiced laughter readily elicits positive affect. *Psychological Science* 12: 252–257.

Baldwin, Mark W. (Ed.) (2005) *Interpersonal Cognition*. New York: Guilford.

Bargh, John A., Chen, Mark and Burrows, Lara (1996) The automaticity of social behaviour: Direct effects of trait concept and stereotype activation on action. *Journal of Personality and Social Psychology* 71: 230–244.

Barkow, Jerome H. (1989) *Darwin and Status: Biological Perspectives on Mind and Culture*. Toronto: University of Toronto Press.

Beattie, Geoffrey (1987) *Making It. The Reality of Today's Entrepreneurs*. London: Weidenfeld and Nicolson.

Beattie, Geoffrey (1996) *On the Ropes: Boxing as a way of life*. London: Victor Gollancz.

Beattie, Geoffrey (1992) *We are the People: Journeys through the heart of Protestant Ulster*. London: Heinemann.

Beattie, Geoffrey (2003) *Visible Thought. The New Psychology of Body Language*. London and New York: Routledge.

Beattie, Geoffrey (2010) *Why Aren't We Saving the Planet? A Psychological Perspective*. London and New York: Routledge.

Beattie, Geoffrey and Sale, Laura (2009) Explicit and implicit attitudes to low and high carbon footprint products. *International Journal of Environmental, Cultural, Economic and Social Sustainability* 5: 191–206.

Beattie, Geoffrey and Shovelton, Heather (1999a) Mapping the range of information contained in the iconic hand gestures that accompany spontaneous speech. *Journal of Language and Social Psychology* 18: 438–462.

Beattie, Geoffrey and Shovelton, Heather (1999b) Do iconic hand gestures really contribute anything to the semantic information conveyed by speech? An experimental investigation. *Semiotica* 123: 1–30.

Beattie, Geoffrey and Shovelton, Heather (2002) Blue-eyed boys? A winning smile? An experimental investigation of some core facial stimuli that may affect interpersonal perception. *Semiotica* 139: 1–21.

REFERENCES

Beattie, Geoffrey and Shovelton, Heather (2005) Why spontaneous images created by the hands during talk can help make TV advertisements more effective. *British Journal of Psychology* 96: 21–37.

Bullock, August (2004) *The Secret Sales Pitch*. San Jose: Norwich.

Cano, Annmarie and O'Leary, Daniel K. (2000) Infidelity and separations precipitate major depressive episodes and symptoms of nonspecific depression and anxiety. *Journal of Consulting and Clinical Psychology* 68: 774–781.

Carter, Sue, Ahnert, Liesolette, Grossman, Klaus E., Hrdy, Sarah B., Lamb, Michael E. and Porges, Stephen W. (2005) *Attachment and Bonding: A New Synthesis*. Cambridge, MA: MIT Press.

Chaplin, William F., Phillips, Jeffrey B., Brown, Jonathan, D., Clanton, Nancy R. and Stein, Jennifer L. (2000) Handshaking, gender, personality, and first impressions. *Journal of Personality and Social Psychology* 79: 110–117.

Cook, Susan Wagner, Mitchell, Zachary and Goldin-Meadow, Susan (2008) Gesturing makes learning last. *Cognition* 106: 1047–1058.

Crane, Frederick and Crane, Erinn (2007) Dispositional optimism and entrepreneurial success. *The Psychologist-Manager Journal* 10: 13–25.

Cunningham, Michael R. (1986) Measuring the physical in physical attractiveness: Quasi-experiments on the socio-biology of female facial beauty. *Journal of Personality and Social Psychology* 50: 925–935.

Cunningham, Michael R., Barbee, Anita P. and Pike, Carolyn L. (1990) What do women want? Facial metric assessment of multiple motives in the perception of male facial physical attractiveness. *Journal of Personality and Social Psychology* 59: 61–72.

Damasio, Antonio (1999) *The Feeling of what Happens: Body and Emotion in the Making of Consciousness*. New York: Harcourt Brace.

Danner, Deborah D., Snowden, David A. and Friesen, Wallace V. (2001) Positive emotions in early life and longevity: Findings from the nun study. *Journal of Personality and Social Psychology* 80: 804–813.

De Vries, Marieke, Holland, Rob W. and Witteeman, Cilla L. M. (2007) Fitting decisions: Mood and intuitive versus deliberative decision strategies. *Cognition and Emotion* 22: 931–943.

Dijksterhuis, Ap. (2004) I like myself but I don't know why: Enhancing implicit self-esteem by subliminal evaluative conditioning. *Journal of Personality and Social Psychology* 86: 345–355.

Dijkstra, Katinka, Kaschak, Michael P. and Zwaan, Rolf A. (2007) Body posture facilitates retrieval of autobiographical memories. *Science Direct Cognition* 102: 139–149.

Duchenne de Boulogne, Guillaume. B. (1990). *The mechanism of human facial expression*. (R. A. Cuthbertson, Ed. and Trans.) Cambridge, England: Cambridge University Press. (Original work published 1862.)

Dudukovic, Nicole M., Marsh Elizabeth J. and Tversky, Barbara

(2004) Telling a story or telling it straight: The effects of entertaining versus accurate retellings on memory. *Applied Cognitive Psychology* 18: 125–143.

Dunnbar, Robin I. M. (1996) *Grooming, Gossip, and the Evolution of Language*. Cambridge, MA: Harvard University Press.

Ekman, Paul and Friesen, Wallace. V. (1969) The Repertoire of Nonverbal Behaviour: Categories, origins, usage and coding. *Semiomia* 1: 49–98.

Ekman, Paul and Friesen, Wallace. V. (1982) Felt, false and miserable smiles. *Journal of Nonverbal Behavior* 6: 238–252.

Elliot, Andrew J., Maier, Markus A., Moller, A. C, Freidman, Ron and Meinhardt, Jörg (2007) Color and psychological functioning: The effect of red on performance attainment. *Journal of Experimental Psychology* 136: 154–168.

Elliot, Andrew J. and Niesta, Daniela (2008) Romantic red: Red enhances men's attraction to women. *Journal of Personality and Social Psychology* 95: 1150–1164.

Frances, Susan J. (1979) Sex differences in nonverbal behaviour. *Sex Roles* 5: 519–535.

Frank, Mark G., Ekman, Paul and Friesen, Wallace V. (1993) Behavioural markers and recognisability of the smile enjoyment. *Journal of Personality and Social Psychology* 64: 83–93.

Fredrickson, Barbara and Branigan, Christine (2005) Positive emotions broaden the scope of attention and thought-action repertoires. *Cognition & Emotion* 19: 313–332.

Freud, Sigmund and Breuer, Josef (1955) *Studies in Hysteria*. Standard edition (vol. 2). London: Hogarth Press. (Original work published 1893–5.)

Friedman, Ron and Elliot, Andrew J. (2008) The effect of arm crossing on persistence and performance. *The European Journal of Social Psychology* 38: 449–461.

Gifford, Robert (1991) Mapping nonverbal behaviour on the interpersonal circle. *Journal of Personality and Social Psychology* 61: 279–288.

Gilbert, Daniel T., Morewedge, Carey K., Risen, Jane L. and Wilson, Timothy D. (2004) Looking forward to looking backward. The misprediction of regret. *Psychological Science* 15: 346–350.

Gilbert, Paul, and Proctor, Sue (2006) Compassionate mind training for people with high shame and self-criticism: Overview and pilot study of a group therapy approach. *Clinical Psychology and Psychotherapy* 13: 353–379.

Gillath, Omri, Mikulincer, Mario, Birnbaum, Gurit and Shaver, Phillip (2008) When sex primes love: Subliminal sexual priming motivates relationship goal pursuit. *Personality and Social Psychology Bulletin* 34: 1057–1069.

Gino, Francesca, Ayal, Shahar and Ariely, Dan (2009) Contagion and differentiation in unethical behaviour. The effect of one bad apple on the barrel. *Psychological Science* 20: 393–398.

Gottman, John (1994) *What Predicts Divorce?: The relationship between marital processes and marital outcomes*. London: Lawrence Erlbaum.

REFERENCES

Gottman, John (1994/1997) *Why Marriages Succeed or Fail and How to Make Yours Last*. London: Bloomsbury.

Gottman, John, Coan, James, Carrere, Sybil and Swanson, Catherine (1998) Predicting marital happiness and stability from newlywed interaction. *Journal of Marriage and Family* 60: 5–22.

Grammer, Karl (1990) Strangers meet: Laughter and nonverbal signs of interest on opposite sex encounters. *Journal of Nonverbal Behavior* 14: 209–236.

Greenwald, Anthony. G., McGhee, Debbie. E. and Schwartz, Jordan L. K. (1998) Measuring individual differences in implicit cognition: The Implicit Association Test. *Journal of Personality and Social Psychology* 74: 1464–1480.

Grill-Spector, Kalanit and Kanwisher, Nancy (2005) Visual recognition: As soon as you know it is there, you know what it is. *Psychological Science* 16: 152–160.

Harmon-Jones, Eddie and Peterson, Carly K. (2009) Supine body position reduces neural response to anger evocation. *Psychological Science* 10: 1209–1210.

Hart, William and Albarracín, Dolores (2009) What I was doing versus what I did. Verb aspect influences memory and future actions. *Psychological Science* 20: 238–244.

Hendrix, Harville (1998) *Getting the Love You Want: A Guide For Couples*. New York: Henry Holt & Co.

Henningsen, David D. (2004) Flirting with meaning: an examination of miscommunication in flirting interactions. *Sex Roles* 50: 481–489.

Hertenstein, Matthew J. Keltner, Dacher App, Betsy, Bulleit, Brittany and Jaskolka, Adrione, R. (2006) Touch communicates distinct emotions. *Emotion* 6: 528–533.

Hicks, Angela M. and Diamond, Lisa M. (2008) How was your day? Couples' affect when telling and hearing daily events. *Personal Relationships* 15: 205–228.

Higgins, Chad A. and Judge, Timothy A. (2004) The effect of applicant influence tactics on recruiter perceptions of fit and hiring recommendations: A field study. *Journal of Applied Psychology* 4: 622–632.

Higuchi, Takahiro, Shoji, Ken, Taguchi, Sumie and Hatayama, Toshitero (2005) Improvement of nonverbal behaviour in Japanese female perfume-wearers. *International Journal of Psychology* 40: 90–99.

Holland, Rob, Hendriks, Merel, and Aarts, Henk (2005) Smells like clean spirit. Nonconscious effects of scent on cognition and behaviour. *Psychological Science* 16: 689–693.

Iyengar, Sheena, Wells, Rachael and Schwartz, Barry (2006) Doing better but feeling worse. Looking for the 'best' job undermines satisfaction. *Psychological Science* 17: 143–150.

Jacobi, Lora and Cash, Thomas (1994) In pursuit of the perfect appearance: Discrepancies among self-ideal percepts of multiple physical attributes. *Journal of Applied Social Psychology* 24: 379–396.

James, William (1890) *Principles of Psychology*. New York: Holt.

Kahneman, Daniel and Miller, Dale T. (1986) Norm theory:

REFERENCES

Comparing reality to its alternatives. *Psychological Review* 93: 136–153.

Kelly, Anita, Klaus, Julie, Von Weiss, Renee and Kenny, Christine (2001) What is it about revealing secrets that is beneficial? *Personality and Social Psychology Bulletin* 27: 651–665.

Klein, Kitty and Boals, Adriel (2001) Expressive writing can increase working memory capacity. *Journal of Experimental Psychology* 130: 520–533.

Kurtz, Jaime (2008) Looking to the future to appreciate the present. The benefits of perceived temporal scarcity. *Psychological Science* 19: 1238–1241.

Kurzban, Robert and Weeden, Jason (2007) Do advertised preferences predict the behaviour of speed daters? *Personal Relationships* 14: 623–632.

Lavater, John C. (1772/1880) Essays on physiognomy; for the promotion of the knowledge and the love of mankind (Gale Document Number CW114125313). Retrieved May 15, 2005, from Gale Group, Eighteenth Century Collections Online. (Original work published 1772.)

Lee, Victoria and Beattie, Geoffrey (1998) The rhetorical organization of verbal and nonverbal behaviour in emotion talk. *Semiotica* 120: 39–92.

Lee, Victoria and Beattie, Geoffrey (2000) Why talking about negative emotional experiences is good for your health: A microanalytical perspective. *Semiotica* 130: 001–081.

Lepore, Stephen J. and Greenberg, Melanie A. (2002) Mending broken hearts: Effects of expressive writing on mood, cognitive social adjustment and health following a relationship breakup. *Psychology and Health* 17: 547–560.

Li, Wen, Moallem, Isabel, Paller, Ken and Gottfreid, Jay (2007) Subliminal smells can guide social preferences. *Psychological Science* 18: 1044–1049.

Luo Lu, Shu-Fang Kao, Ting-Ting Chang and Ya-Wen Lee (2008) Individual differences in coping with criticism of one's physical appearance and Taiwanese students. *International Journal of Psychology* 44: 274–281.

Lynn, Michael and Shurgot, Barbara A. (1984) Responses to lonely hearts advertisements: Effect of reported physical attractiveness, physique, and coloration. *Personality and Social Psychology Bulletin* 10: 349–357.

Mauss, Iris B., Evers, Catherine, Wilhelm, Frank H. and Gross, James J. (2006) How to bite your tongue without blowing your top: implicit evaluation of emotion regulation predicts affective responding to anger provocation. *Personality and Social Psychology Bulletin* 32: 589–602.

McAndrew, Francis, Bell, Emily and Garcia, Contitta (2007) Who do we tell and whom do we tell on? Gossip as a strategy for status enhancement. *Journal of Applied Social Psychology* 37: 1562–1577.

McAndrew, Francis T. and Milenkovic, Megan A. (2002) Of tabloids and family secrets: The evolutionary psychology of gossip. *Journal of Applied Social Psychology* 32: 1064–1082.

McCullough, Michael E., Root, Lindsey M. and Cohen, Adam D. (2006) Writing about the benefits of an interpersonal transgression facilitates forgiveness. *Journal of Consulting and Clinical Psychology* 74: 887–897.

Mehu, Marc, Little, Anthony and Dunbar, Robin (2007) Duchenne smiles and the perception of generosity and sociability in faces. *Journal of Evolutionary Psychology* 5: 183–196.

Morse, Katherine A. and Neuberg, Steven L. (2004) How do holidays influence relationship processes and outcomes? Examining the instigating and catalytic effects of Valentine's Day. *Personal Relationships* 11: 509–527.

Murray, Craig D., Patchick, Emma, Pettifer, Stephen, Caillette, Fabrice and Howard, Toby (2006) Immersive virtual reality as a rehabilitative technology for phantom limb experience: A protocol. *CyberPsychology & Behavior* 9: 167–170.

Murray, Craig D., Pettifer, Stephen, Howard, Toby, Patchick, Emma L., Caillette, Fabrice, Kulkarni, Jai and Bamford, Candy (2007) The treatment of phantom limb pain using immersive virtual reality: Three case studies. *Disability and Rehabilitation* 29: 1465–1469.

Nuttin, Jozef M. (1987) Affective consequences of mere ownership: The name-letter effect in twelve European Languages. *European Journal of Social Psychology* 17: 381–402.

Owens, Kim S. (2004) An investigation of the personality correlates of small business success. *Dissertation Abstracts International* 65: 470B.

Pennebaker, James W., Colder, Michelle and Sharp, Lisa K. (1990) Accelerating the coping process. *Journal of Personality and Social Psychology* 58: 528–537.

Raghubir, Priya and Srivastava, Joydeep (2008) Monopoly money: The effect of payment coupling and form on spending behaviour. *Journal of Experimental Psychology: Applied* 14: 213–225.

Ramachandran, Vilayanur S. (2003) *The Emerging Mind. The Reith Lectures 2003*. London: Profile.

Rauscher, Frances H., Shaw, Gordon L. and Ky, Katherine N. (1993) Music and spatial task performance. *Nature* 365 (6447): 611.

Riskind, J. H. (1983) Nonverbal expressions and the accessibility of life experience memories: A congruence hypothesis. *Social Cognition*, 2, 62–86.

Roseth, Cary, Johnson, David and Johnson, Roger (2008) Promoting early adolescents' achievement and peer relationships: the effects of cooperative, competitive, and individualistic goal structures. *Psychological Bulletin* 134: 223–246.

Scheflen, Albert E. (1965) Quasi-courtship behaviour in psychotherapy. *Psychiatry: Journal for the Study of Interpersonal Processes* 28: 245–257.

Schellenberg, Glenn E. (2004) Music lessons enhance IQ. *Psychological Science* 15: 511–514.

Scher, Steven and Darley, John (1997) How effective are the things people say to apologize? Effects of the realization of the apology speech act. *Journal of Psycholinguistic Research* 26: 127–140.

Schnall, Simone, Benton, Jennifer and Harvey, Sophie (2008) With a clean conscience. Cleanliness reduces the severity of moral judgements. *Psychological Science* 19: 1219–1222.

Seligman, Martin (1998) *Learned Optimism: How to Change Your Mind and Your Life.* New York: Pocket Books.

Sheldon, Kennon M. and Lyubomirsky, Sonja (2006) How to increase and sustain positive emotion: The effects of expressing gratitude and visualizing best possible selves. *Journal of Positive Psychology* 1: 73–82.

Simmons, Rachel A. Gordon, Peter C. and Chambles, Dianne L. (2005) Pronouns in marital interaction. What do 'you' and 'I' say about marital health? *Psychological Science* 16: 932–936.

Simon, Herbert A. (1955) A behavioural model of rational choice. *Quarterly Journal of Economics* 59: 99–118.

Smith, Andrew P., Clark, Rachel and Gallagher, John (1999) Breakfast cereal and caffeinated coffee: Effects on working memory, attention, mood and cardiovascular function. *Psychology and Behaviour* 67: 9–7.

Smith, Andrew P. (1992) Time of day and performance. In: A. P. Smith and D. M. Jones (Eds.) *Handbook of Human Performance.* Vol. 3: *State and Trait* (pp. 217–236). London: Academic Press.

Stepper, Sabine and Strack, Fritz (1993) Proprioceptive determinants of affective and nonaffective feelings. *Journal of Personality and Social Psychology* 64: 211–220.

Tamir, Mayer, Robinson, Michael. D., Clore, Gerald. L., Martin, Leonard L. and Whitaker, Daniel J. (2004) Are we puppets on a string? The contextual meaning of unconscious expressive cues. *Personality and Social Psychology Bulletin* 30: 1–12.

Thayer, Robert E., Newman, Robert J. and McClain, Tracey M. (1994) Self-regulation of mood: Strategies for changing a bad mood, raising energy, and reducing tension. *Journal of Personality and Social Psychology* 67: 910–925.

Thompson, William F., Schellenberg, Glenn E. and Husain, Gabriela (2001) Arousal, mood, and the Mozart effect. *Psychological Science* 12: 248–251.

Thompson, William F., Shellenberg, Glenn E. and Hussain, Gabriela (2004) Decoding speech prosody: Do music lessons help? *Emotion* 4: 46–64.

Vrij, Aldert and Semin, Gün R. (1996) Lie experts' beliefs about nonverbal indicators of deception. *Journal of Nonverbal Behavior* 20: 65–80.

Wells, Gary and Petty, Richard (1980) The effects of overt head movements on persuasion: Compatibility and incompatibility of responses. *Basic and Applied Psychology* 1: 219–230.

Wildschut, Tim, Sedikides, Constantine, Arndt, Jamie and Routledge, Clay (2006) Nostalgia: Content, triggers, functions. *Journal of Personality and Social Psychology* 91: 975–993.

Willis, Janine and Todorov, Alexander (2006) First impressions: Making up your mind after a 100-ms exposure to a face. *Psychological Science* 17: 592–598.

Wilson, David S., Wilczynski, Carolyn, Wells, Alexandra & Weiser, Laura (2000) Gossip and other aspects of language as group-level adaptations. In: C. Heyes & L. Huber (Eds.) *Evolution and Cognition* (pp. 347–365). Cambridge, MA: MIT Press.

REFERENCES

Winston, Joel, Strange, Bryan A., O'Doherty, John and Dolan, Raymond J. (2002) Automatic and intentional brain responses during evaluation of trustworthiness of faces. *Nature Neuroscience* 5: 277–283.

Witvliet, Charlotte V., Ludwig, Thomas E. and Vander Laan, Kelly L. (2001) Granting forgiveness or harboring grudges: Implications for emotion, physiology, and health. *Psychological Science* 12: 117–123.

Witvliet, Charlotte and Scott, Vrana (2007) Play it again Sam: Repeated exposure to emotionally evocative music polarises liking and smiling responses, and influences other affective reports, facial EMG, and heart rate. *Cognition & Emotion* 21: 3–25.

Zechmeister, Jeanne S. and Romero, Catherine (2002). Victim and offender accounts of interpersonal conflict: Autobiographical narratives of forgiveness and unforgiveness. *Journal of Personality and Social Psychology* 82: 675–686.

Zeigarnik, Bluma (1927) Uber das behalten von erledigten und unerledigten handlungen [The memory of completed and uncompleted actions]. *Psychologische Forschung* 9: 1–85.

Zhou, Xinyue, Sedikides, Constantine, Wildschut, Tim and Gao, Ding-Guo (2008) Counteracting loneliness: On the restorative function of nostalgia. *Psychological Science* 19: 1023–1029.

INDEX

Note: Page numbers in **bold** refer to major text sections. The terms 'relationship' and 'partner' refer to romantic/sexual relationships or partners.

INDEX